Life's Healing
CHOICES

REVISED AND UPDATED

FREEDOM FROM YOUR HURTS, HANG-UPS, AND HABITS

John Baker

HOWARD BOOKS
AN IMPRINT OF SIMON & SCHUSTER, INC.

New York   London   Toronto   Sydney   New Delhi

Howard Books
An Imprint of Simon & Schuster, Inc.
1230 Avenue of the Americas
New York, NY 10020

This Howard Books trade paperback edition July 2017

HOWARD and colophon are trademarks of Simon & Schuster, Inc.

For information about special discounts for bulk purchases, please contact Simon & Schuster
Special Sales at 1-866-506-1949 or business@simonandschuster.com.

The Simon & Schuster Speakers Bureau can bring authors to your live event.
For more information, or to book an event, contact the Simon & Schuster Speakers
Bureau at 1-866-248-3049 or visit our website at www.simonspeakers.com.

Manufactured in the United States of America

10 9 8 7

Library of Congress Cataloging-in-Publication Data is available.

ISBN 978-1-5011-5234-4

This book is dedicated to

My Lord and *Savior,* Jesus Christ

To my *family* for loving me, no matter what

To pastors *Rick Warren* and *Glen Kreun*
for trusting and believing in me

To the thousands of *courageous* men and women
who have *celebrated* their recoveries
with me over the last sixteen years

Contents

Foreword by RICK WARREN

Do you ever eat or drink more calories than your body needs? Do you ever feel you ought to exercise but don't? Do you ever know the right thing to do but don't do it? Do you ever know something is wrong but do it anyway? If you answered yes to any of the questions above, you'll know without a doubt that you are a citizen of the human race. As fellow members of the human race, we all deal with life's hurts, hang-ups, and habits. And Jesus, who left heaven to become one of us so that He could minister to those needs, said, "It is not the healthy who need a doctor, but the sick. I have not come to call the righteous, but sinners" (Mark 2:17). At Saddleback Church, we take these words seriously. We've learned that every single person—as a member of the human race—deals with a hurt, a hang-up, or a habit at some level, in some form.

Of course, when you're serious about dealing with broken people, then those people are going to bring a lot of problems with them when they come to church. In 1991, to help deal with these problems, my good friend and the author of this book, John Baker, founded Celebrate Recovery—one of the most successful ministries in Saddleback's history. This ministry, which is a biblically balanced approach to repentance and recovery, is one of the secrets of Saddleback's amazing growth. More than twenty thousand hurting people have participated in Celebrate Recovery at Saddleback, with most of them eventually joining our church and getting involved in ministry. Nearly one-third of those are now serving in our five hundred ministries around the world.

Soon after the onset of Celebrate Recovery, I did an intense study of the Scriptures to discover what God had to say about bringing hope and healing into broken lives. To my amazement, I found the principles of healing—even their logical order—given by Christ in his most famous message: the Sermon on the Mount. My study resulted in a ten-week series of sermons called "The Road to Recovery." Using the principles of that series, John Baker developed the workbooks that became the heart of our Celebrate Recovery program and now has written this life-changing book. He has taken my sermon series and used it as the foundation of this book. In it you will read the 8 Principles from my study and how you can choose to make these teachings a part of your own "life's healing choices."

Now, you may be thinking that this book is only for people with serious addictions, for people whose lives seem out of control. Well, I believe the Bible teaches that all of us have some form of addiction. Sin is addicting and "all have sinned." That means we've all created ungodly and unhealthy methods for handling life. Not one of us is untainted, and because of sin, we've all hurt ourselves, we've all hurt other people, and others have hurt us.

The goal of Celebrate Recovery and this book is not simply to help hurting people recover from past sins and hurts. The goal is to teach them—and you—to make the healing choices that will help you become Christ-like in character. We begin this journey to healing by admitting our need. In the very first beatitude, Jesus said, "God blesses those who realize their need for him" (Matthew 5:3 NLT). When we reach the end of our rope and give up our self-sufficiency, God can move into our lives with healing and growth.

In addition to these revolutionary, biblically based principles, you will also read real-life stories of lives inspired and transformed by the life-changing power of Jesus Christ and the fellowship of other believers. You'll hear about hopeless marriages restored and people set free from all kinds of sinful hurts, hang-ups, and habits as they practice the Lordship of Jesus and live out the Beatitudes.

You will be inspired, and your life will be changed in dramatic ways as you read through the pages of this book.

Rick Warren
Pastor, Saddleback Church
Author, *The Purpose Driven Life*

Finding FREEDOM

from Your *Hurts, Hang-ups,* and *Habits*

One Sunday afternoon a father was trying to take a nap, but his little boy kept bugging him with "Daddy, I'm bored." So, trying to occupy him with a game, the dad found a picture of the world in the newspaper. He cut it up in about fifty pieces and said, "Son, see if you can put this puzzle back together." The dad lay back down to finish his nap, thinking the map would keep his son busy for at least an hour or so. But in about fifteen minutes the little guy woke him up: "Daddy, I've got it finished. It's all put together."

"You're kidding." He knew his son didn't know all the positions of the nations, so he asked him, "How did you do it?"

"It was easy. There was a picture of a person on the back of the map, so when I got my person put together, the world looked just fine."

How is your "person" doing? Are you all put together? The fact is that many of us are a mess. We're scattered all over the living-room floor, with no one to put us together and no idea where to begin the process of healing. Each of our lives is tangled up with *hurts* that haunt our hearts, *hang-ups* that cause us pain, and *habits* that mess up our lives.

Hurts, hang-ups, and habits. There's not a person in the world who doesn't deal with at least one of these on some level—and many of us struggle with all three.

The truth is, life is tough. We live in an imperfect world. We've been hurt by other people, we've hurt ourselves, and we've hurt other people. The Bible says it plainly: "*All have sinned.*"[1] That means none of us is perfect; we've all blown it; we've all made mistakes. We hurt, and we hurt others.

It's amazing how much better the world looks when our person is put together. And that's what we're going to do in this book. With God's help in making 8 Healing Choices, you are going to be able to put the pieces of your world back together.

We'll start with a promise straight from God. There are five ways He promises to help us find freedom from our hurts, hang-ups, and habits.

> "*I have seen how they acted, but I will heal them.*
> *I will lead them and help them, and I will comfort those who mourn.*
> *I offer peace to all, both near and far! I will heal my people.*"[2]

Notice the five promises God extends:

1. If you are *hurt*, God says, "I will *heal* you."

2. If you're *confused*, God says, "I will *lead* you."

3. If you feel *helpless*, God says, "I will *help* you."

4. If you feel *alone*, God says, "I will *comfort* you."

5. If you feel *anxious* and *afraid*, God says, "I will *offer peace* to you."

Trusting in His promises, we find hope for a better future—a life of freedom, peace, and happiness.

HAPPINESS IS POSSIBLE— BUT YOU'VE GOT TO *CHOOSE* IT

Since the beginning of time, men and women have searched for happiness—usually in all the wrong places, trying all the wrong things. But there's only one place where we can find tested-and-proven, absolutely-gonna-work principles that will lead to healing and happiness. These principles come in the form of eight statements from the truest of all books—the Bible—and from the most revered Teacher of all time—Jesus Christ. Jesus laid out these principles for happiness in the Sermon on the Mount in the Gospel of Matthew, chapter 5. Today we call them "the Beatitudes."

Happiness, Jesus says, can be ours, but the pathway to happiness may not be exactly what we're expecting. From a conventional viewpoint, most of the following eight statements don't make sense. At first they even sound like contradictions. But when you fully understand what Jesus is saying, you'll realize these eight statements are God's pathway to wholeness, growth, and spiritual maturity.

"Happy are those who know they are spiritually poor."
"Happy are those who mourn, for they shall be comforted."
"Happy are the meek."
"Happy are the pure in heart."
"Happy are those whose greatest desire is to do what God requires."
"Happy are those who are merciful."
"Happy are those who work for peace."
"Happy are those who are persecuted because they do what God requires."[3]

My Own Personal Choice

I know that the 8 Healing Choices work. Why? Because they worked in my life. I have not always been a pastor. Prior to being called into the ministry, I was a successful businessman. I was also a "functional alcoholic." I struggled with my sin addiction to alcohol for nineteen years. Eventually, I came to a point where I was losing everything. I cried out to God for help, and He led me to Alcoholics Anonymous. Even then I knew that my higher power had a name—Jesus Christ!—and I started attending Saddleback Church in Lake Forest, California. After a year of sobriety I answered God's call to start a Christ-centered recovery program called Celebrate Recovery. Since 1991, millions of courageous individuals have found the same freedom from their life's hurts, hang-ups, and habits that I did. If these 8 Choices worked for someone like me, I promise they can work for you too!

My Partnership with Pastor Rick

After Celebrate Recovery had been going for a year, Pastor Rick Warren, my senior pastor, saw how Celebrate Recovery was helping people in our church family find God's healing from their hurts, hang-ups, and habits. He decided to take the entire church family through a sermon series called the "Road to Recovery." I want to thank Pastor Rick for allowing me to use his "Road to Recovery" series as the foundation of this book.

Pastor Rick's R-E-C-O-V-E-R-Y acrostic identifies 8 Principles. As you read the 8 Principles and the corresponding beatitudes, you'll begin to understand the choices before you.

Choices that Will Change Your Life

1. **R**ealize I'm not God. I admit that I am powerless to control my tendency to do the wrong thing and that my life is unmanageable.

   "Happy are those who know they are spiritually poor."[4]

We finally understand that we do not have the power to control our hurts, hang-ups, and habits on our own. When we admit this, God can begin His healing work in our lives.

2. **E**arnestly believe that God exists, that I matter to Him, and that He has the power to help me recover.

   "Happy are those who mourn, for they shall be comforted."[5]
   As we begin to believe that we are important to God, we find great comfort in knowing that He has the power to change us and our situation.

3. **C**onsciously choose to commit all my life and will to Christ's care and control.

   "Happy are the meek."[6]
   When we commit our lives to Christ, we become a new person. We can finally give up trying to control ourselves and others. We replace our willpower with our willingness to accept God's power.

4. **O**penly examine and confess my faults to myself, to God, and to someone I trust.

   "Happy are the pure in heart."[7]
   In order to have a clear conscience, in order to deal with our guilt and have a pure heart, we need to admit all the wrongs of our past and present. We do this by writing it all down and sharing it with another person.

5. **V**oluntarily submit to every change God wants to make in my life and humbly ask Him to remove my character defects.

"Happy are those whose greatest desire is to do what God requires."[8]

We submit to all the changes God wants to make in our lives, and we humbly ask Him to work in our lives to bring about the needed changes.

6. **E**valuate all my relationships. Offer forgiveness to those who have hurt me and make amends for harm I've done to others, except when to do so would harm them or others.

> *"Happy are those who are merciful."*[9]
> *"Happy are those who work for peace."*[10]

We do our best to restore our relationships. We offer forgiveness to the people who have hurt us, and make amends to the people we have hurt.

7. **R**eserve a daily time with God for self-examination, Bible reading, and prayer in order to know God and His will for my life and to gain the power to follow His will.

We maintain these daily habits of spending time with God in order to keep our recovery on track.

8. **Y**ield myself to God to be used to bring this Good News to others, both by my example and by my words.

> *"Happy are those who are persecuted because*
> *they do what God requires."*[11]

Through God's grace and living these 8 Principles, we have found freedom from our hurts, hang-ups, and habits. Now that we have been changed by God, we yield ourselves to be used by Him as we share our story and serve others.

Jesus's 8 Principles for healing and happiness are the basis for the 8 Choices outlined in the chapters of this book. With the exception of Choice 7, each choice has a corresponding beatitude; Choice 6 actually has two. Regardless of the problem you are struggling with—whether it's emotional, financial, relational, spiritual, sexual, or whatever—regardless of what you need recovery from, the principles that lead to happiness and recovery are always the same, and the choice is always yours.

After reading this book and applying its principles, you will be able to join the many others who can say . . .

+ "I've been living with shame or guilt from my past, and *now I don't have to live with that pain anymore!*"
+ "I've been trapped in a habit or hang-up that is messing up my life, and *now I can be free from its hold on me!*"
+ "I've always been afraid and worried of what may happen tomorrow, and I *now can face my future with peace and confidence.*"

That's the freedom I hope and pray you will find by making the 8 Choices offered in this book: freedom to know peace, freedom to live without guilt, and freedom to be happy—the choice is yours.

OUR JOURNEY TOGETHER

As we take this amazing journey to freedom together, I will lead you, principle by principle, choice by choice, into the healing you desire.

We'll Share Stories of Hope

In the pages of this book, you will find sixteen life-changing stories of people who have completed the eight biblical choices found in this book. The men and women who so honestly tell their stories want to share with you how, with God's power, they found freedom from their hurts, hang-ups, and habits. They'll tell you how they overcame their struggles. Some will share how they were trying to control themselves as well as friends, relatives, and coworkers. Others will share how they struggled with workaholism, overeating, sexual and physical abuse, addiction to drugs and alcohol, sexual addiction, perfectionism, legalism, abortion, loss of loved ones or a job, and much more. *No one is worse or better than the other.*

We'll Focus on the Future

This book is forward looking. We will spend some time looking at the good and bad things that happened in our past. But rather than wallowing in the past or dredging up and reliving painful memories over and over, we will focus on the future. Regardless of what has already happened, due to either your poor choices or the hurtful choices made by others, you and your situation can change. The solution is to start making these healing choices now and depend on Christ's power to help you.

We'll Accept Personal Responsibility

This book emphasizes taking personal responsibility. Instead of playing the "accuse and excuse" game of victimization, it will help you face up to your own poor choices and deal with things you can do something about. We cannot control all that happens to us, but we can control how we choose to respond to what happens to us. That is a secret of happiness. When we stop wasting time fixing the blame, we have more energy to fix the problem. When we stop hiding our own faults and stop hurling accusations at others, the healing power of Christ can begin working in our hearts, our minds, our wills, and our emotions.

We'll Make a Spiritual Commitment

We'll also emphasize spiritual commitment to Jesus Christ. Lasting recovery cannot happen without total surrender to Him. Everybody needs Jesus.

We'll Say "Yes" to a Call to Action

You will not be changed by simply reading this book! You must take action to achieve the changes you desire. At the end of each chapter, you will be asked to complete three action steps. Completing these actions will help you apply the choice you have just read about to your own life. I want to encourage you to take your time and complete each action step honestly and to the best of your ability. Through completing each of the steps, true and lasting healing will occur. The three action steps included in each chapter are "Pray about It," "Write about It," and "Share about It."

1. Pray about It

In this action step, you will be prompted to pray for specific things regarding each choice. If you are not used to praying, don't worry; I have written prayers to help you get started! As you move through this book, you will see how important prayer is in helping you make the changes and healing choices you desire in your life.

2. Write about It

This action will ask you to put your thoughts and insights down in black and white. When a thought passes from the lips to the fingertips, it becomes specific. This is also called journaling. As you progress through each of the choices, you will learn to rely on your writings. We've created a *Life's Healing Choices Journal*, available in all online bookstores. It is specifically made to help you journal your way through these choices, but a spiral bound notebook will work too. What you write in your journal will help you see your areas of growth and the areas you still need further work on.

3. *Share about It*

This book is built on the New Testament principle that we don't change or get well by ourselves. We need each other. Fellowship and accountability are two important components of spiritual growth. In this action step, you will be asked to find a safe person—an "accountability partner"—to share your journey with as you go through these 8 Choices. You will also find some suggestions and guidelines to help you make your selection of this safe person. You will be guided on what to share and how.

As you start reading, I suggest that you take your time. The hurts, hang-ups, and habits that have been interfering with your happiness did not happen or develop overnight. It makes sense that they are not going to simply disappear from your life or be changed by the snap of your fingers. You will discover that you must rely on God's power to help you take the actions necessary to complete the 8 Choices. Only by God's power will lasting life-changes occur.

I invite you to travel with me on this amazing journey!

Realize I'm not God.

R

E   I *admit* that I am powerless to control
         my tendency to do the wrong thing
C   and that my life is unmanageable.

O

V

E

R

Y

"Happy are those who know they are spiritually poor."[1]

Admitting NEED

The REALITY Choice

Part of our human nature is to refuse change until our pain exceeds our fear—fear of change, that is. We simply deny the pain until it gets so bad that we are crushed and finally realize we need some help. Why don't we save ourselves a bit of misery and admit *now* what we're inevitably going to have to admit later? *We are not God*, and we desperately need God because our lives are unmanageable without Him. We'll be forced to learn that lesson someday. We may as well admit it now.

If you answer yes to any of the questions below, you'll know without a doubt that you are a citizen of the human race.

+ Do you ever stay up late when you know you need sleep? yes
+ Do you ever eat or drink more calories than your body needs? yes
+ Do you ever feel you ought to exercise but don't? yes
+ Do you ever know the right thing to do but don't do it? yes
+ Do you ever know something is wrong but do it anyway? yes
+ Have you ever known you should be unselfish but were selfish instead? yes *you should be unselfish with your time and start opening up to others. Actually, take an interest in getting to know them. More important that you need to know him, rather than he needing to know you*

13

- Have you ever tried to control somebody or something and found them or it uncontrollable? *[handwritten: Yes x10. my brother with his day use. And with 1559 with how she feels about me or whether she would stay in my life or her...]*

As fellow members of the human race, we all deal with life's hurts, hang-ups, and habits. In the next pages, we'll look at the *cause* of these hurts, hang-ups, and habits, their *consequences*, and their *cure*.

As we look at the causes and consequences of our pain, our spiritual poverty will become obvious. How can we be happy about being spiritually poor, as the beatitude for this chapter tells us we will be? Admitting the truth that we are spiritually poor—or powerless to control our tendency to do wrong—leads us to this happiness and to the cure we so desperately need.

[handwritten: Don't blame the pornstars for the cause of your problem. Don't blame your phone. Take Responsibility]

THE CAUSE OF OUR PROBLEMS

The cause of our problems is our nature! No, not the trees, rocks, and lakes kind of nature, but our human nature—that is, our sin nature. The Bible tells us that this sin nature gets us into all kinds of problems. We choose to do things that aren't good for us, even when we know better. We respond in hurtful ways when we are hurt. We try to fix problems, and often in our attempts to fix them, we only make them worse. The Bible says it this way: *"There is a way that seems right to a man, but in the end it leads to death."*[2] This verse lets us know we can't trust our human nature to lead us out of our problems. Left on its own, our sin nature will tend *to do wrong, desire to be God,* and *try to play God.*

1. Our Tendency to Do Wrong *[handwritten: Up and gave leave people because they might not want me. blue, but they run on excuses. I'm scared to get hurt. I'm scared to get uncomfortable.]*

We will always have this sin nature—this tendency to do the wrong thing. In fact, we will wrestle with it as long as we are on this earth. Even if you have already asked Christ into your life, even after you become a Christian, you still have desires that pull you in the wrong direction.

[handwritten: uncomfortable. When things are out of my control, I am very uncomfortable. You pull in when you are judging the next person in front of you because what they could be thinking of you, you are pulling in the wrong direction]

14

We find in the Bible that Paul understood this, for he struggled with his sin nature just as we do: *"I don't understand myself at all, for I really want to do what is right, but I don't do it. Instead, I do the very thing I hate. I know perfectly well that what I am doing is wrong . . . but I can't help myself, because it is sin inside me that makes me do these evil things."*[3]

We try to fix problems, and often in our attempts to fix them, we only make them worse.

Do Paul's words sound vaguely familiar to you? Sure they do. We end up doing what we *don't* want to do and not doing what we *do* want to do. For years I thought I could control my drinking. I believed the lie that I could stop whenever I wanted. It really wasn't that bad. My choices were not hurting anybody. I was deep into my denial. As the pain of my sin addiction got worse, I would try to stop on my own power. I was able to stop for a day, a week, or even a few months, but I would always start drinking again. I wanted to do what was right, but on my own I was powerless to change.

2. Our Desire to Be God

Why do we continue making poor choices? Why do we repeat the same mistakes? At the root of our human tendency to do wrong is our desire to be in control. We want to decide for ourselves what is right and what is wrong. We want to make our own choices, call our own shots, make our own rules. We don't want anybody telling us what to do. In essence, we want to be God. But this is nothing new. Trying to be God is humankind's oldest problem. In Genesis 3, even Adam and Eve tried to be in control. God put them in Paradise, and they tried to control Paradise. God told them, "You can do anything you want in

15

Paradise except one thing: Don't eat from this one tree." What did they do? You got it; they made a beeline for the forbidden tree—the only thing in Paradise God said was off-limits. Satan said, "If you eat this fruit, you will be like God."[4] And they wanted to be God. That's been our problem from the very start of humanity. Today, we still want to be God.

3. Our Attempts to Play God

We play God by denying our humanity and by trying to control everything for our own selfish reasons. We attempt to be the center of our own universe. We play God by trying to control our *image, other people,* our *problems,* and our *pain.*

We Try to Control Our Image

We care so much about what other people think of us. We don't want them to know what we're really like. We play games; we wear masks; we pretend; we fake it. We want people to see certain sides of us while we hide others. We deny our weaknesses, and we deny our feelings. "I'm not angry." "I'm not upset." "I'm not worried." "I'm not afraid." We don't want people to see the real us. Why are we afraid to tell people who we are? The answer is, "If I tell you who I really am and you don't like me, I'm in trouble—because then I'm all I've got." *I had that feeling so much in 2009-2013, where I couldn't find who I was. and I just felt constantly drained by people.*

We Try to Control Other People

Parents try to control kids; kids try to control parents. Wives try to control husbands; husbands try to control wives. Coworkers vie for office control. People try to control other people. And along the way we develop a lot of tools to manipulate each other. Everyone has his or her preferred methods: Some use guilt and shame; some use praise and affirmation.

Others use anger, fear, or an old favorite—the silent treatment. All in efforts to gain control.

We Try to Control Our Problems

"I can handle it," we say. "It's not really a problem." "I'm okay, really. I'm fine." Those are the words of somebody trying to play God. When we try to control our problems, we say, "I don't need any help, and I certainly don't need counseling or recovery." "I can quit anytime. I'll work it out on my own power." When a TV repairman was asked about the worst kind of damage he'd ever seen to a television set, he said, "The kind that results from people trying to fix their TVs on their own." The more we try to fix our problems by ourselves, the worse our problems get.

We Try to Control Our Pain

Have you ever thought about how much time and effort you spend running from pain? Trying to avoid it, deny it, escape it, reduce it, or postpone it? Some of us try to avoid pain by eating or not eating. Others try to postpone it by getting drunk, smoking, taking drugs, or abusing prescription medications. Some try to escape through sports, traveling, or jumping in and out of relationships. Others withdraw into a hole and build a protective wall of depression around themselves. Still others become angry, abusive, critical, and judgmental. We'll try almost anything to control our pain.

But the real pain comes when we realize, in our quieter moments, that no matter how hard we try, we're not in control. That realization can be very scary.

Agreeing with God that He's God and we're not leads us into our first healing choice:

CHOICE 1

Admitting NEED

Realize I'm not God.

I admit that I am powerless to control
my tendency to do the wrong thing
and that my life is unmanageable.

The first step is always the hardest, and this first choice is no exception. Until you are willing to admit your need and recognize that you are not God, you will continue to suffer the consequences of your poor choices. As the beatitude says, *"Happy are those who know they are spiritually poor."*[5] Admitting your need is what being "spiritually poor" is all about.

THE CONSEQUENCES OF OUR PROBLEMS

If the cause of most of our problems is our efforts to control everything, then what are the *consequences* of playing God? There are four:

1. Fear

When we try to control everything, we become afraid. Adam said, *"I was afraid because I was naked; so I hid."*[6] We are afraid somebody will find out who we really are—that we're fakes and phonies, that we really don't have it all together, that we're not perfect. We don't let anybody get close to us because they'll find out that we're scared inside, and so we fake it. We live in fear, afraid someone will reject us, not love us, or not like us when they know what we are really like. We believe they will only like the image we work to present. So we are afraid.

No more doing that.

2. Frustration

Trying to be the general manager of the universe is frustrating. Have you ever been to Chuck E. Cheese's? They have this game called Whac-

A-Mole. You use a big mallet to beat down these little moles that keep popping up. But when you whack one, three more pop up. You whack those, and five more pop up. That machine is a parable of life. We whack down one relational conflict and another pops up. We whack down one addiction or compulsion and another one pops up. It's frustrating because we can't get them all knocked down at the same time. We walk around pretending we're God: "I'm powerful; I can handle it." But if we're really in control, why don't we just unplug the machine?

The apostle Paul felt this same frustration: *"It seems to be a fact of life that when I want to do what is right, I inevitably do what is wrong. . . . There is something else deep within me . . . that is at war with my mind and wins the fight and makes me a slave to the sin."*[7] David felt it too: *"My dishonesty made me miserable and filled my days with frustration."*[8]

Frustration is a symptom of a much deeper issue: a failure to acknowledge that we are not God.

God's power is infinite. Our power is finite to the core.

3. Fatigue

Playing God makes us tired. Pretending we've got it all together is hard work. David experienced the fatigue of pretending: *"My strength evaporated like water on a sunny day until I finally admitted all my sins to you and stopped trying to hide them."*[9] Denial requires enormous amounts of emotional energy—energy that could be used in problem solving is actually diverted into problem denying, problem hiding, and problem avoiding.

Most of us try to run from the pain by keeping busy. We think, "I don't like the way I feel when I slow down. I don't like the sounds that go through my mind when I lay my head back on the pillow. If I just keep busy, maybe I can block out those feelings and drown out the sounds." We run from pain by constantly being on the go. We work ourselves to death, or we get involved in some hobby or sport until it becomes a compulsion. We're on the golf course or tennis court or somewhere all the time. Even over-involvement in religious activities can be an attempt to hide our pain. We say, "Look at me, look at all the ways I'm serving God." God does want you to serve Him out of love and purpose. He does not want you to use serving Him or the church to escape your pain.

You must admit that you're powerless to do it on your own—that you need other people, and you need God.

If you're in a constant state of fatigue, always worn out, ask yourself, "What pain am I running from? What problem am I afraid to face? What am I trying to hide? What motivates and drives me to work and work so that I'm in a constant state of fatigue?"

The problem I am afraid to face is that I might not have anything
4. Failure *hard to say to anyone that I am so unpacked out insecure.*
Fearful of economic insecurity

Playing God is one job where failure is guaranteed. You're not big enough. The wisdom of Proverbs tells us, *"You will never succeed in life if you try to hide your sins. Confess them and give them up; then God will show mercy to you."*[10] We need to be honest and open about our weaknesses, faults, and failures.

THE CURE FOR OUR PROBLEMS

The cure for our problems comes in a strange form: it comes through *admitting weakness* and through *a humble heart.*

Admitting Weakness

The Bible says that in admitting my weakness, I actually find strength. *"I just let Christ take over! And so the weaker I get, the stronger I become."*[11]

This is not a popular idea in our self-sufficient American culture that says, "Raise yourself up by your own bootstraps; don't depend on anybody else; do the Lone Ranger thing, be the strong, silent type." The Bible also says that knowing we are "spiritually poor" will make us happy.[12] This is the first step to getting your act together. You must admit that you're powerless to do it on your own—that you are spiritually poor—that you need other people, and you need God.

Making the first choice to healing means acknowledging that you are not God. Doing so means recognizing and admitting three important facts of life: *the pain of seeing my sword like disappear right in front of my eyes.*

1. *"I admit that I am powerless to change my past."*

   "It hurt. I still remember the pain, but all the resentment and shame in the world isn't going to change what happened. I'm powerless to change my past."

2. *"I admit that I am powerless to control other people."*

   "I try to control others. I actually like manipulating them. I use all kinds of little gimmicks, but it doesn't work. I am responsible for my actions, not theirs. I can't control other people."

3. *"I admit that I am powerless to cope with my harmful habits, behaviors, and actions."*

   "Good intentions don't cut it. Willpower is not enough. I need something more. I need a source of power beyond myself. I need God, because He made me to need Him."

A Humble Heart

A second portion of our cure is having a humble heart. God cannot work His change if our hearts are filled with pride. The Bible tells us that "*God opposes the proud but gives grace to the humble.*"[13] God's grace has the power to heal us, enabling us to *change*. Even after all we've talked about in this chapter, it's still difficult for us to admit our need. Our pride continues to insist that we can go it alone. Some of us may still be thinking, "I can do this on my own. I can solve my own problems." No. You can't. If you could, you would have already done so, but since you can't, you won't.

What needs changing in your life? What hurt or hang-up or habit have you been trying to ignore? Choosing to admit that you can't do it alone and that you need God is the first and hardest choice. It's hard to admit, "I have a problem, and I need help." Admitting we have a problem and giving it a name is humbling. Doing it says, "I'm not God, and I don't have it as together as I'd like everybody to think." If you admit that truth to someone else, he or she will not be surprised. Others know it, God knows it, and you know it. You just need to admit it. Stop right now and name the hurt, hang-up, or habit you've been trying to ignore. Then admit to God that you are powerless to manage your life on your own.

Congratulations! You've made the first choice on the road to healing!

Admitting that you have a hurt, hang-up, or habit is just the beginning. To implement this first choice, as well as the seven choices to come, you need to take three actions: (1) pray about it, (2) write about it, and (3) share about it. Working through these action steps is where the real work gets done. This is where the change happens. Some of you may be tempted to skip this part and just move on to the next chapter. *Don't do it!* These three interactive steps, found at the end of every chapter, are your pathway to healing. Make the first choice.

MAKE THE
Choice

Action 1: *Pray about It*

Ask God to give you the courage to admit your inability to control yourself or your world. Pray that you will begin to depend on His power to help you make positive changes. Ask God to take control of your life and help you stop trying to control your image, other people, your problems, and your pain. Let Him know you are weary of carrying the fear, the frustration, the fatigue, and the failures of trying to be the general manager of the universe.

If you do not know all the words to pray and say to God right now, don't worry. You can pray as David did, *"God! Please hurry to my rescue! God, come quickly to my side!"*[14] Or you can pray with me:

Dear God, I want to take the first choice to healing and spiritual health today. I realize I am not You, God. I've often tried to control my problems, my pain, my image, and even other people—as if I were You. I'm sorry. I've tried to deny my problems by staying busy and keeping myself distracted. But I want to stop running. I admit that I am helpless to control this tendency to do things I know are unhealthy for me. Today, I am asking for Your help. I humbly ask You to take all the pieces of my unmanageable life and begin the process of healing. Please heal me. Please give me the strength to choose health. Help me stick with this process for the next seven choices. In Your name, I pray. Amen.

God will hear your cry for help and is ready to provide you with His strength, power, perfect love, and complete forgiveness as you choose to take your first step to healing!

Action 2: *Write about It*

As you begin your journey through the 8 Healing Choices, it is important to write down your thoughts and insights. As God frees you from your hurts, hang-ups, and habits, He will reveal significant insights about yourself and others. Keep a daily journal of what God shows you and the progress and growth you are making day by day. Use the *Life's Healing Choices Journal*, a spiral notebook, or whatever works for you. Just a word of caution: *Keep your journal in a safe place!* What you write in your journal are your private thoughts. As we continue through the 8 Choices, you will learn when and with whom to share your journal notes.

The following questions will help you get started writing:

1. What people, places, or things do you have the power to control?

2. What people, places, or things have you been attempting to control? (Be specific.)

3. Describe how you try to control your image, other people, your problems, and your pain.

4. Write down how the fear, frustration, fatigue, and failures of trying to be the general manager of the universe has affected your relationships with God and others.

5. What specific hurts, hang-ups, or habits have you been denying?

Writing down the answers to these five questions was not easy, but it was a major beginning in your healing process. Now let's look at the third action.

Action 3: *Share about It*

As you move through the 8 Healing Choices, you will discover that you need to share the life-changing truths God is showing you with someone you trust. The wise writer of Ecclesiastes said, *"Two are better than one, because they have a good return for their work: If one falls down, his friend can help him up. But pity the man who falls and has no one to help him up! . . . Though one may be overpowered, two can defend themselves. A cord of three strands is not quickly broken."*[15]

The next few chapters will guide you in choosing this person. You'll be looking for someone you can honestly and openly talk to. This person needs to be nonjudgmental and someone with whom you can safely share your personal journal notes. This person should be willing to share his or her life and struggles with you as well. Once God shows you that safe person, set up a meeting time and ask him or her to join with you in this recovery journey toward healing by being your accountability partner. This person may be a relative, a friend, a neighbor, a coworker, someone in your small group, or someone in your church family.

Be sure the person you choose is of the same sex. You will be sharing very personal details of your life as you go through each of the healing choices. Some of the issues will be inappropriate to share with someone of the opposite sex.

As you work through the next few chapters, if you cannot find a safe person to share with, visit www.celebraterecovery.com to locate a Celebrate Recovery group near you. There you will find people who have worked through the 8 Choices and who will be glad to help and support you as you begin your healing journey. Just remember, this journey should not be traveled alone. You need others to listen to you, encourage you, support you, and demonstrate God's love to you.

If you choose to begin this journey, God will be faithful in giving you spiritual health and freedom from your life's hurts, hang-ups, and habits.

A little background: At Saddleback Church we're committed to being a "safe place," a place where people can talk about and deal with real problems—real hurts, real hang-ups, and real habits—without being blown away by judgmental opinions. We are a family of fellow strugglers. There is not a person in our church who has it all together. We're all weak in different areas, and we all need each other.

One of our most effective ministries at Saddleback is called Celebrate Recovery. This group is made up of hundreds of men and women dealing with all kinds of hurts, hang-ups, and habits. They all work together on the eight Christ-centered healing choices described in this book. At Celebrate Recovery they are called the 8 Principles.

At the conclusion of each chapter, you'll find two personal stories—testimonies from real people in Celebrate Recovery who have chosen to overcome their hurts, hang-ups, and habits through God's power.

These courageous individuals come from very different backgrounds with a variety of problems and issues. As you read their stories, please keep your heart and mind open. You will see how their journey relates to your own life or to someone's close to you.

Marnie's STORY

I wish I could start this story with "Once upon a time" or "There once was a little girl." But, instead, it starts with a broken home, torturous abuse, fits of rage, and those I held dearest to my heart stripped away from me. These are just some of the catalysts that led to my sinful lifestyle, filled with pornography, sex, and lust. My name is Marnie, and I'm a grateful believer who struggles with sexual addiction and anorexia.

My path to recovery started at Saddleback Church in November of 2000. I remember that night well. I crawled into the church building broken and unaware of reality. My view on life had become so distorted, and my actions so out of control, that I don't think the enemy himself could've kept up with me.

I arrived an hour early—unaware that the worship service didn't start until seven o'clock. I remember sitting there listening to the band rehearse while a handful of people walked around and set things up. Tears began to form in my eyes as I looked around, and I struggled to blink them back. I didn't know what I was doing there. Everything within me wanted to get up and walk out. I was still in denial. The same thoughts repeated in my head, *Whatever is wrong with these people is way worse than anything I could have done!* And, *Whatever I've done, I'm sure I can fix it on my own!* But for some reason, I could not bring myself to get up out of that chair and leave.

I was startled when a man came up to me, put his hand on my shoulder, and said, "Excuse me, but this seat is taken." As I looked around the empty room, it took me a moment to realize that he was kidding. Despite my confusion, I found comfort in his words. I felt welcomed and a little less "out of place."

That night happened to be the ninth anniversary of Celebrate Recovery. I watched as people started coming into the room—smiling, hugging, and celebrating. After a brief worship service, I attended Newcomers 101, where I confessed my secrets for the first time. The woman who led 101 that night came and sat beside me, cupped my hands in hers, and told me, "Everything's going to be okay. You've come to the right place." Though I must admit I was a bit skeptical, that was exactly what I needed to hear.

Long before I was born, my family was plagued with turmoil. My parents divorced before my first birthday, and after they separated, they sent my older sister and me to live with my father and grandparents in Hawaii. My father was absent most of the time, so my grandparents were unofficially assigned to care for us. My fondest childhood memories are of the years I spent with my grandparents in Hawaii. They taught me about Jesus, and by their example I learned Christian values. Thankfully, they showed me what it was like to live in a "normal" family. My parents, on the other hand, were the opposites of my grandparents.

My father was a functioning alcoholic, and his negligence as a parent allowed me more freedom than was good for me. I remember crouching in a corner with my sister trying to smoke some of my dad's cigarettes and drink some of his beer. One day while snooping around the house, I found my dad's *Playboy* collection hidden in his dresser drawers. I felt as though I had just stumbled onto a secret, and I ran out of the room. At the same time, I was intrigued by the *Playboy* images.

When I was five or six, I moved back to California to live with my mother. She was physically, verbally, and emotionally abusive. I vividly remember walking in on my mom during one of her fits of rage. She slapped me in the face so hard my tooth punctured my lip. I had a huge, fat lip and black eye the following day. I told everyone I was eating and my fork slipped. My mom would always apologize and say she hated what she had done, but in the next breath, she'd tell me I deserved it. Sometimes I'd have to go to the hospital. I remember the doctors sending my mother out of the room and asking, "Did your mother hit you?" With a stoic face, my response was always a simple shake of the head, *no*.

Throughout my childhood, I was my mother's human piñata. She would choke me and throw objects at me daily. I was beaten with lamps, hangers, and high-heeled shoes. To cope, I escaped into a fantasy life filled with lustful thoughts and pornographic images. I would stay in bed for hours fanaticizing about sexual acts, replaying the same dreams again and again in my head.

A seemingly endless amount of turmoil filled my upbringing. I had to escape the insanity I was living in. So when I turned seventeen—just before the start of my senior year of high school—I emancipated myself. I moved out and was on my own. I was determined to break the cycle of dysfunction I'd lived in all of my life. But as it turns out, I had become a product of my environment.

I married my high school sweetheart in June of 1998. Marriage started off difficult for us. Although we dated for eight years before getting married, as soon as we got married, it seemed that, in an instant, we were miles apart. Our conversations became superficial, we struggled financially, and we lived with his parents. The enemy sank his fangs into me as I viewed my marriage as a mistake. Bitterness, resentment, and anger started to paint an ugly picture as my visions of a "normal" lifestyle fell by the wayside. We went through months of arguments and broken promises. I felt like I was running in place. I felt like I had no voice and no control. Most of all, I felt emotionally bankrupt.

My addictive lifestyle started to take shape when I took a new position at work that required me to travel often. All of this free time away from my husband gave me the freedom to make my own choices, which led to unhealthy behaviors. In my denial, life never felt so good. I was getting attention from men I hardly knew. I began to punish myself for these behaviors by starving my body, both spiritually and physically. Body image became of the utmost importance to me. I put myself on a rigid diet consisting of a handful of grapes each day and excessive amounts of Diet Coke. I started working out obsessively, running between twelve and fifteen miles a day. This lifestyle, coupled with my sexual addiction, left my body weak and out of fuel. I weighed a mere ninety-two pounds; my face was sunken and my skin gaunt. I was rapidly self-destructing. My addiction was now in full throttle.

I became more independent of my marriage every day. I felt in control. I was finally doing something I thought I wanted to do instead of having to live by someone else's rules. But in my heart I knew something was desperately wrong. I struggled with confusion about the Christian values I learned as a child versus what the world views as socially acceptable behavior. I suddenly felt as if I only knew these childhood beliefs intellectually, and my relationship with the Lord was nonexistent. I ignored thoughts about God and replaced them with alcohol, anorexia, and adultery. I was on a suicide mission devoted to a life of deception. My life mirrored the very women I had been warned against in my childhood Bible lessons: Jezebel, Potiphar's wife, and Delilah—yes, Delilah. My life had become a reflection of this woman whose greatest accomplishment in life was destroying the man who loved her most.

As a child, I'd had a lot of practice pretending all was well. So I'd walk into work with a smile on my face, balanced, poised, and professional. Then I would walk into my office, shut the door, and act out with Internet pornography and chat rooms. When with my college friends, I played the innocent codependent Marnie—the "good girl," the Marnie who never drank, but took care of the rest of the bunch when they did.

And believe it or not, I was still going to church. At church, I was the devout Christian, pseudo listening from a concrete bench outside of the worship center, making sure my friends and family knew I was present and accounted for.

But the real Marnie, the uninhibited Marnie, surfaced after work hours. I would spend most of my free time at bars with the "good old boys club." I could tell a good dirty joke with the rest of them. The more I drank, the more I talked. The more I talked, the more I blamed my circumstances for my behavior. I had a completely cavalier disregard and disrespect for myself and for those around me.

I didn't know how to resolve these conflicting pieces of my past. The pain had finally become greater than the fear. I had reached my bottom. As I watched the scenes of my life unfold, I became desperate to find freedom from my life of lies. I picked up the phone and called Saddleback Church. They suggested I try Celebrate Recovery, and I finally did.

During those first few weeks, I began to recall the Christian values taught to me as a child by my grandparents, which I had buried because of my anger and resentment toward God. But He now had my attention, and I began to realize the truth of this Scripture passage: "I don't understand myself at all, for I really want to do what is right, but I can't. I do what I don't want to—what I hate. I know perfectly well that what I am doing is wrong, and my bad conscience proves that I agree with these laws I am breaking. But I can't help myself because I'm no longer doing it. It is sin inside me that is stronger than I am that makes me do these evil things."[16]

Two months after that first night at Celebrate Recovery, a women's

Step Study opened. I picked up a Bible and a set of *Celebrate Recovery Participant Guides,* and began a pilgrimage through the eight steps. I found women I could relate to and who could also relate to me. At first I kept myself at a safe distance. I still guarded my secrets so no one could use what they knew to hurt me. I also felt hideously ugly, and I thought the scars on my heart and soul were visible to everyone.

When I finally shared for the first time, I saw women who listened without judgment. I began to understand that the pains of my past played an important part in my behavior and that I was in a cycle of addiction. All my life I had viewed men as objects and had been living out what I had experienced in my childhood. I had kept so many secrets. Saying them out loud brought truth to my reality; I found comfort in the fact that I could not be perfect. Most important, I saw how far away from my relationship with Christ I had fallen. "Problems far too big for me to solve are piled higher than my head. Meanwhile my sins, too many to count, have all caught up with me, and I am ashamed to look up."[17]

Admitting NEED

Realize I'm not God.

I admit that I am powerless to control my tendency to do the wrong thing and that my life is unmanageable.

CHOICE 1

I began exploring uncharted territory at Celebrate Recovery. It was after working Principle 4, where I "openly examined and confessed my faults to myself, to God, and to someone I trust," that true healing began. It was then I heard God's promise of freedom and stopped acting out. It was then that I realized that "whatever is covered up will be uncovered, and every secret will be made known. So then, whatever you have said in the dark will be heard in broad daylight."[18]

As I laid my sins at the foot of the cross and turned from my addictions, God declared me not guilty. He "blotted out the charges proved against you, the list of his commandments which you had not obeyed. He took this list of sins and destroyed it by nailing it to Christ's cross."[19]

I have reconciled my relationship with my husband, and today we have a beautiful marriage built on honesty and trust. The challenges are still there. Marriage takes work, and my view on marriage is that every couple needs to argue now and then just to prove the relationship is strong enough to survive. We are blessed with the most precious gifts of all, two beautiful girls. My new ministry in life is my family. Where they once played second fiddle to my work and my addictive behavior, they are now my priority.

As for my mother, I have found it in my heart to forgive her. I still do not have a relationship with her, even though attempts have been made throughout the years. I remain steadfast in the fact that she is not a safe person.

My dad has since passed away, but we were privileged to create an amazing ending to our story before he passed. Nine months before he died, I went back to where my life with him began, Hawaii. It was the first time we had seen each other in fifteen years. We made our amends, but more important, he met his granddaughters for the first time. From that moment on it was like no time at all had passed. I look back at the time we spent not talking to each other and I think, *What a waste of fifteen years.* I wish I'd had more time with him in the end, but God gave me those last nine months, and for that I'm eternally grateful. Had we not taken that leap of faith to mend our relationship, I would be grieving his death very differently today. Thankfully, my last moments with my dad are joyful memories.

Reflecting on my life now, I thank God for His never failing truth and understanding. I look back at the journey I had to take through Celebrate Recovery to bring balance to the chaos of my life. I use the tools I learned in CR daily, and I continue my obedience to Christ to live out my life as a wife, mother, and employee.

There was a season of my life when the world made no sense. My allegiance lay in the success of my betrayals and the comfort of my sin. Today, God has taken my tragedy and used it as a testament of my faith. I thank God that, unlike Delilah, my life has not been wasted. God chose to spare me, and I'm no longer defined by my past mistakes and failures. It's only by God's grace that when I look at myself in the mirror today, I no longer see an adulterer, an alcoholic, or an anorexic. I see myself as an incredibly blessed mother, wife, and forgiven child of God. I've learned how to embrace pain and make the choice to abandon the life of deception and destruction.

Remember when I talked about traveling every week without my husband, finding myself in compromising situations, and how my addictions were born out of those situations? Ironically, the pattern of traveling that almost destroyed my life is now being used by God to restore me to wholeness. Today I get to serve as the Celebrate Recovery Conference Director, and it is my privilege to travel every other week to help coordinate Celebrate Recovery One Day Seminars and Summits. My accountability team spans across the nation as I have filled my life with godly women and men from whom I seek guidance every day. And trust me, with an accountability partner in almost every state, there's no hiding anymore.

I am reminded of God's promise in Deuteronomy: "Even though you are at the ends of the earth, the Lord your God will go and find you and bring you back again."[20] The scripture below has become one of my life verses.

There was a time when I wouldn't admit what a sinner I was.
But my dishonesty made me miserable
and filled my days with frustration.
All day and all night your hand was heavy on me.
My strength evaporated like water on a sunny day
until I finally admitted all my sins to you
and stopped trying to hide them.
I said to myself, "I will confess them to the Lord."
And you forgave me! All my guilt is gone.[21]

Drew's STORY

My name is Drew, and I'm a grateful believer in Jesus who struggles with addiction and codependency.

My parents were both raised by parents who were hardworking, salt-of-the-earth types, who were familiar with heavy-handed discipline. Drinking was not just social in their families; it was a part of the day-to-day landscape of everyone's life. Shame and guilt, verbal and emotional abuse, and physical intimidation were all part of their parents' parental discipline toolbox. While it may not have been their wish to pass along such methods, it's true that hurting people hurt other people in the way they were hurt. And so I experienced a good number of those devices in my upbringing.

Though I do have many fond memories from my childhood, my dad's upbringing left him an emotionally hardened perfectionist. Affirmation was nonexistent. Insults, put-downs, and constant reminders that I couldn't do anything right, that I wouldn't succeed, and that I would never amount to anything were normal messages I received in my life. The constant rehearsal of these reminders left me feeling insignificant, inadequate, incapable, and unloved. The result, I felt alone and on the outside in my family and with peers.

Like most children, I desperately wanted the approval of my parents. It became my goal to prove to them I was worthy of it. However, all my efforts failed, regardless of how hard I tried or what I accomplished. Even so, I continually tried to gain their approval, only to be met with disappointment. This happened over and over throughout my teen years and well into my adulthood. I frantically searched to find someone—anyone—to validate me. I was willing to do anything just to fit in somewhere and feel accepted.

Medicating my emotional pain was easy with drugs. I drank a little but didn't like the hangovers, so I thought drugs were a perfect fit. At a young age I also turned to sex. Being involved with someone gave me a certain sense of power because in the moment I felt accepted and loved. However, I failed to see that it too was just an illusion. It was simply another way to medicate myself.

I did do some positive things in my teen years that you would think should have worked in my favor. I was in drama and had a good-paying job at the local grocery store, which allowed me to buy a brand-new sports car while still in high school. My job also provided me with an abundance of spending money. I used the money to buy friends and impress my high school girlfriends. Rather than encouraging confidence, however, my pursuits only bred arrogance. Sadly, I can remember one of my teachers asking what I was going to do after college. I smugly replied, "Why would I want to go to college to be like you? I make more money than you, and I'm still in high school." Arrogance has its price, as I barely graduated from high school and had alienated some of the most caring people I had ever known.

At age nineteen, I met my wife Robin. She too lived with false messages. While we hit it off pretty good, the foundation of our relationship was largely meeting each other's needs in unhealthy ways. By the third year of our marriage, I had done just about everything I could to destroy our relationship. My drug use increased. I was unfaithful and made it clear to her that she could never reach my expectations. Does that sound familiar? Truly, hurting people do hurt others the way they were hurt.

It was also now that I began mixing as many different kinds of drugs as I could in order to get a bigger and better high. The result was unconsciousness and admission to a psychiatric hospital. I remember waking up in a dimly lit room. I couldn't move and felt drool running down the corner of mouth. I think this was the first time I began to realize I was powerless. As I opened my eyes and struggled to focus, I could make out the outline of someone standing over me inquiring, "Why are you here?"

I tried to respond, but could only make gurgling sounds.

"Oh, they must have hit you up with Thorazine or Loxitane," the person said. "You won't be able to move for a couple of days, but eventually it'll wear off. My name's Tom," he continued. "I'm in here for sexual issues."

It occurred to me that the person speaking was not a doctor, but another patient, whose level of sanity was completely unknown to me. I had no ability to respond, defend myself, or even cry out for help should the person behind the strange voice mean me harm. I finally realized, *Drew, your life is unmanageable.*

That moment was sobering, but my struggle to stay in control of my life was far from over. Following my wake-up call in the psychiatric hospital, I experienced about a year of sobriety from drugs. Then I started telling myself all the lies that addicts do: "I can do it once in a while, and I won't get hooked again." "I'll just keep it limited to pot." . . . and so on.

After only a month, I was right back where I was the year before. I was getting wasted first thing in the morning, at lunch, on the way home from work, and all night long. I was mixing as many drugs as I could to achieve a bigger and better high. A deep sense of hopelessness returned. I knew I was back on the path to self-destruction.

Romans 2:4 states, "Don't you see how wonderfully kind, tolerant, and patient God is with you? Does this mean nothing to you? Can't you see that his kindness is intended to turn you from your sin?"[22]

God had been revealing Himself to me for some time, but it had been easy up till then to ignore His voice. I finally decided to pray one of those prayers God loves to hear, "God if You're really there, show me what is wrong in my life."

In that moment, my selfishness, addictions, inability to love, and all the damage I had done became clear. I saw myself nailing Jesus to the cross—one hand at a time—then His feet. Then I saw myself standing in front of the cross, laughing at Jesus as He hung to die. In that moment the words I heard in my heart were almost audible, *"Drew, if you love Me, you'll obey Me."*

I understood then the cost of my actions was the torturous death Jesus experienced on the cross. I realized God's patience and love for me. His invitation to enter into relationship with Him became clear. I no longer wanted to be a crucifier. I understood I needed to make a choice over who was going to be in control of my life.

CHOICE 1

Admitting NEED
Realize I'm not God.
I admit that I am powerless to control my tendency to do the wrong thing and that my life is unmanageable.

I so wanted to make that choice. As I sat in the presence of God, I couldn't help but be honest with Him. I realized just how powerless I was. I loved my sin—the drugs, the porn, and acting out sexually. I confessed to the Lord that I wished it wasn't so. I knew I loved these choices more than anything else, including Him. *"Change my heart, oh God,"* I cried. *"Take away my affection for my sin and replace it with a devoted love for You."*

After praying that prayer, I could feel a deep sense of peace. I understood that God wasn't asking me to measure up to find favor with Him through an act of my own will. He had been waiting for me to invite Him into my life to do the impossible. He wanted to do something for me, in me, and through me that I could not do for myself. In that moment, something very supernatural happened to me. I felt my affection for drugs leave my body. This year I'm experiencing thirty-five years of recovery over drugs.

Dealing with my drug problem was only the beginning. God intended to show me that not only did He love me, but that I could trust Him. He put His finger on my marriage and convicted me of the need to come clean and make amends with my wife about my affair. I argued with God that she would leave. He told me to trust Him. What made this hard was remembering that she had been sexually abused in her past. I knew my actions would only confirm every fear she ever had about men. They can't be trusted.

There's no good way to break someone's heart. I remember having a moment where we were happy and laughing and then soberly changing the subject and confessing my sin to her. As I did, her expression changed from contentment and joy to incredible pain and betrayal. It was like watching a precious piece of crystal shatter in my arms. It was not an easy process of restoration. God needed to do something for us, in us, and through us that we just could not do for ourselves. Although I was truly repentant and wanted to be the man she deserved, she had to rely on God to help her overcome her anger and fear and replace it with forgiveness and trust. I am so thankful she did! I know I didn't deserve her forgiveness or trust. Through her forgiveness, I received an understanding of what it means to experience grace beyond measure. God again showed Himself to be faithful as this year we are celebrating thirty-eight years of marriage.

However, God was not done yet. He started showing me that He created me with unique design and purpose. The Bible tells us, "For we are God's masterpiece. He has created us anew in Christ Jesus, so we can do the good things he planned for us long ago."[23]

For years, the messages of inadequacy I carried made it difficult for me to believe that I had the ability to succeed. Regardless of how much I did or achieved, all I felt was rejection and put-downs. One of the greatest sources of these feelings was that I had chosen not to go to college. The words I had spoken to my teachers long ago had come back to haunt me.

While I was in the grocery business, I was told that I wouldn't be considered for the store manager's training program because I didn't have a college education. Yet despite that, the company had the college graduates train under me due to their lack of experience.

After fourteen years in grocery, God provided an opportunity for us to work in full-time ministry in a Christian residential group home for at-risk teenage boys. Finally, I was getting a chance to work with God's people: *Surely I won't have to worry about put-downs and trying to prove myself*, I thought.

It didn't take long to realize this was a fallacy. At a staff meeting, I shared a thought about a treatment plan for one of our boys. Someone commented, "That may sound like a really good idea, but you don't have any formal training or college."

Instantly invalidated, I had enough! *I'm going to show them!* I thought. Since I've never done things halfway, I decided to go back to school to pursue a PhD in psychology.

I knew getting accepted into grad school meant I would need to get almost perfect grades in college and get research experience. The fact that I'd never cared about grades in high school haunted me. However, I was a man on a mission. I treated school like a business. I was completely focused. The first quarter I received the first 4.0 GPA ever in my life. Semester after semester, I continued to duplicate my success for the next four years. During the last quarter of my senior year, while working on my thesis, I survived on less than four hours of sleep a night. Each morning I left home at 4:30 for the seventy-five-mile drive over a mountain pass to school.

God showed me tremendous favor through college. I got near-perfect grades and completed the research necessary to move forward. I won the president's medallion for the highest grade point average in the School of Sciences. I say this not to brag, but simply to testify of God's abundant grace. It's amazing how God will allow us to have our way, only to show us His ways are higher than ours.

The last week of my senior year, the sun was breaking over the pass during my early morning drive. I saw an eighteen-wheel truck swerving wildly all over the road, heading right for me. Eventually, he straightened up. I noticed he had hit a deer. The deer was completely crushed from the back hindquarter with its entrails hanging out. Yet surprisingly, it was still alive and desperately tried to crawl off the road.

It was only a short way up the road when God began to speak with me. *"Did you see that deer back there? That was you. You believe that by getting the grades, doing the research, and showing everyone they were wrong you're going to be okay. But you're dead and don't even know it."*

Wow, that smarted. The truth can set you free, but it sure can hurt first.

Why did God say that to me? Didn't He know that I was going to have to defend my thesis in a few hours and take my first final? What's with that? The rest of the trip to school, all I could think about was that deer and me, both dead and not even knowing it.

Shaken and rattled, I went to my counseling professor and shared what had happened. As I did, he asked, "So what's really the matter?"

"I told you," I said, and repeated what I had seen.

He repeated himself, "So what's really the matter?"

It was clear he wasn't going to let me off the hook and that he was looking for me to get honest with him and myself.

Eventually, I burst into uncontrollable sobbing and finally admitted that I had spent my entire life trying to get the approval of others, particularly my parents. Again, I began to realize just how powerless I was over my hurts and how much they controlled me. And even though I was in perfect position to pursue a PhD, I also realized with perfect clarity that it wasn't God's plan or purpose for my life. I knew long ago that He wired me to be a pastor. It was as if the Lord let me pursue what I wanted, just to show me it wouldn't fill that hole in my identity. God showed me that it could only be filled by truly understanding who I was in Him and His purpose for my life.

Over the next ten years, I learned to keep good boundaries with my parents. However, I still held on to bitterness toward my father for never giving me the affirmation and approval I believed I deserved. Eventually, after becoming involved in a Celebrate Recovery program at our church, one of my trusted accountability partners challenged me that I needed to ask my dad for forgiveness for the bitterness I was holding on to. At first I was indignant. But God showed me there was still unfinished business that needed to be dealt with. The Lord helped me to realize that because of the brokenness in my dad's upbringing, he himself had never experienced affirmation. I was expecting him to give me something he simply did not possess—much like expecting someone who has been blind his whole life to describe the color green. God not only prompted me to ask for his forgiveness, but also to pour affirmation over him in ways that he had never experienced. I let him know just how much God Himself loved him.

As I shared my amends, my dad was speechless. It was as if he had new understanding of his own existence. He was finally free of the messages he was carrying during his lifetime. Our relationship completely changed on that day. Today, we are extremely close.

After having spent the better part of the last thirty years in full-time ministry, I'm totally amazed by just how much God has blessed me. Previously I was powerless over the sin that held me in bondage and was living without purpose. The Lord has now set me free to fully understand the meaning of Jeremiah 29:11: "'For I know the plans I have for you,' declares the LORD, 'plans to prosper you and not to harm you, plans to give you hope and a future.'"[24]

In the past I would do anything and everything to feel good about myself. I've come to realize that without Christ, it was impossible for me to find relief from the deep-rooted feelings of inadequacy and lack of purpose I lived with. Now, through my relationship with Jesus, I truly know who I am and why I exist.

Thank you for letting me share.

It is my prayer that the honesty and openness of Marnie and Drew help you to consider the hurts, hang-ups, or habits in your own life and how you can make Choice 1: "Realize I'm not God. I admit that I am powerless to control my tendency to do the wrong thing and that my life is unmanageable." Once you make this choice, your life's healing journey can begin!

R

Earnestly believe that God exists,

that I *matter* to Him, and that He
has the power to help me recover.

C

O

V

E

R

Y

"Happy are those who mourn, for they shall be comforted."[1]

Getting HELP

The Hope Choice

It doesn't rain much in Southern California. And it rarely rains enough to cause any flooding. But several years ago it rained so hard that a portion of Lake Forest actually flooded! Glen lives in a low area. The flooding was so bad that the *Orange County Register* sent a reporter, in a boat, out to Glen's neighborhood. The reporter found Glen's wife, Jo Ann, sitting on their roof watching large objects floating by, so he climbed up on the roof to interview her.

As the reporter questioned Jo Ann, he saw a Weber barbecue float by, and then he saw a large golden retriever pass by on top of his doghouse, and finally, a sport utility vehicle! A few minutes later, he saw a hat float by; but after it floated about twenty feet past the house, it started floating back upstream. When it got about twenty feet on the other side of the house, it started floating back down again. The reporter watched the hat go by seven or eight times, and finally he asked Jo Ann, "Do you have any idea how that hat is floating up and down stream?"

47

"Oh, that's just my crazy husband, Glen. He said he was going to mow the lawn today, come hell or high water."

The problem with many of us is that we are still focusing on the lawn while our home is floating away. We have the crazy notion that we are in control.

In the first chapter, we learned that no matter how hard we try to keep everything under control, we are powerless to control our tendency to do wrong and that our lives are unmanageable. In this chapter we'll begin moving out of the role of playing God and into the role of receiving God's power. We will also gain a vision of the hope and help God offers us. But first, we'll look at two of God's blessings in disguise: grief and pain—and when we do, we'll learn how to tap into God's power.

GRIEF: GOD'S PATHWAY TO COMFORT

All of us have broken areas in our lives—things that bring us deep grief and pain. In fact, the things we carry around can be downright devastating. When we carry a hurt for a long time, we eventually find our identity in that hurt and become a victim. We may try to escape our pain by using drugs or alcohol. Or we may try to control all those around us with anger. The list goes on and on.

Just as grief is God's pathway to comfort, pain is God's antidote for denial.

As we work through the 8 Choices of this book, we will come face-to-face with truths about ourselves and our lives that we have tried to hide—and hide from—perhaps our whole lives. We begin to experience hurt and a sense of loss. This is the process of "mourning," and it brings a whole new kind of pain. We mourn over our past mistakes, and we even mourn over our loss of control. In the end, God leads us to His comfort, if we will just trust in Him. As the beatitude for this choice says, *"Happy are those who mourn, for they shall be comforted."*[2]

We Mourn Our Past Mistakes

As you do the work of the 8 Choices in this book, you may begin to grieve over your past and find yourself filled with regret: "I wish I hadn't made those dumb decisions . . . I wish I hadn't responded as I did . . . I wish I hadn't done what I did . . . I wish . . ." It starts to dawn on us that we have hurt people and we have been hurt by others.

We Mourn Our Loss of Control

Even though we never were really in control, we thought we were. Facing up to that fact brings a sense of real loss. Mourning is what happens when we finally face the truth of Choice 1: admitting that we are powerless to control our tendency to do wrong and that our lives are unmanageable.

We Discover God's Pathway to Comfort

As long as we don't get stuck in the mourning process, mourning can serve as the pathway to comfort and to the help and hope God has ready for us. The same promise God gave His people of old, He gives us today: *"To all who mourn in Israel, he will give beauty for ashes, joy instead of mourning, praise instead of despair. For the Lord has planted them like strong and graceful oaks for his own glory."*[3]

PAIN: GOD'S ANTIDOTE FOR DENIAL

Just as grief is God's pathway to comfort, pain is God's antidote for denial. In reality, denial is a kind of sickness and needs a powerful antidote. As strange as it may sound, *pain* is that antidote. C. S. Lewis helps us understand: "God whispers to us in our pleasures, speaks in our conscience, but shouts in our pain. Pain is God's megaphone to rouse a deaf world."[4] Pain is God's way of letting us know something is seriously wrong and needs our attention. If your appendix bursts, and you felt no pain, you wouldn't know your body needed help. The toxins from your appendix would infect your abdominal cavity and could eventually kill you. Pain alerts us to our need for help.

Pain is also God's fire alarm. If a fire alarm went off in your house, I don't think you'd say, "Oh, there goes that stupid fire alarm again! Somebody throw a rock at it and make it stop." Hopefully, you would do something about it. You would call the fire department and get some help. But when our "pain alarm" goes off, instead of dealing with the source of the pain, we often try to cover up the sound. We try to mute the noise with people, work, food, alcohol, sex, and many, many different things. If you ignore the alarm, your house could burn down.

An important point needs to be made here. Just because God *allows* pain to enter your life does not mean that He *causes* the pain, and it certainly doesn't mean that He enjoys seeing you in pain. Pain is often a consequence of our poor choices or the poor choices of others. God allows the natural consequences of these poor choices to play out. This is not the same thing as Him causing our pain. God loves us and wants to lead us out of our pain and into His healing. The miracle is that He brings *good* out of our pain by using it to lead us to His comfort and away from our denial.

With that said, take a look at yourself: How's your pain level? Is God using your pain to get your attention?

Denial—Refusing God's Power to Help

To deny your pain is to refuse God's power to help you recover. You will never find healing from your hurts, hang-ups, and habits until you confront your pain. Unless you've lived a perfect life, it's a sure thing

that you struggle with some kind of issue. How ba
relationship, pain, or memory have to get before you
your denial and admit you cannot handle it by yourself

Remember, if you could have handled that probler
wouldn't still be a problem. If you could handle it, you would have; but
you can't, so you don't.

Sometimes in our denial, we excuse ourselves and we accuse others:
"If my wife would just get her act together, then our marriage would be
just fine." We play the blame game. Do you know how you spell blame? B-
LAME! When we blame others for something we did, we are being lame!

Other forms of denial are just as strange. When someone asks us
how we're doing, we often say "I'm fine" or "So far, so good." Who are we
kidding? We could say the same thing if we'd just jumped off a building
and were halfway down. We haven't hit bottom yet, so we say we're
"fine . . . so far, so good."

Instead of denying your pain, allow it to motivate you to get help, to
start making healing choices, to face the issue that you've been ignoring
for ten, twenty, maybe thirty years. *Don't refuse God's power to help.*

God's Denial Busters

We rarely change when life is cool and comfortable. We change when
we feel the heat. We start to change after our marriage falls apart or after
our kids go off in the wrong direction. One man said, "The acid of my
pain finally ate through the wall of my denial." Unfortunately, we usually
don't change until our fear of change is exceeded by our pain. Most people
never choose to move toward healing until there is no other option.

God uses three denial busters to get our attention, to force us to
move into recovery and away from the choices and circumstances that
have messed up our lives:

ᵗˢ

God uses the pain of an unexpected crisis to shatter our denial: illness caused by years of substance abuse, stress brought on by workaholism, job loss due to inappropriate actions, or a divorce due to infidelity.

Confrontation

God can also use the people in our lives who care for us—people who care enough to say, "You're blowing it." He uses people who love us enough to confront us in truth and love and say, "You're about to lose your health." "You're about to lose your job." "You're about to lose your family."

There is an old saying in Texas: "If one person calls you a horse's rear, ignore it. If two people call you a horse's rear, look in the mirror. If three people call you a horse's rear, buy a saddle." If three people say you need to get some help with a hurt, hang-up, or habit—get some help!

Catastrophe

When the bottom falls out—physically, emotionally, spiritually, financially, relationally—God sometimes just steps back and lets us feel the full impact of our own poor choices. "You want to be God? Okay, have it your way."

Don't ignore your pain. Recognize it as God's denial buster and open yourself up to the hope and power He offers.

Choice 1 says, "I admit it. I'm helpless. I'm powerless." Choice 2 says, "There is a power greater than me, and there is hope. There is a power I can plug into that will help me handle things I can't handle on my own." That is the good news!

CHOICE 2

Getting HELP

Earnestly believe that God exists,

that I matter to Him, and that He
has the power to help me recover.

As we'll see in the remainder of this chapter, Choice 2 is made up of three magnificent truths about God: (1) *He exists*, (2) *I matter to Him*, and (3) *He has the power to help me*. As we begin to understand each truth, we'll see that each one involves a choice on our part—a choice to believe and a choice to receive. Unless we make this choice, His power cannot become real in our lives.

THE TRUTH ABOUT GOD

1. God Exists

The Bible makes it clear that belief in God is essential: *"Anyone who comes to him must believe that he exists and that he rewards those who earnestly seek him."*[5]

Most people do acknowledge that God exists. Why? Because it takes more faith not to believe in a creator than it does to believe in one. If you took your watch completely apart, put the pieces in a paper bag, shook it up, and dumped the bag out on a table, the odds of the pieces coming together randomly as a complete watch would be pretty incredible. And the world is much more complex than your watch. Where there is an effect, there must be a cause. Where there is design, there must be a designer. Where there is a creation, there must be a Creator. *"Since the creation of the world God's invisible qualities—his eternal power and divine nature—have been clearly seen."*[6]

2. You Matter to Him

Since most people believe God exists, the real issue becomes, "What kind of God is He? Do I really matter to Him?"

The reason a lot of us don't know we matter to God is that we don't really know what God is like. And sometimes, when we don't have adequate information, we just make up our own. We say, "God as I understand Him" or, "My idea about God is . . ." Just because we have a certain idea about God doesn't mean it's right. Our personal conception of God is not what matters. What matters is the *truth* of who He is. And sometimes we just don't have the correct information.

Our misconceptions about God confuse our picture of Him. Unfortunately, a lot of people think God is like one of their parents. People who had abusive fathers tend to think God, the Father, is abusive. Those whose mothers were aloof and unloving may think God is aloof and unloving. Those who had reason to fear their parents tend to be afraid of God.

Until we begin to understand God's true character, we can't completely trust Him. It's hard to trust something or someone we do not know about or understand. Fortunately, we have a God who *cares* about us. We matter to Him.

Understanding the following truths about God's character gives us hope when we're in pain:

God Knows about Your Situation

God knows your hurts, hang-ups, and habits. He knows the good and bad. When we have had a tough week or month or life, we may think that no one really cares: "Nobody knows the pain I'm going through in this marriage." We're wrong; God knows. Or maybe we think, "Nobody knows how I'm struggling to break this habit." God knows. Perhaps we think,

"Nobody knows the depression and fear I'm going through." God knows. He knows it all. And He cares. Nothing escapes His notice. King David had plenty of sorrow in his life, and he said of God, "*You have listened to my troubles and have seen the crisis in my soul.*"[7] God sees the crisis you may be going through right now. "*Your Father knows what you need before you ask him.*"[8] "*The Lord is close to the brokenhearted and saves those who are crushed in spirit.*"[9] God is with you in your pain, and He is able to help you overcome your hurts, hang-ups, and habits.

> *Until we understand God's true character, we can't completely trust Him.*

Did you know that God keeps a record of every tear that has fallen down your cheek? "*You know how troubled I am. You have kept a record of my tears.*"[10] Isn't that incredible? You have never, ever shed a tear that God missed. Nothing is beyond His love; nothing is beyond His compassionate gaze. He is with you, and He is aware of everything you've gone through, are going through, and will go through.

Job said of God, "*You keep close watch on all my paths.*"[11] God is watching over you; nothing escapes His eye. Sometimes we wish God didn't have to see all the poor choices we make. The fact is, nothing is off the record with God: "*You know how foolish I am.*"[12] God is not shocked by your sin. He knew it was coming long before you did. He knows why you did it, even when you don't. He knows your good days, your bad days, your foolish decisions, and all your secrets. Amazingly, He still loves you!

God Cares about Your Situation

Not only does God know about your situation, He cares all about it and you: "*As a father has compassion on his children, so the Lord has* compassion on those who fear him; for he knows how we are formed, he remembers that we are dust."[13] God made us, so He knows what we're made of—mere molecules—and He knows that we're frail creatures. God wants to be the Father that many of us never had. He is tender and sympathetic toward us. He says to us, "I have loved you with an everlasting love."[14] He cares about us when we serve Him and when we don't, when we're right and when we're wrong. How can God love and care about us when our lives are so messed up? Because His love for us is unconditional. It is not based on our performance. It is based on His character. This is how much God cares about us: "God showed his great love for us by sending Christ to die for us."[15] There is no greater love than this: that a man "lay down his life for his friends."[16] And this is exactly what Jesus did for you.

3. God Has the Power to Change You and Your Situation

Sometimes God changes you; sometimes He changes your situation. Sometimes He changes both. He's got the power. The magnitude of this power is hard to comprehend, so the apostle Paul prayed for our understanding: "I pray that you will begin to understand the incredible greatness of his power for us who believe him. This is the same mighty power that raised Christ from the dead."[17]

If God can raise Jesus Christ from the dead, He can certainly raise a dead relationship. He can set us free from an addiction. He can take away our guilt and shame. He can help us close the door on the past so those memories stop haunting us. God has the power to change us and our situation.

The Bible goes on to say that nothing is too hard for God: "What is impossible with men is possible with God."[18] The situation you are in right now may seem hopeless. But it's not.

In fact, in our Celebrate Recovery family, we have had millions of people who were in impossible situations. They could not change these situations on their own power. They never thought in a thousand years that they or their circumstances could ever change. But they did! At the end of this chapter you'll find the stories of Scott and Nate—stories that show how God's power helped them change as they completed this second choice.

Now, we'll look at what you can do to make God's power a reality in your own life.

PLUGGING IN TO GOD'S POWER

Believe it or not, *things work better when they're plugged in.* This applies to toasters, vacuum cleaners, coffeemakers—and to us as well. In order to get rid of the pain, we must choose to plug in to God's power, and that means more than just believing. If simply believing in God were enough, most of us wouldn't need this book or these 8 Healing Choices. Belief alone cannot wipe away the pain and devastation of the hurts, hang-ups, and habits in your life. In order to get rid of the pain, you've got to make a choice: you've got to choose to *plug in to* God's power. His power is where your help and healing lies.

God's Triple Power Surge

A lot of Christians have no power in their lives because they're not plugged in. When we're plugged in to His power, God supplies us with all we need: *"The Spirit that God has given us . . . fills with power, love, and self-control."*[19] Power, love, and self-control—God's triple power surge, the very three things we need in order to be healthy, happy, and whole.

Power

We need power to break habits we can't break on our own. We need power to do what we know is right but can't seem to do by ourselves.

We need power to break free from the past and let those memories go. We need power to get on with the kind of life God wants us to live. But we have found that we cannot change on our own power. We need a power much greater than ourselves—we need to plug in to God's power.

Love

We need real love. We want to be able to love people and have them love us back. We need to let go of the fear of getting hurt by the ones we love. We want the ability to establish deep, meaningful, authentic relationships rather than superficial, hurtful, selfish relationships.

Self-control

We also need self-control, but we can't have self-control until Christ is in control of us. When Christ is in control, we understand, perhaps for the first time, what it means to get it all together. When we're not trying to pull ourselves up by our own bootstraps, we'll find that Christ will stand us on our feet.

You can have access to God's triple power surge if you will just stay connected to the power source.

Making the Power Connection—*Believe* and *Receive*

How do I plug in to God's power?

Simple: *Believe* and *receive*.

First, believe the three truths about God that we shared earlier:

1. Believe that God exists.

2. Believe that you matter to Him.

3. Believe that He has the power to help.

Then receive Him into your life. Simply say, "Jesus Christ, put Your Spirit in me." You do that by using a four-letter word—HELP! It takes courage to say this word, but it is your connection to power: "HELP. God, I need Your help in my life."

Receiving God's help can be frightening because we know it means *change*. "I don't know if I *want* help to change," you may say. "I'm scared to death of change." You may not want to change until your pain exceeds your fear of change. But when you are ready to receive God's power, all you have to say is, "God, make me willing to be willing to change." Then He will give you the will and the power to plug in to Him. "*It is God who is at work within you, giving you the will and the power to achieve his purpose.*"[20]

When you do call for help, God has promised to respond: "*When you go through deep waters and great trouble, I will be with you. When you go through rivers of difficulty, you will not drown! When you walk through the fire of oppression, you will not be burned up; the flames will not consume you.*"[21] Where are you hurting today? Are you going through some deep waters? Do you feel like you're going under for the last time? Are you going through the fire? Is the heat on in your life? Do you feel like you're stuck in a rut and just can't find the power to change? Do you feel powerless?

God's power is available to you right now—it's just a choice away. All you have to do is *believe* and *receive*.

When I ran out of myself and had nowhere else to turn, I finally hit my bottom. I found God patiently waiting there for me. He gave me His power to make the changes that on my own I was powerless to make. Stepping out of my denial into God's grace was not easy. Admitting that I was an alcoholic and that my life was out of control was the hardest thing I ever had to do. But when I made this second choice, a huge weight was lifted off my shoulders. The hope and freedom that I began to experience was indescribable! All I had to do was believe and receive while God did the rest.

As you work through the "Make the Choice" section of this chapter, you may end up face-to-face with some real problems—maybe some you haven't wanted to deal with. It might mean taking some risks. It will most definitely mean being honest and trusting God.

MAKE THE
Choice

Action 1: *Pray about It*

Laying down your denial and trusting that God will give you the *power* may be a daily exercise for some time. But God's power is real and amazing. And day by day as we plug in to that power, we will learn to trust Him more and more. Our job is to cry out for help and know He will keep His promise to hear our cries and help us.

Pray on your own, or read this prayer and pray these words in your heart:

Dear God, please help me not to ignore this pain You are using to alert me to my need for help. In the past, as I've ignored the denial busters You've allowed in my life, I have actually refused Your help. I am so sorry for this and ask Your help in facing the truth and trusting You to care for me. You know and care about all the pain and hurt I have in my life. Today I need Your help. I can't do it on my own. I have tried, and I keep coming up empty.

First, I pray for Your power in my life. I need Your power to break habits I can't break. I need Your power to help me do the things that I know are right but can't seem to do on my own. I need Your power to break free from my past. I ask for Your power to get on with the plans You have for my life.

Next, I pray for love. I want real love. I want to be able to love people and have them love me. I pray that with Your love I can let go of past hurts and failures so I can tear down the walls of fake intimacy. God, I ask You to help me have genuine intimacy with You and others. Help me not be afraid of really loving and of really being loved.

God, please grant me Your power, love, and self-control. Help me to continue making healing choices. Amen.

If you prayed that prayer, you just took a very significant step! Don't worry about understanding the how-to's right now; we will look at those in chapter 3. Just know that you are on your way to getting help for when you hurt!

Action 2: *Write about It*

Before you begin, take a minute and reread what you wrote in chapter 1. Sometimes we are in such a hurry to grow, to progress, that we do not take time to reflect on what God has already taught us about Himself or ourselves. Your journal will give you an encouraging picture of your growth as you move through these 8 Choices.

With that said, let's review the following scripture and see what principles we can draw from it: *"When you go through deep waters and great trouble, I will be with you. When you go through rivers of difficulty, you will not drown! When you walk through the fire of oppression, you will not be burned up; the flames will not consume you."*[22]

God promises to be with you today, tomorrow, next week, next month, next year as you face those issues you've been afraid to change all your life. Write out the answers to the following questions:

1. What pain has God been using as a megaphone in your life to alert you to your need for help? Lust & temptation

2. Who or what have you blamed for your problems—either partially or completely? parents · psychologist

need for

3. What pain have you been denying? *My longing and need for someone.*
That I cannot [illegible] thing or everything to happen to me.

4. What denial busters (crisis, confrontation, catastrophe) has
God used to try to get your attention? *Regarding breakup*
Psychos. Hallucination *and gagabos psychwar*
Psychog hallucination

5. In what areas do you feel stuck in the pain of your past—
powerless to change? *My longing for someone like Marssy*
and my regret at the things I did *psychiatric*
use drugs to cause my *stay at*

6. In what area(s) of your life are you now ready to allow God to *the hospital*
start helping you? *My longing for [illegible] lust and*
Relationships.

7. What are you still afraid to turn over to God? *Porn*

8. How are your feelings for your earthly father and heavenly
Father alike? How do they differ? *My heavenly father is*
always present.

Action 3: *Share about It*

This may be the most difficult of the three actions for you to take.
But the good news is that it gets easier as you continue to go through
each of the 8 Choices. God's Word says, *"As iron sharpens iron, so people
can improve each other."*[23]

If you are still looking for a safe person to share your healing journey
with, here are some guidelines that will help you in your search:

1. *Does he or she have a growing relationship with Jesus Christ?* Do
   you see the character of Christ developing in this person?

2. *Does this person's walk match his or her talk?* Some Christians
   can quote the Bible, chapter and verse, but their lifestyle does
   not match their talk. Be certain that the person you choose
   to share your journey with is someone whose life is worthy of
   imitation.

3. *Is he or she a good listener?* Do you sense that this person honestly cares about what you have to say?

4. *Does he or she show compassion, concern, and hope but not pity?* You don't need someone to feel sorry for you, but you do need someone who can be sensitive to your pain.

5. *Is this person strong enough to confront your denial or procrastination?* Does he or she care enough about you and your progress to challenge you? There is a difference between helping others and trying to fix others. You need to be careful to guard the relationship from becoming unhealthy or codependent. You want to be dependent on Christ, not on another person.

6. *Does he or she offer suggestions?* Sometimes we need help in seeing options or alternatives that we are unable to find on our own.

7. *Can this person share his or her own past and current struggles with you?* Is this person willing to open up and be vulnerable and transparent with you?

The journey to a happy, healthy, whole life is not easy. Along the way, you will have to face some problems you have not wanted to deal with. You'll have to take some risks. This journey is not one to be traveled alone. You need someone of the same sex, a trusted friend with whom you can share what God is doing in your life. As you complete this chapter, focus on the hope found in God's love for you and His ability to help you heal.

Scott's STORY

I'm a believer who struggles with alcohol, drugs, and lust; my name is Scott. I'm a man who chose a life of sin for twenty-five years of my life. I abused alcohol, drugs, and sex to drown out all the issues and fears that I faced in life. This behavior all started when I was a young, scrawny kid growing up in an average home with one younger sister.

I was born with a lazy left eye. As an infant I had a couple surgeries, which resulted in having to wear a little set of glasses with a patch over one eye. Other kids at school often picked on me and teased me. A neighborhood boy, who once destroyed my bicycle in a fit of anger, relentlessly bullied me. I passed all that teasing on to my little sister, which led to more trouble for me.

Growing up, I felt like I didn't fit in. I was always trying to keep up with others. I felt "less than," so I sought approval and attention from everyone around me by acting out and being loud. I had many fears as a teen. I had the fear of living life on life's terms and the fear of intimacy when around the opposite sex. I feared not growing up to be the son, husband, and father that I thought my parents wanted me to be.

Raised in the Catholic Church, my religious upbringing was the result of a devout mother who never drank or smoked. She came from a large Catholic family and expected me to act like a good Catholic boy when around family and friends.

My father had a good job, but was a passive man and usually kept his feelings to himself. He didn't say "I love you" often, yet he loved to laugh and have a good time. He was a drinker and occasional cigar smoker. I remember how mad it used to make my mom.

My dad introduced me to alcohol at a young age by allowing me to sip on his beers and mixed drinks, especially at family events. He often traveled with his job and brought home different varieties of beer from around the country. I began collecting the different varieties of empty cans, which slowly led to me having one of the largest collections in downstate Illinois. Alcohol quickly became my idol. There were always a few full cans in the collection that I could sneak away and drink when no one was looking. I loved the feeling that alcohol gave me, which eventually led to a fascination with drugs. I loved smoking pot, popping pills, and experimenting with hallucinogens. I thought they made me cool. The crazier I behaved, the more attention I thought I was getting.

Pornographic magazines in the next door neighbor's basement aroused my sexual appetite as a young teen. He had a porn magazine collection displayed that rivaled my beer can collection. My father would often join him for drinks and cigars while I did my browsing. I started my own collection of magazines. I hid them in the heating vent of my bedroom in fear of getting caught by my mother. I would proudly pull them out when my buddies spent the night. Between both of my collections, my peer approval ratings were climbing quickly. That need for attention drove me to wanting to be the life of the party in high school, having the best music collection, best porn collection, and of course, having all the best drugs. My drinking became more regular as a way to take the edge off of all the rest of the garbage I was putting into my body.

High school was a blur, with parties in the school parking lot every morning, LSD trips, rock concerts, drug- and alcohol-induced blackouts, countless hangovers, and an arrest for drug possession on school grounds.

I was already struggling with drug, alcohol, and nicotine addictions and knew that if I weren't more careful, I'd end up in jail.

I met my first girlfriend while working at McDonald's and introduced her to the party scene. Soon after high school I landed a job with a large insurance firm in our community. I immediately hooked up with older adults who had better drug connections than I'd ever dreamed of. I began selling marijuana and cocaine to feed my own addictions and to make a little more money on the side. Besides, my ego began to grow, and I thought I had it all together. I fell away from my high school friends quickly, and the drug and alcohol use led to wrecking cars, wrecking relationships, and breaking the law.

My girlfriend and I moved in together after high school; and since she had been raised in an alcoholic home, she became my biggest enabler. Drunken arguments and verbal and physical abuse became regular events. But we still "loved" each other and ended up getting married. A couple years later, she became pregnant for the first time but miscarried twin babies after five months. This had a traumatic impact on her, and we both had a lot of guilt because of the lifestyle we were leading. She stopped using altogether, which meant more drugs and alcohol for me. Life went on without much hesitation.

God was already working to catch my attention, though, as she got pregnant again and we had our first daughter on Mother's Day the following year. We ended up having another daughter two years later and a son four years after that.

Work was my life when the kids were young, as my job had me traveling all over the country. I took the party to wherever I went. I was what some refer to as a functioning alcoholic and addict. For many years of this sinful lifestyle, I held a job with that same employer. I was never arrested for driving while drunk. I bought new homes and nice cars, went on great vacations, and preserved the image of a good family man with a wife and three great children. I went to church a few times a year to make an appearance and tried to introduce my children to a religion I wasn't interested in. I was a "poser." I looked like I had it all together on the outside. But, honestly, I was dying on the inside. I was the poster child for self-will run riot. I was lost and alone, trapped inside my body.

Trying to keep up the image and maintain the approval of others, I fell into financial crisis, gambling, lying, and even infidelity in my marriage. I struggled with a lustful pornography addiction and manipulated my spouse into watching just to spice up our dwindling sex life. Unsuccessful sobriety attempts became more regular. I would try staying clean and sober, but it never lasted more than a few weeks, and I'd be right back at it. I was still getting high or drinking before, during, and after work. My coworkers started to notice my behavior and absences. I was angry and frustrated most of the time. I knew I had big problems, but I wasn't ready to admit it to anyone. I was physically, emotionally, financially, and spiritually spent. My marriage was falling apart, and I was close to losing my job. I was sick and tired of being sick and tired and often considered taking my life as a way out.

One morning before work, while sitting alone in my garage, I experienced a moment of clarity as my life passed before my eyes. I didn't believe in the God my mother had taught me about and had no connection with Jesus Christ. I'm convinced today that God was speaking to me clearly that morning. He said: *"Something has to change."*

My father-in-law was an alcoholic and had spent time in treatment. So my wife and I had discussed the possibility of me doing the same. The next morning, I skeptically agreed to check myself in. That was December 26, 1993, the day I took my last drink and my last drug.

I want so much to tell you that life was a bed of roses after I got sober, but it wasn't. I joined the program of Alcoholics Anonymous. I met a man I once knew and asked him to be my sponsor. He began to help me work the 12 Steps for the first time. Recovery is hard work. Ironically, the treatment center I stayed at was right across the street from the church I attended as a child. I spent hours looking out of the third floor window over at the church. I watched people coming and going. I watched the priest standing on the steps on Sunday mornings. I knew that staying sober would be key to my recovery. But I wondered if surrendering to Jesus Christ would bring me the answers that I searched for.

After treatment, I went to ninety meetings in ninety days. After about a year of sobriety, my sponsor suggested I attend a weekend spiritual retreat with a group of other men. That weekend the grace of God poured out all over me! I heard during the retreat that God loved me more than anyone else could love me—even my parents, my wife, and my kids. Those words touched me deeply and the gratitude was humbling. I knew at that moment that my faith was real and earnestly believed that God existed! He was a caring, loving God, not that punishing God I'd learned about as a child. This God would even forgive me for all the years of turmoil I had inflicted on myself and my family. I cried myself to sleep at night during that retreat, mourning my past mistakes and loss of control over my life. The stronghold of my denial broke. I now knew that God wanted me to be happy, joyous, and free! That weekend, I surrendered my life to the one and only true higher power, Jesus Christ. Little did I know how my life was about to change. God used my sponsor as the method of delivering His grace to me, and for that, I will be forever grateful!

Unfortunately, I was powerless over the lives of others around me. My newly found spirituality was difficult for my wife and children to adjust to. As much as I wanted to salvage my marriage, the damage was done. After several years of hope, counseling, and prayer, my nineteen-year marriage ended. I thank God that I was still sober and working a program of recovery as I slowly began to recover from a divorce that I didn't want. I continued to work the 12 Steps, and at the advice of my sponsor's wife, I also spent time in the Al-Anon program to address the codependent feelings and behavior I was experiencing as a result. It was hard to admit my part of the marriage breakup. I had to confess to my selfish, controlling, and manipulative behavior.

Here I was a single father trying to raise three kids and wondering if I'd ever be in a healthy, loving relationship anytime during the rest of my life. I prayed that God would reveal something to me. He answered my prayers. I met a beautiful woman at my place of employment. She was a divorcee with two young children. She loved Jesus and sang in the choir at her church. She had the relationship with Christ that I so deeply wanted. I began to court her. We kept the relationship sexually pure, which was difficult for me considering the sexual dysfunction I struggled with. We knew that God approved of our relationship. We began to pray together that His will be done for us. We courted for over a year and finally married in a small, lovely ceremony in the backyard of our new home. God is so good, and besides Jesus, my wife, Veronica, is the most important person in my life!

Early on, the dysfunction of our previous marriages began to surface through the behavior of our former spouses and the trials that come with a blended family. I also struggled with sexual intimacy and a porn addiction. I knew, though, that God had the power to help me recover that part of my life. I began attending my wife's church and eventually became a member. A couple years into our marriage, the associate pastor, who knew of my recovery background, asked if I had ever heard of a Christ-centered recovery ministry called Celebrate Recovery. He handed me a startup kit, and I was immediately curious.

I was already involved with prison ministry and Bible studies in our home, yet God kept leading me to check out this ministry. I went to my first Celebrate Recovery meeting in a community a half hour away. As soon as I walked in, I felt at home! When I attended the men's small group that night, the leader introduced himself as a believer in Jesus Christ who struggles with alcohol, drugs, and lust. The rest of the men introduced themselves, and I quickly realized that their identity was first in Jesus Christ rather than in the hurt, hang-up, or habit they struggled with. I had been introducing myself as an alcoholic for years in secular programs. But now I was introducing myself as a believer in the one and only higher power, Jesus Christ. I knew this ministry was right for me. I wanted to start it in my own church.

Because of God's unconditional love, He has restored me and loves me based on His character, rather than my performance. He showed His great love for me by sending Jesus to die on the cross for all my sins. Now it was my turn to lay down my life for Him and serve others through Celebrate Recovery. After I attended the Celebrate Recovery Summit conference in 2005, the ministry started at our church in January of 2006. God continues to amaze us through His healing power as we get to witness changed lives, restored relationships, and people recovering through God's power rather than their own.

During a Celebrate Recovery Step Study, I focused my attention on my sexual integrity issues. I was still secretly dabbling in pornography, fantasizing, and lustful thoughts. The Bible says that "anyone who comes to him must believe that he exists and that he rewards those who earnestly seek him."[24] I had been baptized as a child in the Catholic Church, but during that Step Study I was baptized in my church. This was a public expression of my decision to turn my life over in the area of sexual integrity. I still struggle with lust today, but God knows, and He helps me to overcome this hang-up daily.

Over the years, I've had the opportunity to serve with my wife as a State Representative for Celebrate Recovery and now as a Regional Director over nine states. We love serving together and with the many others who have found the healing power of Jesus Christ in recovery. It all started when I made the choice to believe that God exists, that I matter to Him, and that He alone has the power to help me recover!

Getting HELP
Earnestly believe that God exists,
that I matter to Him, and that He has the power to help me recover.

CHOICE 2

God was preparing me spiritually for an intimate marriage, and strengthening me to be the father, husband, and son He wants me to be. He gave me strength to move through a difficult divorce and the troublesome teenage years of my children. And He also gave me strength for the sudden death of my mother, followed by the birth of a grandson who was given up in an open adoption.

My faith was tested as I watched my father die of Parkinson's disease, after spending many years in a local nursing home. I struggled with the challenges of my step-daughter's pregnancy at age sixteen. Through all this, God continues to be my rock, and He always prevails!

I stay involved with weekly prayer groups, my church, and of course, the Celebrate Recovery ministry, as God has brought some wonderful Christians into my life. We share our lives with each other and how God works in and through us, one day at a time. Life still presents ups and downs. But today I have God's peace and serenity, something that I tried to find on my own for so many years.

God can enable any of us to change, no matter how deeply

embedded we may be in this world. The miracle of my new birth took place when I chose to say yes to the stirring of His grace in my soul. When I accepted God's free gift of salvation, I was born again into a new life, where the Holy Spirit filled me and now lives in me. My recovery is about transformation! I love what God's Word says in the book of Ephesians,

Since you have heard about Jesus
and have learned the truth that comes from him,
throw off your old sinful nature
and your former way of life,
which is corrupted by lust and deception.
Instead, let the Spirit renew your thoughts and attitudes.
Put on your new nature, created to be like God
—truly righteous and holy.[25]

Celebrate Recovery has taken my own road to recovery to the next level. I love working the principles and steps, sponsoring other men, working with my accountability partners, and taking part in Step Studies.

I know today that I can't recover by myself. Recovery always happens in relationships, never on my own. I now have a personal responsibility to share the love of Jesus Christ with everyone I meet, whether it's through Celebrate Recovery or simply one-on-one.

I'm a believer who struggles with alcohol, drugs, and lust, and my name is "Child of the One True King"!

Nate's STORY

Hello, my name is Nate. I am a grateful believer in Jesus Christ who struggles with addiction and mental health issues. I started out as a well-adjusted kid in a pastor's home in south Minneapolis, Minnesota. Unlike most of the people I grew up with, my folks were still in a loving marriage. I have three brothers, none of whom were serious troublemakers. We sat in the front row of church during the sermons, next to my mother, whenever she was not singing in the choir. My father was an important person and thus, I felt like an important person.

When I was ten, my father felt called to leave the church we were in and serve the Lord in a small town called Barnes, Wisconsin. While this town was only a three-hour drive from where I had grown up, I might as well have stepped into another world. Downtown Barnes consisted of a building with a convenience store, a restaurant, and a bar. You knew it was downtown because it had a big sign out front that said "Downtown." My fifth grade class in Minneapolis had a higher population than the entire town of Barnes.

I felt isolated. I acted, spoke, and felt treated differently. I tried to adapt; but while I tried to put on a good face, my body started to break down. I frequently missed school because of stomachaches. My moods started going sour. And depression started to set in. Looking back at all of this, I can clearly see what was going on, but at the time, people didn't talk about panic attacks and depression. And besides, I was ten. What mental health issues could a ten-year-old have anyways?

Over the next couple of years, I developed some basic coping skills. I started getting defensive. I didn't let people in. I tried to hide pain and anger behind humor. Until, that is, I discovered that if I misbehaved, I got noticed. It starts out little, but it doesn't stay little when you have the kind of mental health issues I have. It didn't come out until years later that I have borderline personality disorder. A milder form of it, but I have it nonetheless. A borderline personality disorder causes a person's brain to exaggerate the input it receives.

At my current stage of life, I am now able to control the impulses associated with this disorder through the medications I take for my clinical depression. I use mental exercises to filter thoughts and emotions. However, when I was going into junior high, I didn't even know this was an issue, much less how to deal with it. So it ran amok in my psyche. People would pay attention if I threw a spitball across the room. So why not throw my desk out the window?

Having people give me kudos for being naughty once in a while was not enough to offset the debilitating lows that came more and more often. It was then I started using alcohol to ease some of the tension in my brain. It made me feel good. When drunk, I was king of the world— at least until I woke up the next morning. Eventually I turned to drugs, which I liked more because they were easier to hide. Not to mention what I could do with household chemicals.

I could go through all my war stories and list the bad things I did. However, the Bible does a good job of summing up my lifestyle this way: "The acts of the sinful nature are obvious: sexual immorality, impurity and debauchery; idolatry and witchcraft; hatred, discord, jealousy, fits of rage, selfish ambition, dissensions, factions and envy; drunkenness, orgies, and the like. I warn you, as I did before, that those who live like this will not inherit the kingdom of God."[26]

It is simple. I am a sinner.

My behavior became increasingly destructive until right before my twenty-first birthday. I had hit my end. I cut my wrists open with a steak knife and lost enough blood that the doctors said I should not be alive. I spent some time in the acute mental health ward of a local hospital. It was there that I found out just how screwed up I was. The doctors and counselors started to explain what was happening, why it was happening, and what drugs to take for it. It was not the diagnosis, however, that made the largest impact on my life. During one of the many downtime moments, one of the clinicians sat next to me and asked if I would be willing to do some brainteasers. I had nothing else to do so I said sure. What I was not aware of was that he was administering an IQ test. After the test, he paused, looked at me, and said, "You are a waste." I was thinking, *Wow buddy, you should write for Hallmark. That was beautiful.* But he continued: "You are the smartest person in this room right now. If you don't go to college, if you don't make something of yourself, you are a waste."

This stuck with me. For the first time in my life that I could remember, I had someone—with no stake in my life—tell me that I had real value. My parents were open with affection toward me. I grew up hearing over and over that they loved me. But they are parents; they're supposed to say that. This guy had no reason to say that I had value outside of declaring something he saw to be true.

Now, this did not fix me. The first thing I did when I got out of the hospital was to go get high. But it made an impact. It planted a seed. And so over the next couple of years I started using some of the tools I'd picked up, and they did help some. But I was still mixing in my own form of therapy. It wasn't until a series of people started making a spiritual impact in my life that I really started to make a change.

My girlfriend, now wife, had become a follower of Christ. She wanted to make sure I was saved as well. I wasn't so sure. After much back and forth, we finally agreed that she could ask, "How are you doing with the whole God thing?" I would say, "No," and that would end the conversation. Then I started to work fixing railroad cars. It was there I met Ted. Ted was a "Holy Roller." Occasionally I would find myself inside a grain car with Ted, who would sing hymns loudly and off-key while he worked. After what seemed like a constant barrage of God comments, I wore down. I decided I would make a deal with God. I said, "Okay, God. I will give You one more chance. But if You screw it up, I am done." The thing is, though, He honored my request.

He started to work in my life, and I started to make real changes. I stopped getting drunk whenever I could. I started going to church. I even got involved in church. And through the grace of God, I got my life going in the direction it was meant to be going.

I never have liked it when people say, "I found Jesus, and now I am happy all the time." Truth is, in many ways, my life got harder. I lost friends that I had had for years. I had to give up the coping skills that I had since I was a kid. I had to face my problems head-on.

The good part, however, was that for the first time in my life, I wasn't going it alone. The apostle Paul said that nothing can separate us from Jesus's love.[27] Meaning, He is always there. He is always watching. He created us and knows us so well that He knows the number of hairs on our heads. He is the only one who can search me and know me. I can't hide anything from Him. There is no point in even trying. He knows my thoughts. He knows them better than I do. He knows my thoughts before I do. I never have to put on my best face or try not to offend. There is no ritual or customs I need to adhere to. I just get to be me. Really me.

Since coming to Christ, I have had a multitude of events go "wrong" in my life. What seemed to start things off was the miscarriage of my first child. My wife has a bi-coordinate uterus. That just means that her uterus is not shaped the way it should be. She cannot carry a baby the way most women can. When we got pregnant the second time, my daughter was breech. Her feet pointed down the whole time. Combining that with premature labor, what was meant to be one of the happiest times in our lives turned into one of the scariest. I could have easily lost them both.

To make matters worse, I was injured at work a week before my daughter was born. I incurred an annular strain in two discs in my lower back. Now I was out of work, with a family on the way. I had planned on doing a manual job my whole life. Now I had a weight restriction of ten pounds and couldn't lean forward for more than a few minutes at a time. It took about a year before I could finally find work in retail. I did well. I moved into sales and started making decent money. But I was miserable.

I started having panic attacks on my way to work. My depression became intense. My marriage was suffering. And one day I decided, "No more." I tried a few different jobs, but nothing seemed to work out for me. So I took a different route. I began a discussion with my pastor. I began a path in vocational ministry as a youth pastor. This time, I was doing God's work so I knew it couldn't fail.

But one week into the internship, I started getting this unsettled movement in my leg that quickly moved into my entire body. I went to the emergency room and the doctor gave me a strange look. He offered me his highly trained medical opinion: "I don't know." After multiple specialists and countless pokes and prods, the movements were labeled as Paroxysmal Dystonic Choreoathetosis. This is a movement disorder that mimics Parkinson's. They have no idea what causes it, how to treat it, or how long I will have it. At first it was constant, severe, and debilitating. There were times that I looked much like I was having a seizure on the floor, unable to speak, vomiting, and in a whole lot of pain.

So now, not only was I out of work again, I wasn't sure if I would be able to live a normal life at all. My body shook so badly that I had to take motion sickness pills. There is always some uncontrolled movement going on in my body. Sometimes it can be seen. Sometimes it is deep muscle movement that is only noticed by someone else if they touch me. My symptoms have gone down some since their onset, but I still have no idea from one moment to the next what my body is going to do.

The twenty-third psalm says this:

The LORD is my shepherd, I shall not be in want.
He makes me lie down in green pastures,
he leads me beside quiet waters, he restores my soul.
He guides me in paths of righteousness for his name's sake.
Even though I walk through the valley of the shadow of death,
I will fear no evil, for you are with me;
your rod and your staff, they comfort me.
You prepare a table before me in the presence of my enemies.
You anoint my head with oil; my cup overflows.
Surely goodness and love will follow me all the days of my life,
and I will dwell in the house of the LORD forever.[28]

These last few years, I have seen that verse for what it is. I don't have to give up. I can go on because God is with me. Does He take it all away? Not always. But He takes enough.

He gives us places like our church homes, small groups, and Celebrate Recovery. I have been given the chance to share my burdens. Because I took that chance, I know what it means when the psalmist said, "He restores my soul."

A perfect example of that goes back to what I mentioned earlier about going through a miscarriage with my wife. After we got back from the hospital, a good friend showed up at our door. She didn't call first, she just showed up carrying a basket filled with everything she needed to make soup. She let us just be for a while and went about the business of making us a simple meal. She didn't try to fix us. She didn't try to explain it away or cheer us up. We cried, and she let us. She showed us, in a very intimate and tangible way, what it means to be loved by God.

This expression of caring only comes through relationship—relationship fostered through the community found in church, in small groups, and through Celebrate Recovery. In these places I have seen my life change. Now I earnestly believe what Choice 2 says:

CHOICE 2

Getting HELP

Earnestly believe that God exists,

that I matter to Him, and that He has the power to help me recover.

In my early years, I viewed my life as, at best, just a good example of a bad example. I felt that I had no real value, and as a result, that I was nothing worth caring about. I felt that if there were a God, then He certainly wouldn't care about me. But God does exist. He does love me, and I do matter. God doesn't put people on earth to fill space. I have a reason to exist. God has placed me here with a purpose. I still struggle at times and my mental health issues can be brutal to live with, but I will never suffer alone. Matthew 5:4 says, "Happy are those who mourn, for they shall be comforted."[29]

I have a Savior who sees my tears and wipes them away. When I stumble, He picks me up. I am an example of the work that God is doing in the world and the grace that He shows His children. I visit treatment centers in the community, I share my testimony in community workshops and church services, and I have encouraged thousands of people. In 2015, I came on as an intern at my church. I had the opportunity to begin a recovery ministry. In 2016, I came on staff officially at my church as Director of Counseling and Recovery. I have seen more people come into a relationship with Christ than I could have ever imagined. Also, at the end of 2016 I began the task of National Director of Mental Health for Celebrate Recovery. Now I am used by God to reach people all over the world. I'm helping break the stigma that surrounds mental health. While the world looks at people like me as deficient, my God looks at me as extraordinary. My diagnosis is not my identity.

People question me on whether recovery is worth it. I answer with, "My being a part of the family of Christ and my involvement in Celebrate Recovery has made me a better person. It makes me a better husband, father, and friend." And while God has not chosen at this time to heal my body, He has healed my heart, a gift far greater. My body is temporary, but my spirit is everlasting. I can't change what I was before. But by the grace offered to me by God, I am a new creation today. I am always growing, always changing, and always moving forward by the direction of the One who works inside me. I don't know what tomorrow will bring or if I will even see tomorrow. But I know the heart that hungers for the will of God will be led by the will of God.

Thank you for letting me share.

R
E

Consciously choose

to *commit* all my life and will
to Christ's care and control.

O

V

E

R

Y

"Happy are the meek."[1]

Letting GO

The Commitment Choice

Rodney Holmstrom, whose story is at the end of this chapter, shares this with us:

> I can remember as a kid going to the beach and trying to hold down a beach ball under water. I could do it for a while, but soon it became too much to hold down. It took a lot of concentration and constant pressure to keep it held under the water. Over time, it sapped my energy. All I could focus on was holding down that beach ball. I started getting tired, and as the wind picked up, the waters around me got rougher, making it harder and harder to keep it submerged. Eventually, I could hold it down no longer, and the ball shot up out of the water and hit me in the face.
>
> Sometimes in life, we do this with our deep hurts. We try submerging or controlling our life struggles, only to experience greater pain. Then, when life stresses begin to pick up, the pressure becomes too much to handle on our own, hitting us and our family. This only causes more pain and wounds.

I have learned this lesson in my own recovery. Healthy change and growth cannot and will not take place until we are willing to turn our life, will, and life's struggles over to our Higher Power, Jesus Christ.

Allowing God to have control of my life gives me so much energy and freedom. Thank God, we don't have to face these struggles on our own.

That's how some of us try to live our lives. We take desperate measures, trying to keep our life's hurts, hang-ups, and habits buried so they don't come crashing to the surface. We try so hard to keep up a good front—pretending that everything is okay—when in reality, we're struggling with real pain and real issues that we desperately try to ignore.

Then we get stuck. We get stuck trying to keep it all together while our world is falling apart. We get stuck in unhealthy relationships and in addictive habits. We get stuck in grief or sexual relationships. We get stuck, and we cannot get unstuck on our own power—and so despair sets in.

We start feeling *guilty* about our behavior. We wish we could get out of our mess, but we can't. After a lot of failed attempts, we get *angry* with ourselves and others: "I should be able to change. I ought to be able to get out of this." But we can't, and our anger grows. Over time, our anger turns to the *fear* that things are never going to change. We begin to realize that our hurts, hang-ups, and habits are controlling us, and our fear eventually turns to *depression*. We start feeling sorry for ourselves, and we become filled with yet more guilt.

Finally, we give up and say, "I can't change. I quit." The cycle of despair starts all over again!

CYCLE OF DESPAIR

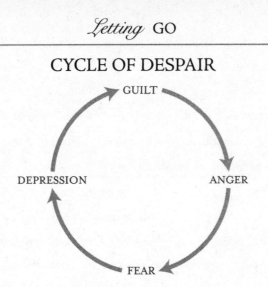

GUILT

ANGER

FEAR

DEPRESSION

How do you break out of the cycle of despair? If you've followed through on the choices in the first two chapters of this book, you're already moving out of this vicious cycle: you've made the "Reality Choice," where you admitted your need. You've also taken the "Hope Choice," believing that you matter to God and that He has the power to help you.

Now you are ready for the "Commitment Choice," where you make the decision to walk across the line. You take a step across that line of decision—a step *toward* God that says you are giving it all to Him and a step *away* from the old way of doing it all yourself. If you haven't made this choice as yet, it will be the most important choice in your life—the choice to accept Christ. For others who have already chosen Christ, this choice will mean a renewed commitment to let go of their lives and give them over to Christ's care and control.

CHOICE 3

Letting Go
Consciously choose to commit
all my life and will to Christ's care and control.

Right now, Jesus is reaching out to you, waiting for you to step across that line and into His open arms: "*Come to me, all of you who are weary and overburdened, and I will give you rest! Put on my yoke and learn from me. For I am gentle and humble in heart and you will find rest for your souls. For my yoke is easy and my burden is light.*"[2]

God doesn't ask you to be weak, but He does ask you to lay down your pride and be meek.

"*Come to me,*" Jesus says. "Your life will be easier, your load lighter. You will have relief, release, and rest. You will be rejuvenated. Give Me the control and care of your life, and watch what I do for you."

What an amazing deal! Why would anybody turn Him down? Yet many have heard this invitation before but never walked across the line. Choosing to step across that line into Christ's care and control is the most important decision you will ever make.

WHAT'S HOLDING YOU BACK?

What's holding you back? What is delaying your decision to surrender your problems and your life to the care and control of Christ? It has been said that our choices determine our circumstances and our decisions determine our destiny. There are five things that keep us from making this third choice: *pride, guilt, fear, worry,* and *doubt.*

1. Pride

Pride often keeps us from admitting we need God's help. "*No one is respected unless he is humble, arrogant people are on the way to ruin.*"[3] This proverb presents a pretty clear picture of those of us who think we can do it on our own: "*A self-sufficient fool falls flat on his face.*"[4]

"*Happy are the meek,*" says the beatitude for this choice. But many equate meekness with weakness. In reality, meekness and weakness are at opposite ends of the spectrum. In fact, the Greek work for *meekness* actually means "strength under control." The word is used to describe a wild stallion that is tamed and taught to be ridden. That stallion still has all its strength, but now its strength is under control, ready for its master's use. God doesn't ask you to be weak, but He does ask you to lay down your pride and be meek. Meekness is surrender; it is submitting; it is agreeing to do what God wants done in your life.

Maybe you're not ready to take this life-changing choice. Your pride may still be keeping you from committing your "life and will to Christ's care and control." Perhaps you need a greater dose of pain. If that's what's needed, God may allow this to happen in order to finally get your attention.

2. Guilt

Guilt is another thing that will keep us from walking across that line and into God's arms. We may be ashamed to ask God to help us: "*Problems far too big for me to solve are piled higher than my head. Meanwhile my sins, too many to count, have all caught up with me, and I am ashamed to look up.*"[5] Have you ever felt that way? Have you ever felt ashamed to look up? Our guilt can make us ashamed to ask God for help.

Maybe you've tried to make deals with God: "God, if You just get me out of this mess, I will never do it again!" You may be embarrassed to ask Him for help. Or you may think God doesn't know all the things you've done wrong and won't ever forgive you. You're wrong; He knows. Even though He knows it all, there is no sin that God cannot or will not forgive. He wants to forgive all your guilt. That's why Christ went to the cross!

3. Fear

Are you afraid of what you might have to give up if you surrender the care and control of your life to Christ? Fear takes many forms.

Sometimes we're afraid to trust God

There's a story about a guy who falls off a cliff. Halfway down he grabs on to a branch, and he's hanging on for dear life—he can see five hundred feet down and five hundred feet up. He cries out, "Somebody help!" Suddenly, he hears the voice of God, "This is the Lord, trust Me, let go, and I'll catch you." The guy looks back down at the five hundred feet below and back up again. Then he calls out, "Is there anybody else up there?"

Sometimes we turn to God only as our last resort—we're afraid to let go and trust Him. Right now you may be hanging on to that branch for dear life, saying, "Things aren't that bad. No problem, really. I'm fine." No, you are not fine. You are just afraid of letting go and trusting Him.

Sometimes we're afraid of losing control

But the truth of the matter is that we're all controlled by someone or something at all times. To some extent you're controlled by the way your parents brought you up. You're controlled by the opinions of other people. You're controlled by hurts you can't forget. You're controlled by your hang-ups and habits.

Part of our control issue is fear of losing our freedom. But do you know what real freedom is? True, lasting freedom is choosing who controls you. When you give the care and control of your life to Christ, He sets you free. God said, *"I have swept away your sins like the morning mists. I have scattered your offenses like the clouds. Oh, return to me, for I have paid the price to set you free."*[6]

Sometimes we're afraid of becoming a religious fanatic

Maybe you've been afraid to open your life to the care and control of Christ because you think He might turn you into a fanatic, a religious nut. But Jesus does the exact opposite: He brings sanity where insanity has had its way.

The Bible tells a story of a man who was filled with demons. He lived in the cemetery, among the tombs, and was so wild and out of control that the local people had tried to bind him up, but he was too strong for them. The demons tormented him—like some of your inner "demons" may torment you—and he cried out day and night and cut himself with stones (it's interesting that cutting has resurfaced as a current destructive way to deal with inner pain). But when he saw Jesus, he *walked across that line to him.* The Bible says, *"When Jesus was still some distance away, the man saw him. He ran to meet Jesus and fell down before him."* After Jesus called the demons out of that man, the people found him *"sitting there fully clothed and perfectly sane."*[7] No . . . Jesus does not turn us into religious fanatics; He puts us in our right minds and makes us *perfectly sane.*

So what are you afraid of? What are you holding on to that makes you think, *I can't let go?* Is it a relationship, an ambition, a habit, a lifestyle, or a possession? God's Word asks this: *"How does a man benefit if he gains the whole world and loses his soul in the process? For is anything worth more than his soul?"*[8]

When you make this third choice, you give up everything to God's control. God takes what you give Him, He cleans it up, and He turns it around. He adds new meaning, new purpose, new significance, and new vitality to your life, and He gives it back to you in a whole new way.

Don't worry about the specifics of what you may have to give up. If you focus on the specifics, you'll never make the greater decision, which is taking the step toward a personal relationship with Jesus Christ. Just come to God and say, "God, I don't even know what I don't want to give up. I just know I don't want to live this way anymore, and I know I want my life to be under Your control. God, here is a blank check. Here's my life." All you have to do is trust Him. He will take care of the rest.

4. Worry

Worry causes us to confuse the *decision-making* phase with the *problem-solving* phase. Consider the process of buying a house. First, you make the initial *decision* to buy the house. That's only the beginning. There are several more *problem-solving* steps that must be taken before you can actually move in. You need to go to the bank and apply for the loan. You need to get an appraisal and complete the escrow. Then you have to contact the moving company and set up the utilities. All of this has to be done before you spend the first night in your new home! If you focus on the "problems"—the individual tasks involved in making your dream a reality—you may never make the decision to buy the house. Make the decision; let God worry about problem solving.

5. Doubt

Have you ever thought, *I want to believe, but my faith is too small?* If so, you need to know the story found in the Bible in Mark chapter 5, about a guy named Jairus.

One day Jairus came to Jesus with a need: "Jesus, I know You can heal people, and my daughter needs to be healed."

Jesus said, "If you have faith, then she will be healed."

Jairus was an honest guy, and so he told Jesus the truth: "Lord, I've got a lot of doubts. I want to believe; help me with my unbelief."

Jesus said, "That's good enough." And He healed the girl.

Maybe you need to say with Jairus, "God, I want to believe that You will help me with my life; help me with my unbelief." *That's good enough.* You don't have to have a big faith to decide to give Christ the care and control of your life. As a matter of fact, *"If you have faith as small as a mustard seed . . . nothing will be impossible for you."*[9]

It's not the *size* of your faith that matters; it's the *who* or *what* you put your faith in that matters. You can have a giant faith and put it in the wrong things—like money and possessions—and come up empty. Or you can have a little faith and put it in our big God and get amazing results.

> *It's not the size of your faith that matters; it's the who or what you put your faith in that matters.*

The bottom line is this: don't let any of these five things keep you from making this third choice. Do not let your pride, your guilt, your fear, your worry, or your doubt stop you from committing your life and will to Christ's care and control. First you make the decision, then you go about solving the problems. Your decision: "I open my life to the care and control of Christ. I don't know how it's all going to work out, but I know it's the right thing to do. So I'm just going to do it."

BEGINNING TO MOVE FORWARD

The Christian life is a decision followed by a process. All this third choice is asking us to do is make the decision. The process will follow! At the end of this chapter, you'll read the dramatic story of the Holmstrom family, and you'll see how their lives changed when they made the decision to ask Christ to take the care and control of their lives. But for now let's see what it means for you to *step across that line and into the arms of Jesus.*

It all begins with a simple two-step process. My dad served in World

War II. When I was in college, I studied the strategies of that conflict. I now understand that this two-step process is similar to the strategy our military forces used in World War II. In the Pacific when they freed an island from Japanese occupation, they used the same strategy on every island, and it worked every time.

Phase 1: Softening Up

First, the planes would fly to the island that had been taken captive, and they would start dropping bombs and various explosives. This part of the strategy was called the "softening-up period." Many of you are in the softening-up period right now. All kinds of explosions are going off in your life, sending fragments everywhere. You're saying, "Life isn't working anymore, and quite honestly, it hasn't been for a long time." You may have come to the point where you're saying, "Yes, I need something beyond myself. My hurts, hang-ups, and habits are softening up my pride, guilt, fears, worries, and doubts. I need help. I need God in my life."

Phase 2: Establishing a Beachhead

In the second phase, the Marines would establish a beachhead. It may have been only twenty yards deep and two hundred yards wide, but they would get a presence on the island. By establishing the beachhead, had they completely liberated the island? No. The beachhead was just the beginning. It was from the beachhead that they began to fight the battles. Sometimes they would move one hundred yards forward, and sometimes they would get pushed back fifty. Sometimes they won the battle, and sometimes they lost. But everybody knew that once they had established a beachhead, total liberation of the island was inevitable. In the history of World War II, once the Marines landed and established a beachhead, they never lost an island. It was just a matter of time until the entire island would be set free.

When you make this third choice, God establishes a beachhead in your life. The Bible calls it conversion, or being born again. Does it mean that everything in your life is perfect? Absolutely not. But it means that God has a presence in your life; He's got a beachhead. For the rest of your life, He will be setting you free from your hurts, hang-ups, and habits—little by little. It's a process. But first you have to trust God to take care of you.

HE WON'T LET YOU GO

Are you worried that in this battle of life you won't be able to hold on? Don't worry. *It's not your job to hold on.* God will do the holding, and He won't ever let you go! God's Word assures us, *"And you also were included in Christ when you heard the word of truth, the gospel of your salvation. Having believed, you were marked in him with a seal, the promised Holy Spirit."*[10] When you put your faith in Christ, you are brought into fellowship with Him—you become *His.* And even beyond that, you are marked with a seal—a sign to all that you belong to Him. He will not let you go! You are His beloved child.

We understand the protective feeling a parent has for his or her child. If you were to help your small child cross a busy street, you would grab hold of his or her hand. As you were walking across the street, your child might, as little children do, want to let go. But no matter how much your child wanted to let go of your hand, you wouldn't let go. Why? Because you are a loving parent.

There are times in your life when you might say, "God, I don't think I want to be under Your care right now." Sometimes you will want to take back control and let go of God's hand. But once we grab on to His hand, God holds on tight. He says, "I'll hold on so you don't have to worry about it."

I made the decision to ask Christ into my heart when I was thirteen years old. When I went to college, I chose to follow my own way. In fact, for the next nineteen years I followed the world's way. But no matter how hard I tried to run, how many times I sinned, or how many poor choices I made, God never let go of my hand. My way left me empty and broken. When I was finally ready to truly repent and surrender, God was right there with me. It was then I truly understood His unconditional love and freely given grace.

Whatever God *asks* you to do, He will *enable* you to do. Just rely on Him as He holds tightly to your hand: "*God who began the good work within you will keep right on helping you to grow in his grace until his task within you is finally finished on that day when Jesus Christ returns.*"[11]

STEPPING ACROSS THE LINE

We've talked a lot about making the choice to commit our lives and wills to Christ's care and control. Let's see how you do that, step by step:

1. Accept God's Son as Your Savior

The first thing you need to do is admit that you need to be saved and accept Jesus as your Savior: The Bible says, "*Believe in the Lord Jesus, and you will be saved.*"[12] What does this mean? It means committing as much of your life and will to Christ as you can, at this moment. Is that good enough? Yes, *that is good enough.*

2. Accept God's Word as Your Standard

Once you make the choice to commit your life and will to Christ, you have—from now on—a manual to live your life by. Some people say, "This life is a test; it is only a test. Had it been an actual life, you would have been given an instruction manual to tell you what to do and where to go."

What they're missing is that we *do* have an instruction manual: it's the Bible. God says it is your standard by which you evaluate life. *"All Scripture is inspired by God and is useful for teaching the faith and correcting error, for resetting the direction of a man's life and training him in good living."*[13]

3. Accept God's Will as Your Purpose

The first thing we need to say as we rise each day is, "Lord, You woke me up this morning. This obviously means You have another day planned for me, a day with a purpose. What do You want me to do with it?" In the psalms, David says, *"My God, I want to do what you want. Your teachings are in my heart."*[14] Inspired by David, you can say, "God, I don't even have to understand everything right now. But, I choose to live my life on Your terms because You made me for a reason. You have a purpose, and I want to fulfill that purpose." As you grow with God, His will becomes your strategy for life.

4. Accept God's Power as Your Strength

This becomes your power statement: *"I can do everything God asks me to with the help of Christ who gives me the strength and power."*[15] No longer do you have to rely on your own energy. God gives you His power to be all He wants you to be.

Are you ready to step across that line? Jesus extends His invitation: *"Look! Here I stand at the door and knock. If you hear me calling and open the door, I will come in, and we will share a meal as friends."*[16] Jesus is standing at the door of your life, saying He wants to come into your life. But He is a gentleman; He will not beat the door down. In this third choice, we need to open the door and let Him in, and the key that unlocks that door is willingness.

Being willing means changing our definition of *willpower*. Our willpower needs to become the *willingness to accept God's power*. We don't need more self-will; we've already tried to run our lives on our own willpower, and it has left us broken and empty. Now it's time to exchange willpower for the willingness to accept God's power to run our lives.

If you are ready to make this choice and commit your life to Christ's care and control, just answer the following questions:

1. Do you believe Jesus Christ died on the cross for you and proved He was God by coming back to life?[17]

2. Do you accept God's free forgiveness for your sins?[18]

3. Do you want to switch to God's plan for your life?[19]

4. Are you ready to express your desire for Christ to be the director of your life?[20]

If you answered yes to those four questions, it's time to make your decision a reality by making the choice.

MAKE THE
Choice

Action 1: *Pray about It*

It's time to ask Christ into your life. You can do that by praying this simple prayer:

Dear God, I believe You sent Your Son, Jesus, to die for my sins so I can be forgiven. I'm sorry for my sins, and I want to live the rest of my life the way You want me to. Please put Your Spirit in my life to direct me. Amen.

Congratulations! If you prayed that prayer for the first time, welcome to God's family! Please do not feel you need to understand everything about the commitment you just made. Understanding will come as you grow and mature in your walk with Christ. For now, let these words be your comfort: Jesus says, *"Are you tired? Worn out? Burned out on religion? Come to me. Get away with me and you'll recover your life. I'll show you how to take a real rest. Walk with me and work with me—watch how I do it. Learn the unforced rhythms of grace. I won't lay anything heavy or ill-fitting on you. Keep company with me and you'll learn to live freely and lightly."*[21]

There's more good news! *"What this means is that those who become Christians become new persons. They are not the same anymore, for the old life is gone. A new life has begun!"*[22] As you complete the remaining five choices, your life will never be the same. Your new life has begun!

If you have previously asked Christ into your heart, use this prayer time to commit to continually seek and follow His will for your life.

Action 2: *Write about It*

Take some time to reflect on the commitment you just made—whether it was your first commitment to Christ or a renewed commitment to continually turn everything over to His care. Committing to Christ is the most important decision you will ever make. You will never be alone again. As you begin your journaling for this chapter, start off by answering the following questions, which will help you organize your thoughts and emotions:

1. Go back to Choice 1, page 24 under "Action 2: Write about It." Reread your answers to questions 1 through 3. Describe how you feel different about them today.

2. How do you feel, now that the burden of trying to control all the people, places, or things in your life has been lifted from you?[23] *It feels freeing because I canbes go of my shames and gave it to God and my people*

3. What does the following phrase mean to you? "*The old life is gone. A new life has begun!*"[24] *my old ideas of who I thought I was or wanted to be is gone*

4. What are some of the first things you will ask God to help you do or stop doing in your new life? *Not cope with behavors that may/that temporary the shame/ but instead go thru the*

5. What are you having a difficult time letting go of? What is *shame* stopping you from turning these things over to God's control? *for the fif dope you so yours tou from thes loss low yers an*

Action 3: *Share about It*

It's important that you share your decision to ask Christ into your life with others. Follow God's direction found in His Word: "*If you confess with your mouth, 'Jesus is Lord,' and believe in your heart that God raised him from the dead, you will be saved.*"[25] Each time you share your decision, it reconfirms your commitment. Your sharing also lets others know the reason for the freedom and joy you now have in your life.

Celebrate the "Good News" of your commitment with the person you have chosen to be your accountability partner. Let him or her know how you are feeling and what led you to turn the care and control of your life over to Christ. Be sure to share the things you are having a difficult time letting go of (your answer to question 5 on page 98).

Ask your accountability partner to pray with and for you. As you pray together, thank God for your willingness to make the one-time decision to ask Christ into your life as your Lord and Savior. Pray that you will daily, hourly choose to seek and follow God's will for your new life.

You've made it through the third choice. You are well on your way to a happier, healthier life—one lived in your Father's will, by His power and not your own.

The Holmstrom Family's STORY

The following is a special testimony of how God healed and restored an entire family as they worked the 8 Healing Choices. You may want to read this one a couple of times.

Rodney: I'm a grateful believer in Jesus, and I struggle with drugs, alcohol, and food issues. My name is Rodney.

I came from a dysfunctional home, one of four boys, with a mom dealing with her own pain, addictions, and baggage. We lived in a home where verbal, emotional, and physical abuse ran rampant. At the young age of ten, I began smoking marijuana, and when that wasn't enough to mask the pain, I turned to alcohol and eventually, cocaine.

Mom moved away when I was just fifteen, and I stayed behind to live with my "friends" who were drug dealers. I was now a homeless, high-school dropout with no hope for a future. I found myself wandering the streets with no sense of purpose. I felt that God didn't know I existed. He wasn't present in my madness and certainly wasn't strong enough to help me out of this mess, or so I thought . . .

I knew I was in a bad situation, so I moved back in with my mom. I believed I was leaving my problems behind. Little did I know, running would not bring me the peace I so longed for.

Now, I'd like to introduce you to my wife, Carol.

Carol: Hi, I'm a believer in Christ who struggles with control issues, codependency, and depression. My name is Carol.

I grew up in what most would consider a normal Christian home. My parents were good people and worked hard to raise my siblings and me. We were at church all the time because of my parents' involvement. At the age of twelve, I walked the aisle to be "saved." It was just an action, and I didn't really know what it meant. I was also involved in the youth group and sang and played the piano in church regularly because of my family involvement.

At an early age, I was exposed to some experiences that would forever shape the way I saw myself. I experienced a nasty breakup with a long-time boyfriend after high school, and I felt my life spiraling out of control. I continued to attend church, but no one had a clue about the pain I was feeling—not only stress from the breakup, but the guilt and shame I had for my poor choices. Even without a personal relationship with Jesus, I knew that the life I had been living was wrong. I desperately wanted to change, but felt stuck in my pain and low self-esteem. I didn't know how to get out.

I finally realized my need for a Savior at nineteen and asked Christ into my life while I was on a mission trip.

Rodney: Mom moved away again, and I was alone once more. I was able to get a place to stay in low-income housing and go back to school. I was trying to find some normalcy in my life for the first time ever. But that was not to be for now.

Unable to pay my rent, I was evicted from that house, which left me homeless once again. I had no place to go. I didn't want to go back to Mom's, as I knew that would probably mean dropping out of school again to work and support my family. So I went to my music teacher, Mr. Taylor. I told him that I was living on my own and going to school. But I was now homeless. I asked him if I could live with him for a while until I figured things out.

His first response was no, which was completely understandable. He was nearing retirement and was in a stage of life where he didn't see taking in a kid as a smart choice. I went back to my house to get whatever I could fit in my backpack, not knowing where I would go or what I would do. I was completely hopeless. That's when I saw my angel—my Jesus in the flesh. I looked out the front window and saw Mr. Taylor pulling into my driveway in his pickup truck. I walked out the front door and there he was, with my moped in hand, placing it in the back of his truck. He said, "You're coming home with me."

It was because of his and his wife's influence that I got into church and accepted Christ into my life at the age of eighteen. My life began to change.

I finished high school and, with my music teacher's help, got a scholarship to attend a local college. It was there that Carol and I met, and nine months after meeting, we married. I thought I had left my problems behind. But I quickly learned that I was bringing my baggage from the past into the marriage. I had a dysfunctional view of what the family should look like, and I had many character defects.

Carol: I brought my own set of issues into the marriage. I had learned to hide my emotions well and had pretty high walls built up around me. I also felt a deep sense of guilt and shame from past decisions that haunted me. A big test came when I nearly miscarried with our son twice during my pregnancy. It would be a few years later before the strain of that time would play itself out in our marriage. But God had a plan, and even though we weren't following Him at the time, He worked through our dysfunction to bring us the first of the two best gifts we have ever received. He worked a miracle and saved our son for His purposes.

Rodney: When life got tough, more poor choices followed. Instead of facing the pain of my past, I hid myself in my work. I had become a workaholic and would be at work for ridiculous amounts of time, barely seeing my wife and son. This caused an emotional separation between us. One day, I came home to an empty house. My wife had left me. Beaten down emotionally, she had nothing left in her tank to give to our relationship. Her leaving devastated me, and I fell into a deep depression and considered suicide. I had hit my absolute bottom in life. My poor choices were to blame, as well as an unwillingness to deal with my past hurts. I could not bear the thought of being without Carol and our son.

Carol: I would spend days crying and rarely got out of the house. I remember kneeling by my bedside and crying out to God, asking Him to fix my husband and fix my circumstances. But I never remember asking Him to fix me. I involved myself in a church, hoping that would fix me and make me happy, but I was looking to the church for my happiness and not to Jesus. During our separation, Rodney tried to convince me to come back and promised that our life would be different, but I always turned him down. But one day, he called and asked if I would go to lunch with him. Everything within me wanted to say no, but yes came out of my mouth. I didn't know it at the time, but looking back on that lunch, I realize that God was giving me a choice. It was Choice 3, "Consciously choose to commit all my life and will to Christ's care and control." I could either go back and fulfill the commitment I made to Him and my husband, or continue to run. As much as I wanted to reject him, I just couldn't. I knew the choice I had to make.

Letting Go

Consciously choose to commit
all my life and will to Christ's care and control.

As we tried to rebuild our marriage, we sought out counseling to mend our hurts and pain—some of them caused by each other. It was a rough road for quite a while, but as we continued to seek Christ, our marriage wounds started to heal. I knew all along that no matter how hard it would be, I had made the right choice.

But I had still not dealt with my own personal issues, which had been there all along. When our second gift was born, a daughter, we decided to name her after the wonderful couple who took Rodney in off the streets as a young man. I'd like to introduce you to our daughter, Taylor.

Taylor: I'm a grateful believer in Christ who struggles with pride and codependency, and my name is Taylor. I grew up in a Christian home, went to church all my life, and accepted Christ at the young age of four. I knew all the "Sunday school" answers and started developing pride at a young age. This pride caused me to be self-conscious, and I began craving the approval of others. That's how I lived my day-to-day life. My choices were based on what my friends wanted to do and what made *them* happy. I would do anything if I could just fit in. I faced rejection often. This began a struggle with depression, with which I still struggle. I didn't know how to seek help for my deep sadness. I was a pastor's kid; I was supposed to be perfect. Right? I shut my parents out and began lying to them and hiding things from them. I sought out guys whose ultimate goal was to take advantage of me, simply because I felt loved by them. I felt trapped, with no possible way to escape the way I was living. I was depressed, I was a liar, and I based my happiness on what others thought of me. I felt like I had nowhere to go.

Rodney: Several years ago, the church approached us about helping with worship at Celebrate Recovery. God had us right where He wanted us. Through this process I learned that I must turn my entire life and will over to Christ's care, as Principle 3 says. By now, I had been sober for several years, and going through the steps of Celebrate Recovery helped me realize the junk I was still carrying around. It was the same junk that led me to use drugs and drinking as a coping mechanism in the first place.

Carol: Through working the 8 Choices, I realized that the things that happened to me as an innocent child were not my fault. I realized I was God's daughter and that He loved me no matter what. I was able to forgive myself after years of carrying guilt and shame for my poor choices. I started to form relationships with women. That is something I never had before. None of my junk was too big or too small for God. He cares about it all.

Taylor: As I started working through the choices, I began to realize that I am *not* perfect, pastor's kid or not, and God began revealing things to me that I had never allowed myself to see before. Choice 3 was a huge step for me. I had to consciously choose to let Christ begin the healing process in me. Before, I was in such denial about the sin and brokenness in my life.

Letting Go

CHOICE 3

Consciously choose to commit

all my life and will to Christ's care and control.

Now, I'd like to introduce you to my brother, Jason.

Jason: I am a grateful believer in Jesus, and I struggle with people pleasing. My name is Jason. I was thirteen when my parents started attending Celebrate Recovery. My parents started a teen program, and it was there that I learned about *Life's Healing Choices*. Once I finished high school, I decided to turn to my own ways. Early on in college, I started drinking and going to parties. I met a girl and we started dating. While drunk one night, I lashed out at her in anger. It scared me to think that I could hurt this person whom I loved. I realized I was not remembering anything I had been taught about these choices. I was reminded that I need help and need to come out of denial and choose to follow Christ's will for my life. I turned back to God and He began working on me.

Carol: For the past several years, I have had the incredible privilege to help lead Celebrate Recovery for pastors' wives groups at my church. I've also led groups for church staff women who want to work through

Celebrate Recovery. I have seen God moving in a big way in these groups. Because of the work God has done in me through these groups, I have been able to truly enjoy watching our children grow into young adults without trying to control them. I love the way God chooses to use Celebrate Recovery to strengthen *all* of my relationships. My marriage has never been healthier. I'm in awe every day that God would bless me with such an incredible, godly man and spiritual leader in our family. I tell people all the time that God used Celebrate Recovery to save our marriage and our family. I believe that wholeheartedly.

Taylor: Thank God that I don't have to do it on my own. The Spirit is daily revealing things to me, correcting me in areas of my life, and then sending me to share this good news with others. My parents have broken the cycle of dysfunction in their families, and now my brother and I get to keep that cycle from repeating itself because of the tools Celebrate Recovery has given us.

Rodney: A few years ago, my mom went home to be with the Lord. By using these 8 Healing Choices, I was able to deal with her sickness and her passing in a healthy way. I find hope and peace in knowing that she is no longer hurting or struggling the way she had for so long. I continue to grow in peace that God is in control. In the final years of her life, I was able to lead my mom to the Lord and had some of the most incredible talks with her. I was able to make amends to her for some wrongs I did that hurt her, and I was able to forgive her for mistakes she made in her life as well. What a gift to get all that off our chests and make peace before we said good-bye.

I am learning to forgive myself for things I have done in my past. I still struggle in my life and still have to guard my heart from time to time so I don't fall into isolation when things go wrong. The difference now is that I know how to identify the early signs of isolation and can call on my network of people, and especially on Christ, to keep me from running to that cave.

Carol: I still struggle, but the difference now is that I can identify telltale behaviors and can go to God for help in working through those issues. I have been able to release control over certain things in my life that were keeping me from fully experiencing God in the way He intended. It's a daily process. I can count it all joy that I have walked the path that I have because the Father uses my hurts to teach me and grow me in my faith.

Jason: The Celebrate Recovery principles are helping me today with my new wife as I continue to grow and be the best husband I can be to her. I know that in this life there will be many struggles and obstacles. But because of the tools I have learned through this process, I can face them head-on and fight them well. I am grateful for changes I have seen in my parents through this program. It has trickled down to me, and I can now use these tools with my wife and future family. They will have a lasting effect on my legacy. I know God must be the center in the relationship for it to work.

Rodney: Celebrate Recovery has taught me that one person's choices can affect a whole family, and when one person has issues, the whole family has issues. Christ used Celebrate Recovery to change my family's lives, and He can change your life too. He can help you achieve your dream for a new and clean life. I am grateful that this ministry *is* a family ministry and that cycles can be broken—starting with *this* generation and continuing in the generations to come.

Today is a new day. It's time to break those cycles and create a new legacy, with Christ's help.

> *Moreover if the Spirit of the one who raised Jesus*
> *from the dead lives in you,*
> *the one who raised Christ from the dead will also*
> *make your mortal bodies alive through his Spirit who lives in you.*[26]

R
E
C
Openly examine

    and *confess* my faults to myself,
    to God, and to someone I trust.

V
E
R
Y

"Happy are the pure in heart."[1]

Coming CLEAN

The Housecleaning Choice

Mary Owen, National CR Director Training Coach, shares this story with us:

> One day our dryer broke, and the technician said it would be ten days before they could fix it. All I could think was, I can't live a whole day without my dryer!
>
> So I asked Mac if he would make me a clothesline. Being the MacGuyver that he is, he had a functional clothesline tied between two aspens in a matter of minutes.
>
> As I walked outside with my basket of wet clothes, I was greeted with a cool breeze rustling the aspen leaves. Fluffy clouds floated in the sky, birds sang from all sides, the hills felt alive. It was like I was in The Sound of Music!
>
> As I hung each article of clothing on the line, I thought of the old saying, "Don't air your dirty laundry." That brought back memories of me keeping secrets for so many years. At that time, evil taunted me with whispers: "No one will love you," they said. "You aren't good

enough. You never will be. You've made too many wrong choices. It won't turn out good. You'd better keep your dirty laundry to yourself."

I don't believe those lies anymore. I don't hide my dirty laundry anymore, either. Celebrate Recovery is perhaps the only place where you will get a standing ovation for sharing how messed up you've been. The applause won't stop, however, because you'll be giving God all the glory for how He has made you white and clean as freshly fallen snow.

All of us have broken dryers. In the fourth choice, we learn that we don't have to let our dirty laundry collect in some back room. In fact, God didn't wait for us to clean up our own act. While we were sinners, Christ died for us! We can't earn it. The only way to a clean heart is to surrender to Him. When we receive the gift of forgiveness, our lives become clean and spotless in His eyes, while our journey continues following Him forward.

"'Come now, let us reason together,' says the LORD. 'Though your sins are like scarlet, they shall be as white as snow; though they are red as crimson, they shall be like wool.'"[2]

Wouldn't it be nice to live our lives in such a way that we could be unafraid of our past catching up with us? Is that even possible?

THE JOY OF A PURE HEART

The beatitude we're learning about in this choice says, "Happy are the pure in heart." A pure heart is one that is free and clean of impurities. It is a heart free of all the junk that weighs us down, washed clean of all the hurts, hang-ups, and habits that plague our lives. Those who are truly pure in heart aren't afraid of their pasts. They don't spend their todays looking over their shoulders at yesterday. But for many of us, the hope of a "pure heart" was given up long ago.

Is the happiness of a pure heart even possible for you? The answer is in the next few pages. In this chapter, we'll learn about *coming clean*. It won't all be easy, but it is broken down into steps—and the results will change your life forever. The truth is that we all have regrets. We've all done things that we wish we could go back and change. But we can't. We feel guilty, and we carry that guilt with us—sometimes consciously, but most of the time unconsciously. We deny our guilt, repress it, and blame other people for it. We make excuses, and we rationalize. But no matter how hard we try to run from it, we feel its effects just the same.

If we are ever to recover from the hurts, hang-ups, and habits in our lives and know the joy of a pure heart, we'll have to learn how to let go of our guilt and shame and how to gain a clear conscience.

> *If we are ever to know the joy of a pure heart, we'll have to learn how to let go of our guilt and shame and how to gain a clear conscience.*

A young man called in to one of those call-in radio talk shows hosted by a psychologist and said, "I'm consumed with guilt and don't know what to do with it. How do I get rid of this guilt?" The answer offered by the talk-show host was very upsetting: "You can't get rid of guilt. You just have to learn to live with it." That is not the answer! This guy actually told the hurting young man to rationalize his guilt. We can rationalize all we want. We can say, "It's okay, everybody's doing it, it was a long time ago . . . ," but in our hearts, we know what we did was wrong.

In this chapter, the good news is that you will find the key to relief from your guilt. If you take the steps needed to complete this choice, you will know the happiness of a *pure heart* as you share the words of the psalmist: *"What happiness for those whose guilt has been forgiven. What joys when sins are covered over! What relief for those who have confessed their sins and God has cleared their record."*[3]

Before we start working on steps to overcoming guilt, it's important to understand the negative effects guilt has on our lives.

I'm done forgiving the battle and I gave it to God as of August 20th 2019, 10 years after the experience the

WHAT GUILT DOES TO US

1. Guilt Destroys Our Confidence

Guilt and confidence cannot exist in the same person. It's impossible. Guilt is the fear that I'll be caught or that people will realize I'm not all that I say I am. Guilt makes us feel insecure because we're always worried that somebody will find out the truth about us. And if they do, will they still like us?

Guilt is like a dark cloud hanging over our head. We're constantly worried that someone will find the skeleton in our closet—that deep, dark secret that only we know about. It is like carrying a heavy weight around our necks. It robs us of our confidence.

2. Guilt Damages Our Relationships

Guilt sabotages our relationships by causing us to respond in harmful ways. We sometimes overreact out of impatience or anger, or we explode without reason because of some buried guilt.

Guilt can also cause us to indulge people unwisely. Parents often feel guilty over poor choices they have made and overcompensate by indulging their children.

Guilt can cause us to avoid commitment. We wonder why we won't let people get close to us. We allow ourselves to get just so close but no closer. One of the main reasons is guilt. Past relationships push their way into the present and taint the future. Many marriage problems are the result of guilt over things that happened prior to or early in the marriage. That guilt from the past causes marriage problems today.

3. Guilt Keeps Us Stuck in the Past

Instead of dealing with the current problem, some people remain stuck in the past. Their guilt over something they did holds them prisoner. Guilt tries to keep us focused on what's behind us by replaying the past in our minds over and over. We replay all the things we wish we could change.

It's like driving a car by always looking in the rearview mirror. A rearview mirror is helpful, because it gives us perspective. Looking at our past gives us perspective too, but if we look *only* at our past, we never get to see the present or look forward to the future. Some people focus on the past to the extent that their rearview mirror gets bigger than their windshield. With this kind of driving, forward progress is nearly impossible. In fact, a crash is likely in the near future.

Spiritual growth is the process of expanding that windshield and shrinking the rearview mirror so you can get on with the present.

Feeling guilty cannot change the past, just like worry cannot change the future. Feeling guilty just makes our today miserable. Over time, guilt can make us physically sick. When we swallow our guilt, our stomachs keep score! And if we don't talk it out with God and others, we will continue to take it out on ourselves and others.

Choice 4 is the one that brings our painful past out in the open so we can deal with it, be cleansed of it, and then move on to health, balance, and happiness. This fourth choice may be a scary one, but it's a step that separates those who just want to *talk* about getting healthy from those who really want to *get* healthy:

CHOICE 4

Coming CLEAN

Openly examine and confess my faults
to myself, to God, and to someone I trust.

Any friend I had, I let go. & I feel guilty about that. I feel shameful about how I went about it in my past work

At the end of this chapter, you'll read the true story of Johnny and Jeni and how their individual lives, as well as their marriage, were dramatically changed as they made this choice.

If you want to change your life, if you want to get well, if you want to grow and let go of your past guilt once and for all, you will have to come clean and make this fourth choice.

The following five steps will help you move past your guilt. While the procedure is fairly simple, it isn't easy to actually *do*, and it requires a lot of courage.

MOVING PAST GUILT

1. Take a Personal Moral Inventory

This may sound a bit scary, but taking a personal moral inventory will be one of the most productive and cleansing things you can do—like cleaning out a closet. When you clean out a closet, you uncover things that may have been stuffed in a dark corner for years. That stuff may even be stinking up your house. But you've ignored it because the thought of closet cleaning is just too overwhelming. However, when you clean out your closet, you also discover some unexpected treasures—favorite pieces of clothing you thought had been lost or some great article you had forgotten about.

That's how it is with our personal "closet" inventory. We may have all kinds of messes stuffed inside us that we've tried to ignore—some that may even be stinking up our lives. However, we'll also discover some great things about ourselves that we'd forgotten or never even realized. Once we actually get around to doing it, taking a personal moral inventory can transform our lives.

We'll get into the specifics of how to do the moral inventory in our "Make the Choice" section, but for now let's look at the following acrostic to help us understand how this inventory works:

M – Make time to begin your inventory

O – Open your heart and your mind

R – Rely on God's grace

A – Analyze your past honestly

L – List both the good and bad choices and events in your life

The inventory begins with *making* some time to be alone with no interruptions. And you need to take your time; don't rush it. Next, *open* your heart and mind to God and let Him reveal what you need to see: *"Search me, O God, and know my heart; test my thoughts. Point out anything you find in me that makes you sad and lead me along the path of everlasting life."*[4] As you begin to see the truth about yourself, you can *rely* fully upon God's grace, knowing that He has forgiven you—no matter what your inventory uncovers. As you *analyze* yourself, you must be ruthlessly honest—no more pretending, covering up, and denying. And finally, be sure to not only look at the negative things in your life but also *list* the good. It's important to keep your inventory balanced.

Why is it important to do this inventory in writing? Because writing forces you to be specific. Thoughts disentangle themselves when they pass through the lips to the fingertips. If you don't put it down in writing, it will remain vague. Just saying, "God, I've blown it in life," is not specific enough. We've all blown it. We need to get specific, and we need to write it down.

When I wrote down my moral inventory, I saw for the first time how, over the years, my poor choices had hurt all those most important to me. It was truly a moment of clarity. I understood how my drinking hurt my wife, my children, and all those close to me. Although it was painful to go through, the end result was worth every minute of it. My past was no longer a secret, and I could choose to continue my healing journey and do my part in restoring all the relationships that I had damaged.

2. Accept Responsibility for Your Faults

Honestly accepting responsibility for ourselves is not an easy thing to do, but God has created us with the ability to see ourselves for who we are: "*The* LORD *gave us mind and conscience. We cannot hide from ourselves.*"[5] Accepting responsibility for our faults begins with one *do* and three *don'ts*.

1. Do be radically honest

The truth of the matter is, we ourselves are the greatest barrier to the healing of our own hurts, hang-ups, and habits. Our healing starts with us being radically honest and saying, "I'm the problem." We can't keep saying, "If I could just change relationships, jobs, or locations, then everything would be fine." The problem with that kind of thinking is wherever you go, there you are!

2. Don't rationalize

We can't keep saying, "It happened a long time ago" or, "It's just a stage" or, "Everybody does it." We need to be honest and face the truth about ourselves. God's grace can cover us, no matter what the truth is. We don't need to minimize our actions by saying, "It's no big deal." If it's no big deal, why do we still remember it twenty years later?

3. Don't blame others

We blame others by saying, "It was mostly their fault." It may have been mostly their fault, but God holds us responsible for whatever part is our fault. It's time to stand tall and accept responsibility for our part in our life's problems.

4. Don't deceive yourself

We just need to admit where we messed up. "*If we claim to be without sin, we deceive ourselves and the truth is not in us.*"[6] If we really want to stop defeating ourselves, we have got to stop deceiving ourselves. God will help us if we just ask Him.

> SPECIAL NOTE: *If you have been physically or sexually abused as a child or adult, I want you to know that I am sorry that you suffered through that abuse. There is no way I can know the pain it caused you, but I want you to know that I empathize with your hurt. When you start writing down your list of wrongs, simply put the words "NOT GUILTY" for the abuse that was done to you.* No part of that sin committed against you was your fault. *Renounce the lie that the abuse was your fault. Do take responsibility for how you may have hurt others because of your reactions to your past abuse.*

Don't you think it's time to finally deal with your guilt so you can get on with life? As you complete your moral inventory, you will be able to look at your list and say, "Yes, that's me—the good, the bad, and the ugly. I accept responsibility for my faults."

3. Ask God for Forgiveness

"*If we freely admit that we have sinned, we find God utterly reliable and straightforward—he forgives our sin and makes us thoroughly clean from all that is evil.*"[7] You can't find a better promise than that! If we freely admit it, God will forgive us.

God's nature is the basis for forgiveness. There is no sin so severe that God cannot forgive: "*No matter how deep the stain of your sins, I can take it out and make you as clean as freshly fallen snow.*"[8]

A woman came in to see her pastor and said, "I'm depressed. I've been in bed for weeks, and I no longer have the energy to get out of bed and live."

Sensing her deep pain, the pastor asked her, "Is there something in your life you really regret?"

She began to pour it out. "Yes. My husband travels. I had an affair and got pregnant and had an abortion. I have never told my husband about it."

The pastor shared God's promise that no matter how deep the stain of our sins, God can take it out and forgive us.

Distressed, she replied, "It just doesn't seem fair. Somebody's got to pay for my sin!"

"Somebody already has," the pastor assured her. "His name is Jesus Christ. That's why He died on the cross. He died for that sin and every other one you've committed and confessed and ones you're going to commit."

She cried and asked, "How do I ask God for His forgiveness?"

You may be asking the same question. Here's how:

1. *Don't beg.* You don't have to beg for God to forgive you. He wants to forgive you. God wants to forgive you more than you want His forgiveness. He is a forgiving God.

2. *Don't bargain.* Don't say to God, "If You'll just forgive me, I'll never do this again." If you say you will never do it again, and that's your area of weakness, you're probably setting yourself up for failure. You don't have to bargain with God to get His forgiveness.

3. *Don't bribe.* Don't say to God, "If You will forgive me, I promise to do a bunch of good things. I'll go to church; I'll tithe; I'll help the poor." God doesn't want you to try to bribe Him. He wants you to admit your faults and sins to Him and turn from them to the purpose He has for you.

4. *Do believe.* Do believe that He will forgive you. He forgives our sin and makes us thoroughly clean from all that is evil.

When we freely admit that we have sinned, we will find God utterly reliable. To admit or confess means that we agree with God about the

Sometimes I wish I was able to see the extent of my sin. Lord / Jesus, I ask you to show me the extent of my sin w/o any reservations.

sin in our lives. We are saying, "God, You're right. What I did or am still doing is wrong." That's what it means to confess. And you will be forgiven!

4. Admit Your Faults to Another Person

[handwritten: When did I do? How did I mess up my life so bad? I'm having flashbacks to 7th/8th grade, and I was a great kid.]

God tells us that it is absolutely essential to share our moral inventory list with another person: *"Admit your faults to one another and pray for each other so that you may be healed."*[9] How does this verse say we are we healed? By admitting our faults to one another.

Why can't we just admit our faults to God? Why must another person be involved? Because the root of our problems is relational. We lie to each other, deceive each other, and are dishonest with each other. We wear masks and pretend we have it together. We deny our true feelings and play games largely because we believe, "If they really knew the truth about me, they wouldn't love me." We become more isolated than ever.

> *When you risk honesty with another person, all of a sudden, a wonderful feeling of freedom comes into your life.*

We keep all of the junk of our past inside, and we get sick. There's a saying: *We are only as sick as our secrets.* The hurts, hang-ups, and habits that we try to hide end up making us sick, but "revealing your feelings is the beginning of healing."[10] *[handwritten: (Be kind to your innerchild) (Rissa)]*

When you follow God's instruction to *"admit your faults to one another,"*[11] when you risk honesty with another person, all of a sudden a wonderful feeling of freedom comes into your life. You begin to realize that everybody has problems, and many have the same ones you do. There is something therapeutic about admitting your faults to another person. It's God's way of freeing you.

Maybe you're beginning to open your heart to the possibility of sharing your inventory list with one other person, but have some questions: <u>Whom will I tell?</u> <u>What do I say?</u> When do I do it? We're going to answer those questions right now.

Whom Do You Tell?

How do you choose whom to tell? Do you just go out and broadcast your sins to everybody? No. Telling the wrong person or people could cause big trouble. You don't just indiscriminately tell your problems to anyone. You need to find a safe person to share your inventory with. Hopefully, you found that person as you completed the action steps in the first three chapters. If not, here are some additional suggestions that will help you find the right person:

1. *Ask someone you trust*—someone who can keep a confidence and is not a gossip. You don't want to finally share the secrets you've bottled up for years and then read about them in next week's *National Enquirer!*

2. *Ask someone who understands the value of what you're doing*—someone who values and understands the journey of a changed life.

3. *Ask someone who is mature enough not to be shocked*—someone who has been transparent with you about his or her life.

4. *Ask someone who knows the Lord well enough to reflect His forgiveness to you*—a pastor, your accountability partner, your ministry leader, a trusted friend, or a Christian counselor. Most genuine Christians would be honored to have you share your inventory with them.

What Do You Say?

1. *Before you say anything, find a place to meet without interruptions.* You will be sharing some tough issues, and it may not be easy to get the words out. You need plenty of time, and you don't need any distractions.

2. *Be up-front in saying that you need to share your moral inventory*

list. You may start off by saying, "I just need someone to listen to me as I verbalize some things I know are wrong in my life—some of the things I've done and felt; my hurts, hang-ups, and habits."

3. Be specific. The secret you most want to conceal is the very one you need to reveal. The revelation of that most painful secret will bring you the most healing. Then you will experience God's abundant grace and finally be free! You will experience relief and freedom like never before. By taking this action, you step out of the darkness of your secrets and into Christ's freeing "light of life." *"When Jesus spoke again to the people, he said, 'I am the light of the world. Whoever follows me will never walk in darkness, but will have the light of life.'"*[12]

Completely leaving Sabrina in the dust because of fear. Then blaming her. Then blaming God.

When Do You Do It?

There's one answer to this question: *As soon as possible.* Don't procrastinate.

You may be thinking, "I'll finish the rest of the book, and then I'll come back and share my moral inventory with another person." Or, "I need to think about this one for a while. Maybe I'm not quite ready to take this step yet."

That's okay. You may just need a little more pain.

God is waiting to free you from your past. He's waiting for you to come clean so you can move toward healing and joy. Make this healing choice, do it now, and God will bless you and protect you!

5. Accept God's Forgiveness and Forgive Yourself

"All have sinned and are not good enough for God's glory, and all need to be made right with God by his grace, which is a free gift. They need to be made free from sin through Jesus Christ."[13] This passage tells us that we all have missed the mark. We all have done things for which we need God's

forgiveness. We're all in the same boat. We've all sinned. We've all made poor choices. We all have hurts, hang-ups, and habits, just in different areas and degrees.

Forgiveness takes place invisibly. What actually happens when God forgives us? How does forgiveness work?

1. God forgives instantly

He doesn't wait. The moment you ask, you're forgiven. It's done. He never makes you wait or suffer for a while. He loves you way too much. Humans do that, but God doesn't. This is the confidence we can have: "Let us, then, feel very sure that we can come before God's throne where there is grace. There we can receive mercy and grace to help us when we need it."[14] Doesn't that sound exactly like what you need?

2. God forgives freely

He freely takes away your sins. You don't deserve it; you can't earn it; you can't work for it. It's free. "All need to be made right with God by his grace, which is a free gift. They need to be made free from sin through Jesus Christ."[15] God is the one who makes us right—by His grace and for free.

3. He forgives completely

God's forgiveness is not in stages; it is not partial; it is absolutely complete. He wipes our sin out. The Bible says, "Therefore, there is now no condemnation for those who are in Christ Jesus."[16] How great it feels to live with no condemnation, to live with the knowledge that God loves us in spite of all our faults!

Now all that's left is to do it. In the three action steps for this chapter, we'll help you deal with your guilt, come clean through a personal inventory, and accept God's gracious, full, and free forgiveness.

SPECIAL NOTE: *If you are experiencing a lot of pain and distress over completing your inventory because writing down the events of your past is just too difficult to do on your own, I understand. I suggest you go to www.celebraterecovery.com and find a Celebrate Recovery near you. There you will find help and support in completing your inventory. You will find people who have dealt with the same hurts, hang-ups, and habits that you are going through. You will find a safe place!*

MAKE THE
Choice

Action 1: *Pray about It*

Facing your past and being honest about your guilt is not easy. You need God's help to take each step in this choice. Prayer is the best way to tap into His power. You can pray your own words or use these . . .

Dear God, You know my past—all the good and bad choices I have made and all the good and bad things I have done. In working through Choice 4, I ask that You give me the strength and courage to list the items called for in the "Write about It" section below so that I can come clean and face the truth. Please open my eyes to the truth of my past—the truth of how others have hurt me and how I have hurt others. Please help me reach out to others You have placed along my pathway to healing. Thank You for providing these individuals to help me keep balanced as I do my inventory. As I come clean in this choice, I thank You in advance for the forgiveness You have given me. In Christ's name I pray. Amen.

Action 2: *Write about It*

Take a minute to review what you wrote in chapters 1–3 in the "Write about It" sections. It's important that you complete each chapter to the best of your ability before moving on to the next. The Bible encourages us in our efforts: *"Let us examine our ways and test them, and let us return to the Lord."*[17]

Take an 8½ x 11 piece of paper and divide it into five columns. You will need several sheets of paper to complete your moral inventory:

THE PERSON	THE CAUSE	THE EFFECT	THE DAMAGE	MY PART
1. Marissa	1. left me	1. Made myself say "Never will"	1. Left me lonely.	1. Ignorance Jealousy
2. *(illegible)*	2. *(illegible)*	2. I trust someone	2. Killed my self esteem	2. Envy
3. *(illegible)*	3.	3. again	3. Made me feel unworthy of love	3. Ego

Never will I let someone in again   Fear

Column 1: *The Person*—In this column, list the person or object you resent or fear. Go as far back as you can. Remember that resentment is mostly unexpressed anger, hurt, or fear. *I didn't know what I wanted in a friendship anymore. (relationship)*

Column 2: *The Cause*—It has been said that "hurt people hurt people." In this column, list the specific actions someone did to hurt you.

Column 3: *The Effect*—In this column write down how that specific, hurtful action affected your life in the past and continues to affect it in the present. *It continually has me looking inward, not expressing outward. It's kept me to myself. It made me worse people*

Column 4: *The Damage*—In this column write down which of your basic needs were injured. *Social*—Have you suffered from broken relationships, slander, or gossip? *Security*—Has your physical safety been threatened? Have you faced financial loss? *Sexual*—Have you been a victim in abusive relationships? Has intimacy or trust been damaged or broken?

Column 5: *My Part*—In this column you need to honestly determine and write down the part of the resentment or any other sin or injury that you are responsible for. Ask God to show you your part in a broken or damaged marriage or relationship, a distant child or parent, or maybe a job loss. List the people you have hurt and how you specifically hurt them. *The things I did then beginning of time, being rebellious, not listening to others who had their best interest at heart*

PLEASE NOTE: *If you have been in an abusive relationship, especially as a small child, you can find great freedom in this part of the inventory. You will see that you had no part, no responsibility, for* I saw myself staying confused & deemed useless, as no longer being good for anyone. I didn't know what I wanted in life anymore.

the cause of the resentment. By simply writing the words "NONE" or "NOT GUILTY" in column 5, you can begin to be free from the misplaced shame and guilt you have carried with you.

me being a bad person. so that's why all they happend is misplaced

Action 3: *Share about It* *Shame and guilt*

In your "Write about It" action step, you spent some serious time listing some difficult truths. Now it's time to share those truths aloud with your trusted friend. In your next meeting, go through your five columns and share it all. This is the second part of Choice 4—that you "openly confess your faults to someone you trust."

Take your time and have the courage to go through each column in your list:

1. *The Person*—the one or ones you resent or fear

2. *The Cause*—the reason you hurt

3. *The Effect*—both past and present effects of the hurt

4. *The Damage*—how you were hurt (socially, sexually, or made to feel insecure)

5. *My Part*—here you take ownership for your role in the problem, large or small

Remember, saying the words aloud untangles the thoughts in your head, giving them shape and enabling you to face them productively. After you've shared these five topics, take a minute with your friend to thank God for His full forgiveness.

SPECIAL NOTE: *Be careful to safeguard your inventory; this list is no one's business but yours, God's, and the special person you choose to share it with.*

128

the things I have done
or said. I wrong represented
the things that happened
in the past, and the
mean I, and the wrongs
the destructions the
harm that was caused
in them. On myself and others

STORIES OF
Changed Lives

Johnny and Jeni's
STORY

The following is a testimony of a courageous young couple. They both share how making each of the eight *Life's Healing Choices* not only changed their lives but strengthened their marriage and family.

Johnny: Hello, my name is Johnny, and I am a believer who struggles with alcoholism and codependency. For as long as I can remember, I have had a relationship with God. As a preschooler I heard stories about Jesus and how much He loved me. I was instantly drawn to Jesus and wanted to learn more about Him. I asked my parents to take me to church on Sundays so I could hear more about Him. As I got older, I remained in youth group activities, but that church taught a legalistic way to approach God. This fed my already developed guilty conscience. Even as a young kid I would lie awake feeling guilty. I also had an advanced ability to worry. I came to believe that I needed to *earn* God's love. And I had no idea how I would do that.

On top of my guilt and worry, I have always had a need to go against the grain. This desire to rebel coupled with my need to do the right thing made things very uncomfortable for me. When I was fourteen, my parents separated and I found the perfect excuse to act out. No one would blame me for rebelling now; rather, they would expect it. Among my friends, your parents' separation was worth at least a few wild parties. I tried pot for the first time and began having sex with

129

my girlfriend. It was a wild freshman year. Fortunately, after thirteen months, my parents reunited. My mom, my sister, and I began attending Saddleback Church.

Jeni: My name is Jeni, and I'm a believer who struggles with codependency and being an adult child of family dysfunction.

When I was young, my dad was a youth pastor and choir director, which resulted in frequent moves. This was a source of tension between my parents, and they argued a lot. I was only in first grade when my parents divorced. Since my mom left my dad, he was the hero. I felt bad for him because he got left behind. After the divorce, we immediately moved in with Mom's next boyfriend, who ended up being her next husband. He had a temper. There was a lot of arguing in the home, but family life felt somewhat stable. I was angry that this new stepdad had a place in my life, and I'd argue with him often. He became the scapegoat for all of my anger. My mom wanted a happy little family, and I was not willing to comply.

They divorced and my mom quickly went into a relationship with another man.

I didn't like him, and he didn't like me. He also didn't like the fact that my mom had any kids at all. Again, I would argue with him every chance I got. He left my mom, and she had an emotional breakdown. She was depressed, didn't eat, and was hospitalized. I was in junior high and the oldest of the three kids. Being strong for my siblings and my mom while she was in the hospital was the hardest thing I'd gone through thus far. I remember being terrified and so sad. I'd never seen my mom so weak, and it scared me. Over time, my relationship with my mom became codependent, and she was emotionally manipulative.

When she was released from the hospital, we moved yet again to Southern California. She spent a lot of time going out at night looking for a new "stepdad" for us. As a single parent, my mom worked a lot. I felt like the second parent—I was the one cooking and taking care of everyone, including her. Then she married the next stepdad.

I began being two different people, depending on whether I was with my mom or dad. My mom's house didn't have many rules or boundaries— it was a fend-for-myself atmosphere, and felt chaotic. At my dad's, there was more structure, and I could be a kid again. Mom's unstable; Dad's stable.

Around age ten or eleven, my dad became less and less involved in my life. I was confused and felt abandoned. To this day, I feel as if I have to earn his approval—be this perfect kid. *Envy fear Jealousy ego*

Resenting youth/young adults groups and at church
They don't care for my presence The damage says Nobody cares
It makes me stay home isolate you will flock for me
I think I'm unworthy/disloved

Johnny: Around the time we began attending Saddleback, my dad told me he was an alcoholic. At first I didn't believe him. I told him I didn't think he was. I hadn't ever even seen him drunk. He assured me he was, and then he did something extraordinary. He apologized. He said he was sorry for the drinking and the separation. He said he and Mom were going to renew their marriage vows. He asked me for my forgiveness, which I gave him immediately.

When my parents began going to Celebrate Recovery, I got deeply involved with the youth group at Saddleback and did the CR classes 101-301 with my family. I had found a church home and was able to experience the grace of Jesus Christ.

But soon, my old need to rebel kicked in. I found my first drug of choice: Camel cigarettes. This quickly led to a pack-a-day habit that stayed with me for years. Here I was, a leader in the youth group, the

It damages my self-esteem self-centeredness is an obvious trait Fragmented/fearful

leader of the teen group at CR, and "secretly" smoking a pack a day. I knew that smoking wasn't something I should be doing in those roles, but that only made it more appealing. I began lying to cover it up and found out quickly that I had a gift for lying. I did it so well that I actually began to believe my own lies.

During this time, I did my first Step Study. I was sixteen years old and determined that I would never struggle with alcohol. But when I graduated from high school, I decided to move to Los Angeles and try my hand in Hollywood.

I was twenty-one and on my own for the first time. I was in walking distance of four bars. I began to take full advantage of not having to drive home. Soon I was going to the bars most nights of the week. Sometimes with friends, sometimes alone. When I wasn't drinking, I was trying to get acting jobs. I had an agent and went on some auditions, but nothing ever came of it. I never even had a callback. Within that first year of trying, I realized that I wasn't cut out for it. For the first time in my life, I started to feel depressed. I began drinking more and more. Soon I was drinking every night. At this time, I would not have said I was an alcoholic. I was twenty-one and having fun. I was just doing what I was supposed to do.

There was a small problem, though. I was still coming home every weekend and volunteering at church. I was living two different lives. At church I was the good boy who was raised in the church. Out in the world I was a totally different person. There were only a few people who knew both sides of me.

But this double lifestyle was a huge source of shame for me. I was a total hypocrite, and I knew it. I tried many times to stop drinking on my own. I went to a camp with the college group and made a pact with one of my drinking buddies that we would stop drinking together. That lasted about a week. Then we were right back drinking together. I still did not consider myself an alcoholic.

It was around this time that I met Jeni. She and I began dating, and I could tell that she was not going to be interested in "drinking Johnny." I did all that I could to put that side of me away when we were together and play it down as much as possible. I told her that I rarely drank and that when I did, it was just a beer or two. I kept the extent of my drinking a secret, even when she became my fiancée.

I had multiple lives as well. Sometimes 2 or 3 drinks less in a day. Depending on who I was talking to, and who I was seeing. I didn't know better. I was quite lost. And didn't really know myself.

Jeni: Johnny and I met in college ministry. <u>After a brief period of being friends, we started dating and later married.</u>

Johnny drank while we were dating, but I didn't know how much.

Johnny: In December of 1999 I went to my friend's house to celebrate my birthday. It was three days until Christmas, and we started to have some drinks. At 3:30 in the morning, I left to drive home. It was about half a mile from door to door. I made it almost all the way home. The problem is that at 3:30 in the morning, three days before Christmas, I was the only car on the road that wasn't a police car. I was pulled over and given the field sobriety test and failed. I told the officer who drove me to jail that my fiancée would break up with me when I told her I was arrested for a DUI. Thankfully, I was wrong about that. She was gracious and forgiving and let me know she still loved me.

Jeni: I was shocked when Johnny called me at work to tell me about his DUI. I thought, *How did I end up with a guy who got arrested for drunk driving?* To me, drinking was always associated with chaos and out-of-control behavior. But I loved him, so I found it easy to forgive him.

Johnny: After my DUI, I never drank again . . . yeah, right. I wish that were true, but I justified my actions in many ways: I didn't have a problem with alcohol. I just needed to be smarter about driving after I drank. I never again got behind the wheel of a car after drinking, but I certainly did drink again. By the way, when I was arrested, I used my one phone call to call my dad to help me get out. I have never been so nervous and so ashamed in my life. Oh, and I haven't mentioned it yet, but my dad is the author of this book and the pastor and founder of Celebrate Recovery! He didn't lecture me. He told me he loved me and that I probably needed to look at my actions and see why I was making those choices. He left the decision up to me.

Jeni and I married in May of 2000, and we recently celebrated our fifteenth wedding anniversary. I am truly blessed to have her in my life. At first, we rarely had alcohol in the house. I would sometimes convince her that we should have margaritas or needed some kind of alcohol to cook with. Sometimes she would agree, and I would have a few drinks. Jeni never drank, and I never got drunk in front of Jeni. I knew she wouldn't stand for it. One night I went to the kitchen while she was asleep and had a few before going back to bed. This was the first time I drank behind her back, but it wouldn't be the last.

Jeni: After we married, Johnny continued to drink, and I saw the evidence in his out-of-control behavior. But I was afraid to confront him because I thought he would leave me. Going into my marriage, I didn't know what a stable family looked like, but I did know what I didn't want my family to look like. One resolve I had was that I wasn't going to fight with Johnny. I didn't want to treat him like I'd treated my stepdads—arguing and yelling. In my past, arguing and confrontation always equaled divorce.

Johnny and I had opposite work schedules—I worked during the day, and he at night—which made it easy for him to hide the drinking. I didn't know the full scope of his drinking, but knew some of it. I thought I was saving my marriage by not confronting him. I was angry with myself for not calling him out on it, and angry with him for choosing this behavior.

Johnny: I worked nights as a waiter and had trouble sleeping after a busy shift. I convinced myself that drinking was the only way I could sleep. It is amazing how fast you can convince yourself of the things you want to believe. I came up with all kinds of ways to disguise my drinking from Jeni. I would usually get home as she was getting ready to fall asleep, so it wasn't hard to sneak beer or some other kind of alcohol into the house. But when Jeni got pregnant with our first daughter, I was finally aware my drinking might be a problem. It was harder and harder for me to enjoy drinking as I thought about impending fatherhood. I didn't want my kids to see me drink the way I saw my dad drink. What especially got to me was the thought that Jeni might go into labor after I had started drinking, and I wouldn't be able to drive her to the hospital.

So I decided I needed to stop drinking. I accepted the fact that I was an alcoholic and that it was time to give it up. After I quit drinking, I thought I'd become sober. But what I was instead was a *dry drunk*.

When Maggie was born, it had been about eight months since my last drink, but I wasn't going to meetings or working the program. Thankfully, I was able to draw on my past Step Study experiences and

Nothing better to do. No excuses.

apply the principles as I dried up. But I didn't have accountability; and although I didn't drink anymore, I found myself thinking about drinking every day. When Maggie wouldn't sleep or cried a lot, which I have come to find newborns do quite well, I would fanaticize about drinking. It was time for me to get involved in Celebrate Recovery, so I could live and enjoy my sobriety.

I found a sponsor, began attending Step Study and Open Share groups, and started applying the principles of recovery to my life, as well as I could.

Coming CLEAN

CHOICE 4

Openly examine and confess my faults
to myself, to God, and to someone I trust.

Jeni: I'm thankful that he got into recovery when he did, because I didn't have a lot of time to build up resentment. When Johnny did get into recovery, it was real and genuine. He came to me on his own and admitted for the first time that he had a drinking problem and that he needed to get into recovery. I thought, *Oh good, I don't need to call him out on it.* He was so good about including me in the process. His recovery was very healing for both of us. Recovery became an active part of our lives.

Johnny: When Maggie was about six months old, I felt God speak to my heart and tell me that He wanted me to become a pastor. I yelled, "NO!" at the top of my lungs and for some reason turned off the radio. It was like I thought He was talking to me from there. But He didn't let up. I had been running a restaurant, but I lost the joy and desire of doing that and felt called to start working in ministry. I told Jeni, assuming she would say I was crazy. But she didn't. She said, "Great, what do we do next?" I applied for jobs at the church and was told no over and over. I didn't get discouraged; I knew that God had something special planned for me.

That's when my dad asked if I would be willing to come work at Celebrate Recovery. I started answering phone calls and emails that came in from all over the world asking about Celebrate Recovery. I began leading groups at Celebrate Recovery in Lake Forest, and I traveled with the team that trains other churches how to do the Celebrate Recovery program. I learned so much about recovery and how it applies to me. I also knew this was exactly what God had planned for me. I began seminary and eventually became the pastor of Celebrate Recovery at Saddleback Church.

Jeni: When Johnny started working for Celebrate Recovery, he began to toss around terms like *codependent* and eventually suggested that I'm a codependent and that I should check it out.

Johnny was right. My relationship with my mom was extremely codependent. I considered her my best friend. I often put her before Johnny; her opinions were more important to me than anyone else's opinions. When my mom experienced yet another failed relationship, she went into another tailspin and jumped right into a new relationship with a dangerous man. I thought, *I'm married now; I don't have to be a part of her chaos.* So I tried to put some boundaries in place with my mom and her latest relationship. I told my mom that her latest boyfriend could not come to our daughter's first birthday party. She threatened not to come. I told her if she did not come, it would forever change our relationship. She chose not to come. A couple of months later, I received a threatening text from this man and made the decision to remove myself and my family from my mom. I was nine months pregnant with my second child when this happened.

We stayed separated from each other, with no connection at all for five years. She missed the births of my second and third children. This was devastating to me.

After a year of counseling, we were able to reconcile. For the first time, I told my mom how her actions had affected me. She said I seemed like a different person, as I had never talked to her about these things before. After we reconciled, I struggled with discerning appropriate boundaries and feared that I would slip back into old habits.

During all of this, I was realizing that, *Yes; I need the Celebrate Recovery program.* But I was overwhelmed with being a mom to three young kids. Then the guilt would set in, because I knew that other pastors' wives were active in their husband's ministry. I would wrestle with God about it, get some peace, then go back to feeling guilty.

Three years ago, at the Celebrate Recovery Summit, Johnny's mom, Cheryl, said to me, "I think you should go through a pastors' wives Step Study."

And she wanted me to pitch the idea to the other Saddleback pastors' wives. I felt intimidated and unworthy because I had not gone through the study myself, and I suggested that Cheryl talk to the women about it. But she gently pushed back and said I should pitch it because I would be doing it. So I did. And the group started meeting in September 2013. Since then, I have led three Step Studies for the pastors' wives at our church.

Since completing my first Step Study, I'm learning to let go of my need for others' approval. I've always known in my head that God loves me and that His opinion is the only one that matters, but this is the first time I have actually been okay with not everyone liking me.

When I first worked on Principle 1, Step 1 and the idea of being powerless, I wrote and shared, "I am powerless to heal from my childhood hurt and anger alone." This was an important revelation for me. Though I had vaguely understood that truth, getting it down in words impacted me powerfully.

The Bible encouraged me, "With man this is impossible, but with God all things are possible."[18] It was the first time I began to realize how much I hadn't dealt with this hurt.

CHOICE 4

Coming CLEAN

Openly examine and confess my faults

to myself, to God, and to someone I trust.

Step 4—the "housecleaning" inventory—was my favorite part. I had the most "aha" moments during this step But I was also terrified that I would somehow do it wrong. Looking back, this is where the real grieving process started. I had never looked at the patterns and their impact on my life. I hadn't realized how the events in my past were affecting my choices in my present adult life.

And I realized that I had never really forgiven my mom or grieved the divorce of my parents—which shocked me. This, combined with working through my character defects, helped me learn that I was stuck in a victim mentality, which was why I was easily hurt by others. I learned that my response to that hurt was to pull away or walk away from that relationship. I realized that I had a certain sense of pride in doing things on my own and not asking for help. Part of that stemmed from my control issues—after all, trying to control my environment is how I survived growing up.

I also learned that I was using harmful sarcasm with my children and worried that I was beginning to be manipulative. I was doing the exact things my mother did when I was a child, and I didn't want to fall into the same pattern.

In particular, I had an issue with one of my kids and her temper. If you ask me, I would say she got it from Johnny. If you ask Johnny, he will tell you the truth and say she got it from me. Because my mom and I did not have good boundaries, I went into parenthood with the fear that I would have unhealthy boundaries with my kids too. My daughter's strong-willed nature triggered the fear in me that I would not be able to parent well. I, in turn, would have an unhealthy response. After our interactions, my sarcastic response would leave us both defeated. It hurt her and I felt guilty afterward. I kept looking for an answer. Then I ran across this verse in the book of James, "Everyone should be quick to listen, slow to speak and slow to become angry."[19] It was the exact opposite of how I had been interacting with my daughter.

Throughout the study, this verse and the idea of being a better listener kept popping up in regards to other relationships. I wondered why the idea kept popping up. I believe the reason is that being quick to listen, slow to speak, and slow to get angry is the antidote to my control issues. It's hard to *both* control the situation and listen. Listening counters my selfishness, because I have to put the other person first.

By the end of the Step Study, I enjoyed answering the questions about my victories. By overcoming my victim mentality, I could see *my* part in relationships where I have been hurt. I've been able to identify relationships where I've been jealous and own my part in it. I have been able to forgive my mom. We have built a new relationship—one that is healthier. I am so thankful that she is an active part of my life now. My relationship with God has deepened as I am now relying on Him to conquer my character defects on a daily basis—trusting in Him to help me heal from these hurts in my life.

I have a restored attitude over the relationships in my life. My ability to forgive, to right my attitude, and to be a more loving parent to my kids has been so freeing.

Johnny: Watching Jeni go through recovery has been one of the highlights of my life. She has jumped into her recovery and encourages and challenges me to keep focused on mine. I hadn't even thought about how recovery could apply to my parenting style until she brought it up! I believe God will use Celebrate Recovery to heal my family for generations to come. I feel so fortunate that Jeni and I get to continue the legacy started by my parents. Jeni and I both are committed to ending the cycle of dysfunction in our family. Since beginning recovery, I have completed many Step Studies and have continued to work on key areas of my life, including my own codependency. One of my favorite things about Celebrate Recovery is that we don't have to pretend. We don't have to try and fake it. With these people, I can admit that I have character defects and that certain issues still pop up that need to be dealt with.

For those of you who think pastors should be perfect, I have news for you—we aren't. Although I haven't had the desire to take a drink in years, I still know that as soon as I think I can do this by myself, I'm in for a relapse. I also know there are many other issues in my life that still need to be dealt with. In my last Step Study I didn't focus on my alcoholism; instead, I worked on my codependency issues.

One of my biggest victories is that I am no longer two different people. I'm not leading two different lives. I'm not just sober. *I'm whole.* There is such joy in not hiding things from the people closest to me, especially Jeni. I don't have to worry that she will find me out or waste the energy keeping my story straight.

I love getting to serve at Celebrate Recovery. Every Friday night I get to see lives changed right in front of me. As someone whose life has been changed by Jesus through Celebrate Recovery, I can think of no better joy than getting to help other people find the same life change. I have been honored to become a speaker at the Celebrate Recovery Summits and One Day Seminars. I have even gotten to write some books!

I never would have thought I would get to do such things. I am far from perfect. If you don't believe me, just ask Jeni. I am banged up. I make huge mistakes. I routinely need to apply the principles of recovery, especially making amends and offering forgiveness. But God has decided to use me anyway. I don't tell you that to brag, but to tell you that no matter where you are in your journey, He can do the same thing for you.

God has used not only my past pain and struggles for His purpose, but also the struggles of my family. Whether you have been in recovery fourteen days and the going is tough, or you have fourteen years of experiencing victory over your hurts, hang-ups, and habits, when you share your experiences with those around you, both you and they will be encouraged.

Jeni: Before Celebrate Recovery, I knew that everyone has hurts in their lives; but I had no idea how much I would learn about myself through the Step Studies. It's an amazing journey. I felt like God lovingly held my hand during this process. As a whole, I've had victory over anger, resentment, bitterness, and jealously. When I was younger I was drawn to this verse: "He comforts us whenever we suffer. That is why whenever other people suffer, we are able to comfort them by using the same comfort we have received from God."[20] It gave me comfort that one day God would use the hurt in my life to help others. I love that Celebrate Recovery gives me the chance to do this.

One of the things I love most is that instead of sitting on the sidelines, I can now serve in ministry with my husband. One of our favorite verses is this:

> *Make every effort to add to your faith goodness;*
> *and to goodness, knowledge; and to knowledge, self-control;*
> *and to self-control, perseverance; and to perseverance, godliness;*
> *and to godliness, brotherly kindness;*
> *and to brotherly kindness, love.*[21]

R
E
C
O
Voluntarily submit
E
R
Y

to every *change* God wants to make
in my life and humbly ask Him
to remove my character defects.

"Happy are those whose greatest desire is to do what God requires."[1]

Making CHANGES

The TRANSFORMATION Choice

The following story is from my wife, Cheryl, about an interesting experience we shared together.

It was time. We had put it off long enough because we did not want to deal with the inconvenience and the pain—to our wallet. It was time to remodel the house. Oh, we had some choices. We thought about moving and letting someone else deal with fixing up the house. Or we could just live with it the way it was. Or we could go through the hassle of making the changes that would make our home look better and be more enjoyable for us. We decided that we did not want to sell our house, and that it was time to make some big changes.

But when the floors were torn up, the fireplace demolished, and doors removed, I began to wonder if we had made the best choice. Thirty years ago, our children's small feet had padded across those floors. They had hung their stockings by that fireplace, and we had chronicled their growth on the back of one of those doors. Some of our past came crashing down in the remodel, and sometimes it hurt.

Days went by while the guys "prepped" the walls or put in new electrical outlets. The saws and drills made a lot of noise, yet we couldn't see much progress. This was discouraging. We "camped out" in different areas of the house while cleaning out cabinets and closets. It was a good opportunity to sort through things and make choices about what we wanted to keep and to throw out the things we didn't need. But this was not easy!

But gradually and eventually, we saw progress. The new floors were put in and the cabinets in the kitchen were installed and painted. Our house was looking better and felt cleaner. We began to see that the results were going to be worth it.

When the remodel was complete, we looked at each other and wondered why we had put off the process for so long. The reconstruction had included some good times, some bad times, and plenty of funny moments. But it was now worth it! We had a beautiful, comfortable new home, and we were ready to make new memories with our kids and grandkids.

Most of us get to a place in life when we know that we need to make changes. We often put those changes off for as long as we can. Change is hard. Maybe you have tried to move away from your problems by relocating or taking a new job. You may need to let go of some things or people from your past. It might be time to sort through your life to decide "what to keep and what to throw away." It can be painful and discouraging when you are working so hard and seeing so little progress. But you aren't alone. You have Jesus Christ to help you get through the inconvenience of hard choices and pain. If you stay with the process and are willing to make small, new choices every day, you might just look back and say, "What took me so long?"

Because you have already worked through Choices 1 through 4, you are now ready for the *transformation* choice. You are ready to submit to God and allow Him to change you. The Bible has this to say about the transformation choice: *"Offer yourselves as a living sacrifice to God, dedicated to his service and pleasing to him. . . . Let God transform you inwardly by a complete change of your mind."*[2] God is ready to transform you by changing your mind; He is just waiting for you to submit to His loving hand.

The beatitude paired with this choice says, *"Happy are those whose greatest desire is to do what God requires."* And one of the things He requires is *change*, and that change begins with your submission to His power. Will the changes be easy? Will they happen overnight? Of course not. But the promise of this beatitude is that when your greatest desire is to do what God requires, you'll be *happy*.

> God loves you too much to leave you the way you are.

You know God has forgiven you; now He wants to change you. He loves you too much to leave you the way you are.

In this chapter we will learn how to *cooperate with God in His process of changing us.* But first, we'll look at the *origin of our character defects* and *why it is so hard for us to get rid of them.*

WHERE DO OUR CHARACTER DEFECTS COME FROM?

Our character defects come from three sources: biological, sociological, and theological. We'll examine these three sources through our *chromosomes*, our *circumstances*, and our *choices*.

147

1. Our Chromosomes

Do you know that your mother and father each contributed 23,000 chromosomes to your development? From your parents, you inherited some of their strengths and some of their weaknesses. You inherited many positive traits from them, but you also inherited some of their negative characteristics. You inherited some physical defects, as well as some emotional defects. This explains your predisposition toward certain problems.

However, this predisposition doesn't give you an excuse to act out inappropriately. You are still responsible for your own behavior. For instance, you may have a tendency toward a hot temper, but that doesn't give you an excuse to go out and punch somebody. You may have a tendency to be lazy, but that doesn't mean it's okay for you to lie on the couch all day. You may have a tendency, genetically, toward certain addictions, but that doesn't excuse you for choosing to become addicted to prescription drugs. Our genetics, or our natures, contribute to our character defects; and while they don't provide us with excuses, they do provide some understanding.

2. Our Circumstances

The circumstances of how you were raised and what you saw as you grew up, even your current circumstances, contribute to your character. Much of how you behave and relate you learned from watching others. When you were very young, you learned from watching your parents. As you grew you learned from watching others—your peers, your teachers. You developed certain patterns and habits; many of them were attempts to protect yourself, to handle hurt and rejection, and to cope.

The truth is, many of your current character defects are actually self-defeating attempts to satisfy your unmet needs. You have a legitimate need for *respect*. If you didn't get respect early in life or don't feel you have it now, you may settle for attention instead. You've figured out how to get attention in various ways, some positive and some negative. You also have a legitimate need for *love*. If you didn't get the love you needed as a child (and perhaps you still feel unloved), you may have learned to settle for superficial relationships or one-night stands. You also have a need for *security*, but if you grew up in an insecure environment or are in one now, you may be seeking security through the accumulation of possessions.

Our circumstances, past and present, help us understand the character defects that haunt us today.

3. Our Choices

The choices you make are the most significant source of your character defects, because they are the one thing you can do something about. You can't control or change who your parents are. You can't go back and change the environment of your childhood. But you can, with God's power, change the choices you make.

You develop your hang-ups because you repeat negative choices. And if you choose to do something long enough, it becomes a habit. Once it becomes a habit, you're stuck. When a person makes the choice to take that first drink, he or she never thinks addiction will eventually follow. But after a series of choices to continue to abuse alcohol, the habit or addiction begins to own that person's life. Our choices may have been influenced by our chromosomes or our circumstances, but ultimately we are responsible for the choices we make.

WHY DOES IT TAKE SO LONG TO GET RID OF OUR CHARACTER DEFECTS?

Why is it so hard to change the defects in our lives? There are four main reasons:

1. Because We've Had Them So Long

It's human nature to want to hold on to what's familiar, even when that familiar thing is causing us pain. Most of us have had our hang-ups and habits for a long time—they may have taken years to develop. Many were developed in childhood. Many are painful and self-defeating, but we hold on to them because they are familiar.

They're comfortable like an old pair of shoes. They may have big holes in the soles and they allow our feet to get wet, but we hang on to them because we're used to them; we feel comfortable in them. Since we've had them for so long, we have a hard time letting them go.

2. Because We Confuse Our Defects With Our Identity

We often confuse our identity with our character defects. We say, "That's just the way I am." We identify ourselves by our defects when we say, "It's just like me to be a workaholic or overweight or anxious or passive. It's just like me to be fearful or lose my temper or to lust."

Our words and thoughts become self-fulfilling prophecies. If you say, "I'm always nervous when I get on planes," what's going to happen the next time you get on a plane? You're going to be nervous.

Sometimes we so closely identify ourselves by our defects that we worry, "If I let go of this defect, will I still be me? This has been a part of me for so long, who will I be if I ask God to remove it?"

In the small group meetings at Celebrate Recovery, when someone shares, they introduce themselves by saying, "Hi, I'm Bob, a believer who struggles with anger." Or, "I'm Nancy, a believer who struggles with overeating." Notice that their identity is in their belief in Christ. Their hurts, hang-ups, and habits do not define them. We all need to be sure that we do not allow our character defects to become our identity.

3. Because Every Defect Has a Payoff

We have a hard time letting go of our defects because each one has a very real payoff. The payoff may be temporary relief from pain. It may be attention or control. Our defects may give us an excuse to fail or allow us to compensate for the guilt in our lives.

If a negative behavior is repeated, you can be sure there's a payoff. The payoff may be self-destructive, but it brings some sort of perceived benefit.

A mom who is struggling with her anger might politely say to her children, "Kids, come to dinner." When they don't come, she asks them again. When they still don't come, she yells, "Kids, come down to dinner, or you are going to get me mad, and you know what happens then!" Then they come. Unconsciously, the kids have set up their mother to yell and get mad, and Mom has figured out that yelling works. There's the payoff.

4. Because Satan Discourages Our Efforts to Change

Satan constantly tries to fill our minds with negative thoughts. He is the accuser. He whispers in your ear, "This will never work; you can't do it; you'll never change." Some of you have been reading this book and thinking, "This is good stuff. I'd really like to get rid of this habit. I'd like to stop hating that person. I'd like to stop hurting from that past experience out on the schoolyard. I'd love to change." Then you put the book down, and Satan starts in on you: "Who do you think you are? You think you're going to change? Forget it! Other people can change, but not you. You're stuck. It's hopeless. Don't even think about it." And worse than that he says, "If you change this about yourself, who will you be? If you change, you'll self-destruct; something bad will happen to you."

The Bible says that Satan is a liar: *"There is no truth in him. When he tells a lie, he shows what he is really like, because he is a liar and the father of lies.*"[3] But counteracting Satan's lies is the truth that sets us free. Jesus said, *"You will know the truth, and the truth will set you free."*[4] As you grow in God's truth and voluntarily submit to the changes He has in store for you, you will discover the happiness of doing what God requires.

At the end of this chapter you'll read the stories of Sabrena and James and how they found freedom when they faced the truth about their character defects and voluntarily submitted to the changes God wanted to make in each of them. For now let's discover the exciting news of how we can cooperate with God as He works the change process in our lives through Choice 5.

CHOICE 5

Making CHANGES

Voluntarily submit to every change
God wants to make in my life and humbly
ask Him to remove my character defects.

HOW DO WE COOPERATE WITH GOD'S CHANGE PROCESS?

Remember the illustration we opened the chapter with—about remodeling our house? Again, the only way to change the direction of our lives—long-term—is to accept that change is needed. That's what the *transformation* choice is all about. Remember also the verse that says, *"Be transformed by the renewing of your mind."*[5] Transformed. Renewed mind. If we want to change our lives, we've got to allow God to renew the way we think. Our thoughts determine our feelings, and our feelings determine our actions.

What character defects are you trying to stop by using your own willpower? Are you tired yet? Have you figured out that you can't do it on your own? Only by God's power can your mind can be changed.

After I made the fourth choice, all of my sins and the wrongs of my past were no longer a secret. I was finally willing to allow God to change me by removing the defects of my character. I was willing to allow God to transform my mind—its nature, its condition, its identity.

I thought my major defect of character was my sin addiction to alcohol. But I learned that it was only a symptom. God showed me that my biggest character defect was my nonexistent self-esteem. As a young boy in high school I never felt good enough for anyone—my teachers, my coaches, my parents, my girlfriends, my teammates, anyone. I attempted to cover up that poor self-image with the world's largest ego. Believe me, that is not a very comfortable way to go through life. I carried my character defects with me until I finally got into recovery.

In this fifth choice, God changed me. He helped me rebuild my self-worth based on His unconditional love for me. I stopped trying to measure up to the world's standards and always failing and falling short. Today I attempt to live my life pleasing to God. Not much changed in my life—just everything! If you would like to read my entire story, go to www.celebraterecovery.com.

The following seven focus points will show you how to *cooperate* with God as He works to change your autopilot and gets you heading in the right direction.

1. Focus on Changing One Defect at a Time

You may have thirty different things you know need changing, but the wisdom of Proverbs tells us, *"An intelligent person aims at wise action, but a fool starts off in many directions."*[6] Trying to tackle all thirty problems at once is like those little bugs that fly around in all directions, never making any real progress but stirring up a lot of motion. Ask God to help you focus on changing one defect at a time. Otherwise you'll feel overwhelmed and discouraged, and you won't be able to change anything at all.

We can't think about living an entire lifetime of victory, but we can focus on victory for just one day.

Focus on one specific change at a time, such as your anger, anxiety, workaholism, dishonesty, or tendency to control people. In "Action 1" at the end of this chapter, you'll look through your moral inventory from chapter 4 and ask God which item on the list is causing the most damage to your life, today. He can help you focus on one defect at a time.

2. Focus on Victory One Day at a Time

God didn't promise to give us all the groceries we need for the entire year so we can stuff our refrigerator full and then forget about Him. When Jesus taught His disciples to pray, He said, "*Give us today our daily bread.*"[7] He didn't say, "Give us this month our daily bread." He didn't tell them to ask for one week, one month, or the rest of their lives. Why? Perhaps for two reasons: first, God wants us to lean on Him day by day; and second, He knows we can't handle looking forward to a whole lifetime all in one chunk. We need it broken down. We can't think about living an entire lifetime of victory, but we can focus on victory for just one day.

It's like the old saying: "How do you eat an elephant? One bite at a time." You take a lifetime problem, remembering you didn't get it overnight, and you break it down into bite-size pieces. You seek victory one day at a time. God gives you enough strength to change for one day. He takes care of you one day at a time, as you put your trust in Him.

We live in a world of instant everything: mashed potatoes, coffee, microwave popcorn, even information. And we want instant spiritual maturity. One day we are a total mess, and we want to be Billy Graham the next. It doesn't happen that way. There's another old saying: "Life by the yard is hard, but by the inch, it's a cinch." You grow by inches. You experience victory day by day. Jesus tells us, *"Don't be anxious about tomorrow. God will take care of your tomorrow too. Live one day at a time."*[8]

Don't set a deadline for yourself; just work on it one day at a time. Some character defects you'll be working on for the rest of your life.

Ask God to help you just for today: "Lord, just for this day, I want to be patient and not get angry. Just for today, protect me from going to those Internet sites. Just for today, help me think pure thoughts instead of lustful ones. Just for today, I want to be positive instead of negative." Ask God to help you just for today, and take it a little bit at a time. This keeps you from making rash vows like, "I promise never to do it again, from here to eternity." Such promises doom you to failure. Remember, one day at a time. Bite-size pieces.

Each night thank God for whatever change or victory He has worked in your life, no matter how small.

3. Focus on God's Power, Not Your Willpower

Can you remember your last New Year's resolutions? Even if you can remember them, have you followed through and actually done them? Probably not. Studies show that within six weeks, approximately 80 percent of us will break our New Year's resolutions.

You already know that willpower isn't enough. If your own willpower worked, you would have already changed. The truth is, your self-will can't help you change because *you* don't have the power to do it. In fact, depending on your own strength will actually block your recovery. It's like trying to turn that big boat by your own willpower when it's set on autopilot to go the opposite way. You struggle and you try, but in the end you are defeated because you just get worn out with the effort of fighting those strong opposing forces. As soon as you get tired, as soon as you let up just a little, the autopilot will pull you right back on the course you've always been on.

God's Word gives us some profound insight: *"Can . . . a leopard take away his spots? Nor can you who are so used to doing evil now start being good."*[9] Forget it. You'll never change by your own willpower. Here's the good news: *"I can do everything through him who gives me strength."*[10]

Try to imagine God literally taking away your character defect. Let's say you are working on your temper. Imagine taking your temper out and opening up the garbage can. Imagine putting your temper into the garbage can, sealing the lid, and taking the garbage can out to the curb. Then imagine the garbage truck pulling up by the side of the road. See the sign on the side that says, "God & Son, Doing Business with People Like You for 2000 Years."

Watch them pick up the garbage, dump it in the truck, and smash it down. Then watch as the truck turns around and speeds off, taking your defect with it. Some days you will need your garbage picked up about every hour. Talk to God about it: "God, it's going into the garbage." Then let God take it away. Willpower doesn't work. You have to trust God's power, not your own. He can help you change your character defects if you submit to Him and pray, "Lord, I know I can't change on my own power, but I'm trusting You to change me."

4. Focus on the Good Things, Not the Bad

The Bible says, *"Fix your thoughts on what is true and good and right. Think about things that are pure. Think about all you can praise God for and be glad about.*"[11] What you focus on is what you move toward. What you focus on dominates your life. If you focus on the bad, it will dominate your life. If you say, "I'm not going to think about sex, I'm not going to think about sex," guess what you are going to think about? Sex! So what's the answer? You change the mental channel of your mind. If you're watching an inappropriate show on TV, you don't just sit there and keep saying, "I'm not going to watch this; I'm not going to watch this." No, you pick up the remote control and change the channel.

This is where the power of God's Word comes in. Did you know that there are more than seven thousand promises in the Bible? These promises are the perfect channel to change to. When you get these promises into your mind, you can change your channel to something good at any time. You can change your channel by learning to memorize Scripture. Memorize one verse a week, and by the end of the year, you'll have fifty-two verses memorized. When they're in your mind, you can change the channel on any negative thoughts the enemy or others give you.

Did you know that every time you think a thought—positive or negative—it sends an electrical impulse across your brain, and that impulse creates a path? Every time you think the same thought, the path gets deeper and reinforces that brain pattern. Some of us have negative ruts in our minds because we've thought the same negative things over and over. But we can also create positive pathways in our mind. Every time we think about a scriptural truth, we reinforce that positive brain pattern. The only way to replace the negative ruts is to think God's Word over and over.

As you focus on what you can be and what God wants you to be, you will move in the right direction. Whatever has your attention has you. Jesus tells us, *"Stay alert, be in prayer, so you don't enter the danger zone without even knowing it. Don't be naive. Part of you is eager, ready for anything in God; but another part is as lazy as an old dog sleeping by the fire."*[12]

Stay focused on the good and not the bad. According to what Jesus said in the verse above, that means staying alert to the danger that's out there and being diligent in our positive focus instead of being *"as lazy as an old dog sleeping by the fire."*

5. Focus on Doing Good, Not Feeling Good

If you wait until you feel like changing, you'll never change. The enemy will make sure you never feel like it. But if you'll go ahead and do the right thing, your feelings will eventually catch up with you. It's always easier to act your way into a feeling than to feel your way into an action. If you don't feel loving toward your spouse, begin to act loving, and the feelings will come. If you wait until you feel like it, you may have a long wait.

The old phrase "Fake it 'til you make it" applies here. Do the right thing even though you don't feel like it. Do it because it's the right thing to do. Eventually, your feelings will catch up. Anytime you try to change a major part of your life—a character defect, flaw, personality trait, or weakness— it won't feel good at the start. In fact, it will feel awkward. Even more, it will feel bad for a while. Why? Because it won't feel normal. Sometimes we are so used to feeling abnormal that normal doesn't feel good.

Let's say you're a workaholic, and you decide to *do* the right thing whether you *feel* like it or not. So you go home at five, and you don't take work home in your briefcase. The first time you try this, it feels really weird. The first time you try to relax, you find that you don't know how to relax because you've worked so hard for so long. If you're an overeater, a drinker, or a smoker, the first time you try to break your habit, you feel weird because there's nothing in your mouth. It'll feel funny for a little while, and it may not feel right. But if you do the right thing, over and over, eventually your feelings will catch up with your behavior.

As we focus on doing what's right, we must draw on the power of the Holy Spirit, whom God has placed in all believers. Scripture makes a powerful promise about our reliance on the Holy Spirit: *"If you are guided by the Spirit you will be in no danger of yielding to self-indulgence."*[13] The guiding of the Holy Spirit works in direct opposition to self-indulgence. So as we *do* what's right, His power works in us to bring our heart and feelings in line.

6. Focus on People Who Help, Not Hinder You

The Bible says, *"Do not be fooled: 'Bad friends will ruin good habits.'"*[14] In other words, if you don't want to get stung, stay away from the bees. If you know what type of people tempt you, just stay away from them. If you're struggling with alcoholism, don't say, "I think I'll go down to the bar with a friend just to eat some peanuts." Bad idea. If you're struggling with pornography, you don't hang out with a friend who has pornographic magazines lying all over his apartment. You don't get around people who mess you up.

On the other hand, you *do* need to hang around people who will help you make positive changes in your life. Again, the Bible has words for us: *"Two are better than one. . . . If one falls down, his friend can help him up. But pity the man who falls and has no one to help him up! . . . A cord of three strands is not quickly broken."*[15] There is power in numbers. If you fall you'll need the kind of friends who can help you up.

7. Focus on Progress, Not Perfection

Some of you may be thinking, "I've been reading this book for a while now, and I don't see a whole lot of change yet." Don't worry about it. It's progress we're after, not perfection. Life change is a process. It's a *decision* followed by a *process.* To the Philippians, the apostle Paul said with total confidence, "*I am sure that God, who began the good work within you, will continue his work until it is finally finished on that day when Christ Jesus comes back again.*"[16] If you have turned the change process over to God and have resolved to cooperate the best you can, God *will* work change in you through the power of His Holy Spirit.

Don't fall into the trap of thinking that God will only love you once you reach a certain stage. God loves you at each stage of recovery and growth. God will never love you any more than He does at this very minute. And He will never love you any less than He does right now. A father does not expect his seven-year-old to act like a seventeen-year-old. The seven-year-old still makes messes and acts like a child, but the father is pleased with and loves his seven-year-old child.

God is pleased with whatever growth and progress you have made. Just as a parent thrills at his or her baby's first steps, your heavenly Father thrills at each and every step of your growth—no matter how small. It's the direction of your heart that pleases Him as you say, "God, I voluntarily submit to the changes You want to make in my life. I humbly ask You to remove my character defects."

MAKE THE
Choice

Action 1: *Pray about It*

In this chapter we've talked a lot about character defects—where they come from, why it takes so long to get rid of them, and how we can cooperate with God to change them. You may be feeling a bit overwhelmed, so let's just pause and take a breath. We're not trying to fix everything at once. Remember the question, "How do you eat an elephant?" You do it one bite at a time. That's how you'll face your character defects—one defect at a time. So in this action step, we're going to put into practice one of the seven ways to cooperate with God. The first focus step listed earlier is "Focus on changing one defect at a time." Look back at the moral inventory list you made in chapter 4. Through prayer, ask God to help you review this list and choose a place to start. You can pray, using your own words or by following along with the prayer below:

> *Dear God, thank You for Your forgiveness. Now I am ready and willing to submit to any and all changes You want to make in my life. By Your grace, I am ready to face it and deal with the defects one by one.*
>
> *I have defects that have hurt me and defects that have hurt others. I've lived with some of these defects for so long that they have become a part of who I am. I have tried by my own power to fight against my defects and have failed over and over. I now ask, by Your power and the power of Your Holy Spirit, You transform my mind, my heart, and my actions.*

I need Your help in knowing where to start. I cannot handle all my defects at once. I can only face them one at a time. Show me, Lord, where I should begin. Help me as I look over my inventory list. Which character defect is the most damaging to my life? Where do I need to start? I am ready to follow Your lead. Amen.

Action 2: *Write about It*

In addition to writing in your journal, this action step will provide you with some Bible promises to help you focus on the *good* things, not the *bad.*

To begin, you'll need several 3 x 5 index cards. On one side of the card write a positive Scripture verse. On the other side write a practical application of the verse in the form of a personal affirmation. Here's an example:

On side one, write:

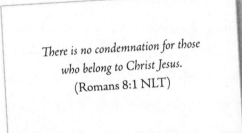

There is no condemnation for those
who belong to Christ Jesus.
(Romans 8:1 NLT)

Turn it over and write:

God does not condemn me for my
_____. He loves me just as much on
my bad days as on my good days. I can
make it through today without _____,
because Christ gives me His strength

Here's another example:

Side one:

> Where God's love is,
> there is no fear,
> because God's perfect love
> drives out fear.
> (1 John 4:18 NCV)

Side two:

> Today is going to be a better day than yesterday, because God is helping me get stronger. Yesterday, I was worried about _____. Today, I'm not afraid because God loves me!

Some other verses you might use are:

+ *If anyone belongs to Christ, there is a new creation. The old things have gone; everything is made new! (2 Corinthians 5:17 NCV)*

· *Those who know your name will trust in you, for you, LORD, have never forsaken those who seek you. (Psalm 9:10 NIV)*

· *Trust in the LORD with all your heart and lean not on your own understanding; in all your ways acknowledge him, and he will make your paths straight. (Proverbs 3:5–6 NIV)*

· *Commit to the LORD whatever you do, and your plans will succeed. (Proverbs 16:3 NIV)*

· *Come to me, all of you who are tired and have heavy loads, and I will give you rest. (Matthew 11:28 NCV)*

- *Do not worry about anything, but pray and ask God for everything you need, always giving thanks. And God's peace, which is so great we cannot understand it, will keep your hearts and minds in Christ Jesus. (Philippians 4:6–7 NCV)*

- *Without faith no one can please God. Anyone who comes to God must believe that he is real and that he rewards those who truly want to find him. (Hebrews 11:6 NCV)*

Write out a whole stack of these. Every night when you go to bed, read the verses and affirmations and think about them. When you wake up in the morning before you get out of bed, read them again. Put them in your pocket or purse and read them throughout the day. As you think positive thoughts, your autopilot will be reprogrammed and new positive ruts will be created in your mind. In about four to five weeks, you will begin to notice a difference in how you feel.

As you write in your journal . . .

1. Keep a record of how this simple exercise changes the way you feel about God, yourself, and others.

2. Write about the defect God has guided you to focus on first. Then record the progress (and setbacks) you are experiencing as you cooperate with God to focus on changing this one defect.

3. Spend time journaling about your efforts to "focus on *doing* good, not *feeling* good." It helps to write down the daily struggles and victories you have as you try to do the right thing, even when you don't feel like it.

As the weeks pass, you will see in black and white how you are overcoming certain defects of character. You will also begin to see other defects that you and God still need to work on. Having it all written down helps as you share your progress with your accountability partner.

Action 3: *Share about It*

If you shared your moral inventory list (your hurts, hang-ups, and habits) with your accountability partner, you've taken a big step in this sharing relationship. If you haven't shared it yet, you need to do so before you go any further. It is important to complete one choice completely, to the best of your ability, before moving on to the next. This is especially true with sharing your moral inventory. Your accountability partner can't help you work on your defects of character if he or she does not have all your information.

If you have shared your moral inventory, then you are ready to:

1. Share the one defect God has guided you to focus on changing first. Be honest about the character defect, how it has hurt you and how it has hurt others.

2. Share the progress God is making in your life in changing this defect. Be honest about your level of cooperation.

3. Share about your efforts to act yourself into a better way of feeling. Share the negative feelings you're trying to replace, and share the positive actions you're taking even though you don't yet have the feelings to match.

Remember the promise in Proverbs, "*As iron sharpens iron, so one man sharpens another.*"[17]

Sabrena's STORY

Hi, my name is Sabrena, I'm a grateful believer in Jesus Christ, and I struggle with codependency and fear.

Born and raised in the San Francisco Bay Area, I am the oldest of two girls. My childhood and teen years were full of chaos, confusion, anger, sadness, loneliness, depression, and fear. My parents' issues, which resulted from their own traumatic childhoods and personal choices, impacted their ability to face life's struggles and parent in healthy ways. My father struggled with alcohol addiction, and my mother struggled with codependency. My dad eventually quit drinking, but not until I was in my twenties, and already out of the house and married.

I began to withdraw emotionally at a young age, building a wall between my family and me and, later, with others. I had no idea how to manage or express the pain of my emotions in healthy ways. I did not feel stable, safe, protected, or nurtured in my home. This contributed to emotional abandonment issues. A distorted belief began to take root in my soul—I believed that I didn't matter.

When I was around eight years old, I met a girl who lived around the corner from me. She lived with her uncle and aunt, and she became my best friend. Her family became my family, and her home became a safe place. I started going to church with them and found more "family" there. I learned about God, His love for me, and His desire to have a relationship with me through His Son, Jesus. Since my parents were not believers, I had never heard about Jesus dying on the cross for me so I could go to heaven. I found love and acceptance in this family, this church, and from God, and I accepted His gift of eternal life when I was around twelve years old. However, I did not decide to follow Him for many, many years. I was too busy seeking my self-worth through anyone and anything else I could.

I developed many compulsions and addictions to control my emotions, stress, and internal chaos. Food became my first "drug of choice," causing me to become overweight when I was around nine years old. I loathed myself when I looked in the mirror and began a thirty-year struggle with body image issues. In the insanity of my addiction, I engaged in extreme dieting, bingeing, and exercising. I became obsessed with my looks and "fixing" my weight and body.

I also began picking at my skin obsessively—especially my fingers. I picked at them until they bled and were shooting with pain. Yet still, I would continue.

I became codependent, a people pleaser; and I was terrified of hurting others' feelings, making them angry, or facing any confrontation. My fear of abandonment was at the root of my behaviors. I became a giver and allowed everyone in my life to be takers. However, I did fight this tendency by becoming opinionated, "independent," and outspoken. It was simply a mask to try to override my fear. I involved myself in too many activities, saying yes to anyone who asked me to do anything. My social life became everything to me, so I had lots of friends, but I kept people at arm's length to protect myself emotionally.

Perfectionism was a big part of my codependency. I got a lot of attention for both the "good me" and the "bad me," and I was trying to figure out who I wanted to become. In a dysfunctional home, everyone is just trying to survive. Although praise and discipline are necessary, without nurturing and acceptance it is difficult for a child to build self-worth. I never gained self-worth apart from what I did or didn't do. It was how I looked or didn't look, or how I performed, that mattered.

I also developed a distorted view of sexuality and sex. Before the age of five, a teenage male who was visiting our home fondled me. Nothing else happened, but I looked up to this boy and admired him. What he did confused me. As a pre-teen, I developed earlier than other girls, and got attention for my looks and my body, which I absorbed like a sponge. As a teen, I saw porn magazines and movies and became addicted to porn, acting out whenever I was alone.

My relationships with boys did the most damage to my views on sex. When I began dating, boys rejected or ridiculed me because I wouldn't "mess around." Boyfriends dumped me because I wouldn't go "far enough." With each boyfriend, I would go a little further than the one before, but I resisted having sex because I was determined to wait until marriage. However, when I was in the tenth grade, I had little fight left in me. One night, the boy I was dating at the time humiliated me because I was saying no. In one sarcastic, biting sentence from him, I hit my breaking point. I went numb, dropped my hands to quit fighting him off, and didn't say another word. The numbness within me was overwhelming. He broke up with me shortly after, having gotten what he wanted.

I immediately resumed dating a boy I had dated before, but this time I gave him what he wanted. I despised myself and felt that God was so disappointed in me. I lived in shame constantly. I didn't know I could feel any worse about myself, until one day when I said no to sex, and the boy kept pushing. I kept fighting, and, eventually, he forced himself on me. He felt terrible afterward, and I had no idea at the time that this was date rape. I just remember how I felt, more ashamed and filled with more pain.

From these experiences, I was learning that sex equaled being used and that women were intended to be objectified. This distortion created the perfect environment for the insanity of all my relationships. And my home life, my codependency, my need to look and be perfect, and my desperate need to be loved and accepted added insanity to insanity. Every time I was used and/or abandoned by a boy, my emotional wall got higher and thicker. I also allowed these boys to believe that everything was about them. I believed the lies that if I made everything about them and pleased them, I would receive love. I had no sense of myself, of what I wanted or needed, or of what I accepted or didn't accept. Over time I became more and more desperate to be loved by someone who wouldn't leave me or use me.

I started dating Allen my junior year of high school, and I had hope again. As much as I had built a wall around my heart, and as many times as I had been abandoned, I still had hope that maybe I would finally matter to someone. We began a physical relationship very quickly. He wasn't a Christian. I had pushed down the Holy Spirit long enough that I barely heard Him anymore. Allen's father struggled with alcohol and anger, and his mother, with codependency. We both thought that since we didn't drink, we were safe from our families' dysfunctions. Instead, we became a repeat of our childhood families; we just didn't drink. What *had* been passed down to us were the other issues: anger, control, and codependency. We each thought the other would be the savior to heal our brokenness.

We married at nineteen. The pastor counseled me that marrying a non-believer wasn't what God wanted for my life. I ignored his advice, because I just knew that God had put Allen in my life so I could "save" him. I didn't know that only God can save people, that it wasn't my job.

Only two months after getting married, I found out I was pregnant. I sat on the floor and bawled after hanging up from the nurse who happily congratulated me. I knew Allen did not feel ready for a child, and he wanted me to have an abortion. I was the Christian in the relationship, and I knew this was wrong, but I didn't fight. I had quit fighting for myself a long time before and had never laid down any boundaries. I didn't know how I would ever live with the shame, but I couldn't face the confrontation or lose Allen. So I had the abortion. It was one of the lowest, saddest times in my life. Although I have asked God for forgiveness and know He has forgiven me, I will never, ever forget the child I didn't fight for.

Over the next seventeen years, I lost myself completely. I died slowly inside, and over time I decided I would never escape the pain that had always been there. I became so tired and defeated. I realized life was never going to change. There was not a drop of hope left in me. I came to feel nothing but despair. I had thought that I would escape my childhood pain in this marriage, but I now knew that would never happen.

However, during all those years of marriage, God was working. I had always lived my Christian life on the fence. I had been living for God only as far as it didn't offend Allen. One day when I was doing a Bible study at home, God knocked me down from that fence. I told Allen that God created me to live for God one hundred percent. I could no longer be afraid of what it would do to my relationship with him. There was such a drastic change in me over the next several months, that Allen was greatly impacted—in a good way. Within six months, he was saved during a newcomer class at our church.

The Holy Spirit made up for lost time with Allen. The change in him was no less than miraculous and could only have come from God. Within a year, Allen's anger subsided drastically, and God completely removed my sexual addiction. Only He could have removed a struggle that I had tried and tried to control for twenty years. I also believe these behaviors were a compulsion to relieve my high anxiety and stress, to which Allen's anger highly contributed.

Even with these amazing changes happening to us, I sadly began to realize that the damage, which had built up over a long time, wasn't going away. I still loved Allen, but I had not been in love with him for a long time. The wall that I had begun to build after so many years of anger, control, and codependency was miles thick. We had to do something. We got marital counseling, but all of our time was spent getting Allen to understand his issues with anger and control. Frustrated and angry, I had not been able to work through my hurt and pain.

Around this time, I was an administrator for the Student Ministries at our church. One of our pastors asked me to visit a local Celebrate Recovery with him and others so we could learn how to start one. I quickly decided this group was what I needed and began attending the first night of our launch. Allen also attended to "support" me so *I* could get the help *I* obviously needed so *we* could get better. He believed he was all done, so now *I* just needed to get fixed. Of course, God didn't allow either of us to just sit back and point the finger for long.

I didn't go to Celebrate Recovery for Allen or our marriage, I went for me. And slowly, God began to show me, through this amazing program, that *I* was the reason I was miserable. I had bookshelves full of "self-help" books that I had been reading since my twenties, Christian and secular alike, including books on codependency and adult children of alcoholics. I knew I was codependent and had other issues, but I never fully realized my responsibility for my choices. In my mind, it was Allen's fault that I was codependent. When he stopped being controlling and angry, I would stop being codependent. I saw my responses to his issues as justified and completely natural! I had very little awareness of the connection between my issues and my childhood. I had forgiven my parents long before, understanding they had experienced their own trauma, and had "moved on" from the other relationships in my life as well. All of those things were in the past! What I didn't realize was that even though I wasn't holding on to the past, it was still holding on to me. It had shaped who I was: how I thought, felt, communicated, acted, interacted, and especially how I dealt with my emotions.

The 8 Principles, or Choices, and the 12 Steps became a catalyst for true, life-changing transformation within me, especially Choice 5:

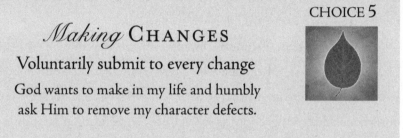

CHOICE 5

Making CHANGES

Voluntarily submit to every change God wants to make in my life and humbly ask Him to remove my character defects.

I spent years trying to change myself and overcome my issues, including time in the rooms of Al-Anon and Overeaters Anonymous. And I had also prayed for Allen during those years—that *he* would change. And believe me, he needed to change! But in Celebrate Recovery, I learned that I needed to allow *God* to change *me*, not anyone else, in order for *my* life to change. Slowly, God began to show me, through the leading of the Holy Spirit, my part in my misery and pain.

As a helpless child without choices, I had developed coping skills to deal with my emotions and the chaos in my life. But as I grew up and began to make choices on my own, I continued to avoid my emotions with these unhealthy choices. My behavior patterns no longer protected me. Instead, they damaged me and my relationships. Yes, many others had contributed to my pain, but, contrary to what I believed, I had choices. So, as scary as it was, I started to look at the changes God wanted to make in *my* life, and began to recognize *my* character defects.

I had always lived for other people. I became an expert in manipulation so that I would have some feeling of control over my life. I would get angry, cry, pout, or ignore others when I was hurt or angry, instead of being honest and direct. Setting limits and boundaries in healthy ways was never modeled for me. So, I didn't know how to do it. Codependent "punishing behaviors," as I call them, were all I knew. They often worked in the moment, so that's what I used.

In recovery, I realized that I was just as selfish as the boys in high school who used me, or my husband who "controlled" me or lashed out in anger at me. I was using them as much as they were using me. In my denial, I believed they were selfish and I wasn't. But just like anyone else with an addiction or compulsion, I did these behaviors hoping *I* would feel better, that *I* would be happy. I was trying to get from them something I didn't have inside myself, something they didn't have the power to give me: the knowledge that I did matter. As long as I believed I didn't matter, I wouldn't. I then enabled others to believe the same. I chose to allow their selfishness because of my own selfishness.

As I have learned to accept myself and my choices, my wall has slowly, very slowly, come down. I have learned to trust others, especially and most importantly my husband. This became possible because first, I trusted God—no one has to be my savior anymore because He is—and second, I learned to trust myself. I have learned that sacrifice isn't saying "yes" out of shame, guilt, or compulsion to make others happy when I really want to say "no." I can say no. I am also able to say yes from my own free will. Jesus didn't die for me out of shame, guilt, or compulsion, but out of love, with complete confidence in Himself and His choice. I can trust God and myself and I know I am learning true sacrifice, acting out of love, giving freely with no expectations of others to fill me and satisfy me.

For most of my life, I gave away the free will God gave me, and as a result I became chained to my addictions and compulsions. I know I am not perfect and that I will always be a work in progress. But through Celebrate Recovery, the chains that bound me are breaking and falling away. Through Celebrate Recovery, I have gained freedom, and I have learned to live by Matthew 5:37:

> *Simply let your "Yes" be "Yes,"*
> *and your "No," [be] "No";*
> *anything beyond this comes from the evil one.*[18]

My name is James, and I'm a grateful believer in Jesus Christ who struggles with shame and anger. I celebrate recovery from sexual sin and pride.

The person I am today is not the same person I was when I walked through the doors of Celebrate Recovery. When I walked through those doors, I was a broken man. I was living a lie, and I had no idea what God's path was for me. I didn't know what it meant to have a relationship with someone, especially Christ. This is the story about who I was and who I am now.

I had a severe speech impediment as a child; it was so bad that I couldn't even say my own name. When I would stutter at home, my little brother would often hold my throat just so I could talk, which for some reason always helped. I was relentlessly bullied as a child due to my speech impediment. This made school brutal. I couldn't find much solace at home because my parents divorced when I was young. They told me I had to choose which parent I would live with. I chose my dad, but he worked a lot and wasn't home much.

The bullying and loneliness I felt as a child made me feel like I was lost in a black box where I couldn't find the exit. I knew I needed to get out, but I didn't know how. The divorce made life difficult at home. I had family members in my life that would say things like, "I wish you'd never been born."

However, God had His eye on me because He put someone else in my life. Due to my stutter, I had weekly appointments with a speech therapist and counselor. I took solace in the time we spent together because she helped me gain confidence in myself and overcome my stutter.

In middle school, I involved myself more in church. I went to a church camp for most of the summer. At summer camp, I had several friends and no bullying at all. I felt transformed in this environment, and I accepted Christ into my heart. I felt an amazing connection to God and started learning what it meant to have Jesus as Lord of my life.

But I was heartbroken when I had to quit speech therapy because of changes in the school district. I no longer had the support of my counselor, and I soon lost touch with my Christian friends. And I started being bullied again.

When I went into high school, I found the "cool kids" and craved their attention. I spent most of my time with them and felt so close to them that they began to feel like my new family. I felt accepted and not threatened by my peers for the first time since church camp. I was no longer bullied. I realized that my new friends liked me more when I copied everything they did. I got even more attention from them when I took things to the extreme and went even further than they did. Looking back on this period of my life, I realize that these so-called friends took advantage of me. I never got back what I gave them.

Midway through my senior year of high school, an adult introduced me to pornography by falsely accusing me of looking at it. He kept showing it to me and would accuse me of downloading it. Needless to say, I became interested in what I saw. It became an obsession that slowly replaced my spiritual closeness with God. My dad found out about my obsessive pornography use. I was not allowed to use a computer for the rest of my senior year of high school. An adult that I had talked to about my problems even told my computer teacher about my struggle with pornography. My computer teacher told the entire class. I felt betrayed and embarrassed. I began to question authority. I told myself that I never wanted to feel that way again. So my new addiction became performance.

As I succeeded in work and college, I became addicted to the feelings associated with high achievement, and I developed an unhealthy pride in myself. I worked full time throughout college and eventually moved out of my dad's house into my own place. Since I never dealt with my pornography obsession, one of the first things I did was buy a computer and continue my addiction. As with most addictions, I had to take things to the extreme. I began wasting a lot of my time deep in my addiction to pornography. I remember saying that I would stop when I had a long-term girlfriend. And if that didn't happen, then I would stop when I got married.

Around this same time, I was diagnosed with Polycystic Kidney Disease. This is an incurable genetic disease. I felt like my life was unmanageable, and I was reminded that my time on earth is short. I immediately recalled the time in my life when I was closest to God. If my time on earth was going to be short, I wanted to experience life like I did when I was close to God! He, again, had His eye on me. I realized how much my relationships impacted my life, and I turned this area over to God. In 2004, God answered my prayers, and I met Brynea! I was amazed at her honesty, her commitment to God, and of course her beauty. She had a close relationship to God and was the first woman I wasn't able to manipulate.

We married in 2006. The first year was tough because she worked overnight, and I worked during the day. Sometimes we would only see each other when we passed each other on the highway. Two years into our marriage, I was ashamed and guilt-ridden because I had passed the line I said I wouldn't cross—looking at pornography while married. I took advantage of the time my wife worked overnight to indulge myself. I felt like I was living a double life, because during the day I was working at an addiction treatment facility as a counselor. At night I was indulging in my own addiction. I was really good at helping everyone except myself.

During this time, one of my family members was reaching their rock bottom and wanted recovery. I knew my church had Celebrate Recovery, and I thought it was just what *they* needed. My family member and I went, and a man gave his testimony about his addiction to pornography. The man shared about how his behavior led to infidelity, job loss, a failed marriage, and finally the loss of his relationship with his children. I heard about how God transformed him through Celebrate Recovery!

I came home convinced that I was tired of the old me. I felt compelled to confess my hidden lifestyle to my wife. When I did, she immediately thought there was something wrong with her. She took the blame, and I let her. However, I started attending Celebrate Recovery every week, and as I heard other men take responsibility for their behavior, I began to do the same. I told her that it was my fault and began to take responsibility for my behavior. I told her it was something I had to work through with Christ's care and control.

There were times when I didn't feel like going to a Celebrate Recovery meeting. But it seemed the days that I really didn't want to go were the days I really needed to be there because God had a lesson for me. For example, I remember hearing a woman giving her testimony and describing her tendency to want to fix her husband. I immediately thought, "Brynea needs to be here. She does that." I came home and told her, "You need to be there because you have lots of problems too." Of course I got no response to that rude invitation. When I decided to focus on myself and let God work in Brynea's heart in His timing, she started seeing changes in me. She wanted to see what Celebrate Recovery was all about.

We started attending together, and our marriage got stronger. We both went through a Step Study. We began the difficult process of honestly completing a moral inventory. Our Celebrate Recovery family became our Forever Family as we experienced many of life's challenges and victories together. When we started doing the work, it stuck and gave us a taste of what we wanted for the rest of our lives. I later asked her what would have happened if I had continued my lying and addiction to pornography. She said she would have left me. It was then that I realized that turning over my hurts, hang-ups, and habits to Christ's care and control is a lifelong and generational change. The changes can't just be short-term! I found out that those changes only happen when I make Choice 5:

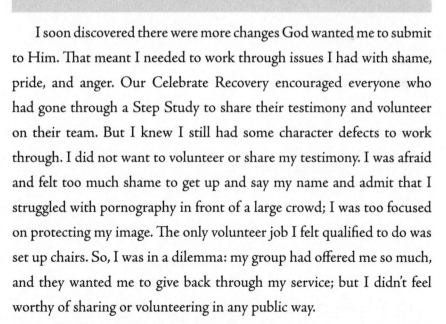

CHOICE 5

Making CHANGES

Voluntarily submit to every change

God wants to make in my life and humbly ask Him to remove my character defects.

I soon discovered there were more changes God wanted me to submit to Him. That meant I needed to work through issues I had with shame, pride, and anger. Our Celebrate Recovery encouraged everyone who had gone through a Step Study to share their testimony and volunteer on their team. But I knew I still had some character defects to work through. I did not want to volunteer or share my testimony. I was afraid and felt too much shame to get up and say my name and admit that I struggled with pornography in front of a large crowd; I was too focused on protecting my image. The only volunteer job I felt qualified to do was set up chairs. So, I was in a dilemma: my group had offered me so much, and they wanted me to give back through my service; but I didn't feel worthy of sharing or volunteering in any public way.

I was able to get around this dilemma, however, when we decided to move to Washington, DC, which offered Brynea better opportunities for her career. We knew we needed to find a Celebrate Recovery to attend, but there weren't any groups that were close enough to us. I talked to Brynea about approaching our church leadership about starting a Celebrate Recovery. Because of my struggles with pride, she suggested I wait until someone approached me. Not long after this, a potential leader who wanted to start a recovery group contacted me. I thought this would be great. He would lead the group; I would set up chairs and finally be able to attend a CR group. However, there was a little confusion because he was given my name as someone who might want to *co-lead* the group, not just sit back and be a participant. I reluctantly agreed, and soon four other people, who were interested in starting the group, joined us.

The month we wanted to start, it was evident that the enemy didn't want us to be successful. My car was totaled, my rental car was towed, and I got a call from a doctor who said I might have kidney cancer. I immediately looked at the survival rates for kidney cancer and believed the worst. Being thousands of miles from my family made it even harder. We shared our struggles with the other leaders, and they prayed for us and we prayed for them. It seemed that each one of them was also facing difficult situations. One of the leaders had a child pass away and another leader was diagnosed with breast cancer. The next month, we had our first meeting.

I got a second opinion on the diagnosis. The second opinion came back that it wasn't cancer and my kidneys were in great shape! The person diagnosed with breast cancer experienced an amazing healing, and the leader whose son died felt supported and loved by our group.

As I began to lead the Celebrate Recovery group, I got to spend a lot of time reflecting on my recovery journey. I realized that before Celebrate Recovery, I had tried so many different things to deal with my addiction to pornography and all of them failed. I realized they failed because I was just treating the symptoms and not dealing with the core issue. The core issue of shame led me into the fantasy world of pornography, that later led me to be angry at my failure while prideful in my public persona. I remember watching some old videos of myself and feeling sick to my stomach seeing how prideful I was.

I submitted to every change God wanted to make in my life and humbly asked Him to remove my character defects. When I finally shared my story, it lessened my shame, and I soon experienced recovery from pride and great traction in many of my other character defects. At this point I had a realization: *The person I am now is radically different from the person I was then.* The key for me was learning that my identity is in Christ and not in my addictions or character defects! I served as ministry leader for my group in DC and served as the first Celebrate Recovery state representative for the DC area. This position involved helping DC Metro area churches launch new Celebrate Recovery groups, while supporting existing groups and helping them achieve healthy growth in Christ. After three years in DC, my wife got an amazing job offer that took us to Arizona. Our biggest concern was that we would struggle with finding the family we had through our Celebrate Recovery group and our church. But, God is good because Celebrate Recovery is alive and strong in Arizona! I had the pleasure of serving as the Celebrate Recovery state representative for Phoenix.

I now have the opportunity to serve on the National Celebrate Recovery Team as the regional director for the mountain region. I share this because I'm continually amazed at what God is doing. The only ministry job I had felt worthy to do was setting up chairs. But God had a different plan, and His plans are always better than my own! Through Celebrate Recovery, I can travel across the country and find more of my Forever Family whom

God wants me to meet. Through Christ's care and control, I have overcome the cancer of pornography and many of my character defects.

Today I am a different person from who I was when I walked through the doors of Celebrate Recovery. I believe my change will have generational impact. However, I have not arrived; I'm still a work in progress—and always will be. God is still teaching me lessons, and sometimes those lessons are learned through the pain of life. Last year, my wife had a miscarriage; this came after a while of trying to have children and was a very painful experience. It happened a few days before Father's Day. We had to return several items that we planned on using to announce our pregnancy to our parents who had waited over nine years for us to have children. It happened to be the day before we were scheduled to give our testimony at a local Celebrate Recovery group. My first thought was to cancel, as that's what the old me would have done. But I needed to be with my Forever Family. We shared, and it was amazing. We talked about how God never wastes a hurt and we read the following scriptures, which so comforted us.

> *For I know the plans I have for you,*
> *declares the LORD, plans to prosper you and not to harm you,*
> *plans to give you hope and a future.*[19]

> *The thief comes only to steal and kill and destroy;*
> *I have come that they may have life, and have it to the full.*[20]

> *Delight yourself in the Lord and he will give you*
> *the desires of your heart. Commit your way*
> *to the LORD; trust in him and he will do this:*
> *He will make your righteousness shine like the dawn,*
> *the justice of your cause like the noonday sun.*
> *Be still before the LORD and wait patiently for him.*[21]

We continued to wait patiently for God, and this year my wife found out she was pregnant again right around the same time she did last year. We got to announce our pregnancy to our family on Father's Day and then to hundreds of our Forever Family at the Celebrate Recovery Summit! My wife is having a healthy pregnancy, and we are expecting our first child soon.

Through Celebrate Recovery, I now have a life that is worth living.

R
E
C
O
V
E

Evaluate all my relationships.

R   Offer *forgiveness* to those who have hurt me,
     and make amends for harm I've done to others,
Y   except when to do so would harm them or others.

"*Happy are those who are merciful to others.*"[1]

"*Happy are those who work for peace.*"[2]

Repairing RELATIONSHIPS

The RELATIONSHIP Choice

When it crashed against the hard tile floor, I stuck my head out of my office and yelled across the living room into the kitchen, "What was that?!"

A small panicked voice shouted back, "Nothing, Daddy! Nothing!"

I was elbow deep in paying bills. Wanting to just get this monthly labor-intensive chore wrapped up, I rolled my chair back up to my desk and dove back into the dizzying circus of budgets and bank accounts. Minutes later, a little girl's fist knocked against the door frame, interrupting my concentration.

"Honey, Daddy's really busy."

I looked up and met the tear-filled brown eyes of my seven-year-old. She was holding a blood-soaked napkin around her finger and her face wore a mix of guilt, fear, and pain.

"Lily! What . . . what happened?!"

She just burst into tears and grabbed me around the neck. When we got the cut cleaned up and properly bandaged, she had settled down enough for me to get the story out of her.

She told me that she knocked a bowl off the counter, breaking it into several pieces. Quietly getting out the glue and picking the shattered fragments off the floor, she tried to fix it without me knowing. When she reached for the bowl, a broken edge sliced into her pinkie.

She said, "I just didn't want you to be mad, but it hurt too much. Oh, Daddy, I'm sorry!"

Lily hugged me hard and began to cry again. As I hugged her back, I felt a protective, fatherly emotion that banished busted dishes and unfinished bills into irrelevant oblivion. All that I felt were the honest tears of my child on my shoulder and the joy of knowing my love was comfort enough to calm her guilt, fear, and pain.

Making amends is always about getting our heart right before our heavenly Father. We ask forgiveness of others for what we have done, and we seek to forgive others for what they have done to us. We must never forget who, ultimately, is the source of all redemption. Amends is not an exercise in fixing those we hurt or for those who have hurt us. Our part of the amends is all we can truly focus on. Our Higher Power alone can restore the shattered past. Our work is to bring the broken pieces to God, allowing Him to heal and comfort, reconcile and redeem.

> Godly sorrow brings repentance that leads
> to salvation and leaves no regret.[3]

In Choice 6, we'll work on making "corrections" in some of our relationships by doing some relational repair work. And we'll do that by working through a two-part process: We'll start off by *forgiving* those who have hurt us, and then we will work on *making amends* to those we have hurt.

There are two beatitudes that guide us in our sixth choice:

"Happy are those who are merciful to others."
"Happy are those who work for peace."[4]

When we are *merciful* to others, we are willing to forgive them, whether they deserve it or not. That's what mercy is about—it's undeserved. And when we *work for peace*, we put out real effort to make amends where we have wronged another, and we work to bring harmony back into that relationship. This choice and these beatitudes are all about repairing relationships. In this chapter we'll look back on our lives for the purpose of evaluating, not regretting. We'll learn how to repair the damage that others have done to us and that we have done to others.

Let's begin with forgiving others for the wrongs they have done against us. But *why* should you do this and *how* do you do it? These are good questions.

REPAIRING RELATIONSHIPS BY FORGIVING THOSE WHO'VE HURT YOU

Why Should You Forgive Others?

There are at least three reasons, and believe it or not, the benefits are all yours.

1. Because God Has Forgiven You

If God has forgiven you, shouldn't you forgive others? The Bible says, *"You must make allowance for each other's faults and forgive the person who offends you. Remember, the Lord forgave you, so you must forgive others."*[5] When you remember how much God has forgiven you, it makes it a whole lot easier for you to forgive others. The Bible also says, *"Get rid of all bitterness, rage and anger, brawling and slander, along with every form of malice. Be kind and compassionate to one another, forgiving each other, just as in Christ God forgave you.*[6] You forgive as Christ forgave you. You will never have to forgive anybody else more than God has forgiven you.

When you have a hard time forgiving someone else, it's usually because you don't feel forgiven. It is a fact that people who feel forgiven find it easier to be forgiving. If you don't feel forgiven, look again at these two verses: *"Remember, the Lord forgave you . . ."* and, *"Forgive each other, just as in Christ God has forgiven you."* If you accepted Christ in Choice 3, you are *forgiven!* It is a done deal. Now He asks you to turn around and forgive others.

2. Because Resentment Doesn't Work

The second reason you need to forgive those who have hurt you is purely practical: resentment doesn't work. Holding on to resentment is *unreasonable, unhelpful,* and *unhealthy.*

Resentment is unreasonable. The Bible says it plainly: *"To worry yourself to death with resentment would be a foolish, senseless thing to do."*[7] Why is holding on to resentment foolish and senseless? The practical answer is that *"you are only hurting yourself with your anger."*[8] Resentment hurts you much more than the person you resent. Think about it. When you are angry and resentful toward someone, you're not hurting them; you're hurting yourself. You're the one who's stewing, spewing, stressing, and fretting. You're the one who's losing sleep and being distracted from the joys of life. It's not bothering them at all! They're sleeping great. They probably aren't even aware of all the huffing and puffing that's going on inside you. They're oblivious to it all.

Someone may have hurt you ten, twenty, thirty years ago, and you're still hurting yourself over it. It's still making you miserable, but they've forgotten all about it. From a purely practical point of view, resentment is totally unreasonable—it's an irrational waste of energy, making no sense at all.

Resentment is unhelpful. Resentment cannot change the past, the problem, or the person who hurt you. It doesn't even hurt the person who hurt you; it only hurts you. Resentment certainly doesn't make you feel better. Have you ever known anyone to say, "I feel so much better being resentful"? Of course not! Resentment just makes you mad and unhappy.

Resentment is unhealthy. "*Some people stay healthy till the day they die. . . . Others have no happiness at all; they live and die with bitter hearts.*"[9] Resentment is like a cancer that eats you alive. It's an emotional poison with physical consequences. Have you ever said, "That guy is a pain in the neck"? Did you ever stop to think that your resentment against him may actually be causing that real pain in your neck?

> *Nothing drains you emotionally like bitterness and resentment.*

Did you hear the one about the guy who walked into his doctor's office and said, "I need some more pills for my colitis"? The doctor asked, "Who are you colliding with now?" Resentment has emotional and physical consequences. It can lead to depression, stress, and fatigue. Nothing drains you emotionally like bitterness and resentment. Continuing to replay the hurt you received from that teacher, relative, business associate, or former husband or wife allows them to continue hurting you emotionally and physically today! It simply prolongs the hurt. It's a kind of emotional suicide. In the beatitudes paired with this chapter, Jesus shows us a better way: "*Happy are those who are merciful to others*"[10] and, "*Happy are those who work for peace.*"[11] Mercy and peace.

3. Because You'll Need Forgiveness in the Future

We will all need God's and others' forgiveness in the future. *"When you are praying, first forgive anyone you are holding a grudge against, so that your Father in heaven will forgive you your sins too."*[12] Resentment blocks you from feeling God's forgiveness. The Bible says you cannot receive what you are unwilling to give: *"Forgive us our debts, as we forgive our debtors."*[13] It can be dangerous to pray the Lord's Prayer. In it, you are praying, "Lord, forgive me as much as I forgive everybody else." You want nothing short of His complete and full forgiveness, so the obvious implication is that you must extend nothing less to those who have sinned against you.

The story has been told about a man who went to John Wesley and said, "I can never forgive that person. Never."

John Wesley replied, "Then I hope you never sin. Because we all need what we don't want to give." Don't burn the bridge you need to walk across.

How Do You Forgive Others?

Forgiving others is not easy. How do you forgive those who have hurt you? These three Rs can show you how: *Reveal, Release,* and *Replace.*

1. Reveal Your Hurt

You have some options when it comes to dealing with your hurts. You can *repress* them and pretend they don't exist, but they do. You can *ignore* them and try pushing them out of the way. That never works because those hurts always pop out in some form of compulsion. You can *suppress* them and say, "It's no big deal; it doesn't matter. They did the best they could." No they didn't. These people hurt you. Or you can do what works: You can *admit* them. You can reveal the truth that you hurt.

You can't get over the hurt until you admit the pain. Why is it that we don't want to admit that the people we love have caused us pain? Perhaps it's because we have the misconception that you can't love somebody and be angry with them at the same time. The truth is, you can.

A woman in a counseling session insisted, "I forgive my parents; they did the best they could." But the more she talked, the more obvious it became that she really hadn't forgiven them. She was angry with them, and she was denying her anger. The truth was, her parents hadn't done the best they could. None of us do the best we can. Your parents didn't, and if you're a parent, you are not doing the best you can. We're all imperfect, and we all make mistakes. When this woman was able to admit that her parents didn't do the best they could, then she was able to forgive them.

If you want to close the door on your past and get closure so certain people don't hurt you anymore, you can do it. But there's one thing you have to remember: there is no closure without disclosure. First you must admit it, or *reveal* it, by owning up to the truth: "That hurt. It was wrong, and it hurt me."

Once you've revealed the hurt, then you will be in a position to *forgive.* You can't forgive a hurt you won't admit.

2. Release the Offender

The second step in forgiving an offender is *releasing* him or her. You may have some questions about how this works.

When do I release the offender? The answer is that you do it now; you don't wait for the offender to ask for forgiveness. You make the choice to do it independently of the other person. You do it whether the person asks for forgiveness or not, and you do it for your sake, not the other person's. You do it for the three reasons we looked at earlier in the chapter: because God has forgiven you, because resentment doesn't work, and because you'll need forgiveness in the future. So you release your offender and forgive for your own sake.

How often do I have to do it? Jesus was asked this very question by Peter: "'How often should I forgive someone who sins against me? Seven times?' 'No!' Jesus replied, 'seventy times seven.'"[14] Jesus is saying that our forgiveness must be continual. Forgiveness is not a one-shot deal where you say, "I forgive you," and it's done. Those feelings of resentment are going to keep coming back. Every time they do, you've got to forgive again until you have fully released the offender, even if it takes a hundred times or more.

How will I know that I have fully released an offender? You'll know when you can think about him or her and it doesn't hurt anymore. You'll know when you can pray for God's blessing on his or her life. When you can begin to look at and understand the hurt he or she feels, rather than focusing on how you have been hurt—remembering that hurt people hurt people. You keep forgiving and keep forgiving, until thoughts of the person or offense aren't associated with hurt. You may not be able to completely forget, but you can release the offender and let go of the pain.

Is it always wise to release the offender face-to-face? Not always. And in some cases it's not even possible to go back to the people who have hurt you. To bring up old hurts may not be productive for you or kind to them. If your parents hurt you, they may not even know about it, and for you to go back to them forty years later and bring up old pain would just blow them away. You may not be able to find some of the other people even if you wanted to. They may have remarried, moved away, or even died.

What do you do in those situations? There are two techniques you can use. One is the empty chair technique. You sit alone with an empty chair and you imagine the person you need to forgive sitting in the chair, and you say, "I need to say some things to you. Here's how you hurt me," and you lay it out. "You hurt me this way, this way, and this way. But I want you to know I forgive you because God has forgiven me, because resentment doesn't work, and because I will need forgiveness in the future. I am releasing you."

Another technique is to write a letter that you will never mail. In this letter you put down in black and white how you have been hurt: "This is how you hurt me." You've been carrying your hurt so long. Now is the time to unload it, and you can do that by letting it out in a letter. At the end you say, "But starting today, I forgive you because God has forgiven me, because resentment doesn't work, and because I will need forgiveness in the future." And you do it for your own sake. You release your offender so you can experience freedom.

3. Replace Your Hurt with God's Peace

At some point, all this free forgiveness may start to sound unfair. If I forgive this person—especially if I forgive my offender without him asking for forgiveness or without me ever confronting her face-to-face— then he or she gets off scot-free. I've been hurt, and this person suffered no consequences.

We need to relax and let God settle the score. He can do a whole lot better job than we can, anyway. The Bible says, "*We will all stand before God's judgment seat. It is written: 'As surely as I live,' says the Lord, 'every knee will bow before me; every tongue will confess to God.' So then, each of us will give an account of himself to God.*"[15] We see here that God is going to settle the score. He's going to call things into account; He's going to balance the books; and one day, He's going to have the last word. He'll take care of it. He's the judge. He's just. When we learn to release our offenders and allow God to be in charge of settling scores, then we will discover the wonderful blessing of His peace. The Bible tells us to "*let the peace of Christ rule in your hearts.*"[16] You get to choose what rules your heart. It can be the misery of unforgiveness or the peace of Christ.

The fact is, relationships can tear your heart into pieces. But God can glue those pieces back together and cover your heart with His peace.

When you forgive those who have hurt you, God is free to do the needed repair in your heart.

Below is one of the best actual examples of forgiveness that I have ever seen. It is a letter written by my good friend John Eklund to his mother.

Dear Mom,

This is long overdue. I am not sure what's taken me so long to write you. Well, that's not quite true. There are many reasons. I've started writing to you in the past, but I'd get stuck and quit. Maybe I wasn't ready before now. It's probably best that I waited. I've been working my recovery. I have finally found the clarity to be honest with myself . . . to be honest with you. It's been twenty years since I walked out of your apartment—an angry, lost, wounded teenager—jumped into my car, and took off. I have never looked back until now. I have regrettably blamed you for the many messes I have made in life. Maybe I blamed you because then I wouldn't have to clean them up. The divorce in grade school, the moving from house to house, the many relationships you got into and out of had effects beyond what I think you were willing to admit. Your decisions impacted many people. Your decisions impacted me, and I hated you for it. I protected and forgave you until something broke that night nearly two decades ago. It seems like I have been limping emotionally since then.

Anger toward you has always seemed a safe place to store and release my pain. I am not sure when it stopped working. I imagine it never really did work. In looking back at twenty years of hating you,

I have seen a heart hardened toward a mom who was just as broken and lost as I was. I've also seen a heart hardened toward everyone, including God. I think it makes sense to me now what Jesus said in Matthew 6, that if I do not forgive, I won't be forgiven. It's not that God can't forgive me, it's that my heart is not breathing when I have unforgiveness. I am not inhaling grace, I am not exhaling grace. Without forgiveness, my heart has been dead.

Sometimes I see someone who reminds me of you. I often look at my daughters and wonder what it would be like for them to know their grandma Chrissy. In some ways I still can't believe you're gone. You were so alive—larger than life. Your laugh was loud and unashamed. I hear your laugh in Rose, my youngest. I am sorry, Mom. I will not blame you for my choices. I believe your choices, even the bad ones, are being redeemed in my life for God's glory. I am sorry I wasted the time we had here together being angry. My comfort and hope is that we will see each other again where there will be no more pain and no more tears.

My sponsor and I are going to decide what to do with this letter. You are never far from my thoughts. I love you, Mom.

Before we move on to the second part of repairing relationships, let's review Choice 6:

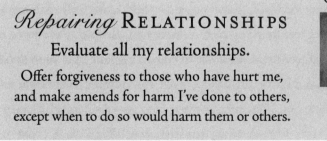

CHOICE 6

Repairing RELATIONSHIPS
Evaluate all my relationships.
Offer forgiveness to those who have hurt me,
and make amends for harm I've done to others,
except when to do so would harm them or others.

With this in mind, let's move on to the second part of relationship mending.

REPAIRING RELATIONSHIPS BY MAKING AMENDS TO THOSE YOU'VE HURT

Repairing relationships is a two-part process: we've talked about *forgiveness*; the second part is *making amends*. Not only have people hurt you; you have hurt other people. *Why do we need to make amends* and *how do we it?*

Why Do You Need to Make Amends?

As painful as making amends may seem, it is absolutely essential. Dealing with the root of your problems means dealing with unresolved relationships. Until you do this, recovery can't happen.

When I got to this choice, I had a lot of work to do. I had quite a long list of names of people to whom I needed to make my amends. Over the years of making poor choices, I had hurt a lot of people. They ranged from former employees and employers, to friends and neighbors. But the most special amends I needed to make were to my family. I had caused them a lot of pain and heartache, but they graciously accepted my amends, and after a period of time our relationships were restored. Today those relationships are stronger and more loving than I could ever have hoped for or deserved.

After I completed making my amends, God truly blessed me and my recovery. He gave me the vision of starting Celebrate Recovery—a Christ-centered recovery ministry for people struggling with all kinds of hurts, hang-ups, and habits. It is a safe place for individuals and families to find His healing grace.

Making amends is such a big deal that the Bible says, *"If you are* standing before the altar in the Temple, offering a sacrifice to God, and you suddenly remember that someone has something against you, leave your sacrifice there beside the altar. Go and be reconciled to that person. Then come and offer your sacrifice to God."[17]

One of our beatitudes for this choice says, "*Happy are those who work for peace.*" Making amends is "working for peace." The Bible places a high priority on getting things right in our relationships.

The Bible also says, "*Watch out that no bitterness takes root among you, for as it springs up it causes deep trouble, hurting many in their spiritual lives.*"[18] One of the reasons you can't let go of that hurt, get past that hang-up, or get over that habit is that when you hold on to unresolved relationships, bitterness takes root in your heart and causes all kinds of trouble. These unresolved relationships must be dealt with if you're really going to get on with your recovery and enjoy the happiness that comes from being merciful and making peace, as our beatitude says.

We've talked about *why* we need to make amends; now we'll talk about the hard part: *how to do it.*

How Do You Make Amends?

The Bible has a great piece of advice on keeping peace with others: "*If it is possible, as far as it depends on you, live at peace with everyone.*"[19] Keep this in mind as you work through the steps of making amends to those you've hurt. Do what you can. The Scripture says, "*If it is possible, as far as it depends on you . . .*" You are only responsible for what you do; you are not responsible for how the person you approach responds to your amends.

How do you make amends to the people you've hurt? We'll show you how:

1. Make a List of Those You've Harmed and What You Did

We'll do the actual hands-on work for this choice in the "Make the Choice" action steps, but let's think about a couple of things as we introduce this idea.

First, a word of caution: As you start listing the people you need to make amends to, your mind may immediately jump to "How on earth am I going to pull this off?!" Don't worry about the "how-to's" right now. Don't travel down that mental road of "How will I ever ask forgiveness of my ex-spouse?" or "How can I pay back the money I stole from my dad?" Just write the names down; the how-to will come later.

Second, some of you may be saying, "I can't think of anybody I've hurt." In the "Make the Choice" section, you'll find some questions to help get you started. Getting the names and offenses down in black and white is an important first step in making things right with those you've wronged.

2. Think about How You'd Like Someone to Make Amends to You

Most of us have heard these words from Jesus before: *"Do to others as you would have them do to you."*[20] So stop and think, "If someone were going to come and apologize to me, how would I want it done?" Here are four things that might affect how you'd want it done.

Timing: There is a time to *let* things happen and a time to *make* things happen. There are right times and wrong times to make amends. You don't just drop a bomb on somebody. You don't just bring up a sensitive topic when they're rushing out the door or as they're laying their head down on the pillow: "By the way, I've got some stuff to deal with, and it involves you." You do it according to what works best for the other person, not when it's best for you. Ecclesiastes says, *"There's a right time and right way to do everything."*[21]

Attitude: Think about how you would like somebody to apologize to you. Here are three things to consider.

First, do it *privately*. Choose your time and place carefully, and consider what will make the other person the most comfortable.

Second, do it with *humility*. Sincerely and simply say what you did wrong. Don't make any justification for your actions or attitude; offer no excuses. Just humbly acknowledge your part in the problem and assume whatever responsibility belongs to you. The other person may have had a part in the problem too, but you're just trying to clear up *your* side of the ledger.

Third, do it *without expectations*. Don't expect anything back from the person you're trying to make amends to. If the other person doesn't acknowledge his or her responsibility or apologize too, who cares? The actual heart change is not about them. It's about you doing what's right.

Appropriateness: There will be some situations when contacting the one you've hurt would be unwise. Remember the qualifier in Choice 6: "except when to do so would harm them or others." In some situations, trying to make amends would be inappropriate because it would open up a whole can of worms and probably make the situation worse.

> "If someone were going to come and apologize to me, how would I want it done?"

You could harm an innocent party, as well as the person you intended to make amends to. You wouldn't want to go back to an old boyfriend or girlfriend who is now married. If you were involved in an affair, it would be inappropriate to have further contact with that person. The more serious your offense, the less likely it would be appropriate to make amends face-to-face. So what do you do? Once again, you can use the empty chair or unmailed letter technique. The wisdom of Proverbs says, *"Rash language cuts and maims, but there is healing in the words of the wise."*[22] Consider the situation, consider the person, and try to make amends in the way that's best for him or her.

Restitution: Make restitution wherever possible. If you've borrowed something and not returned it, return it. If you owe somebody some money, pay it back—even if it takes a long time. Making restitution gives you freedom and confidence.

The Bible tells about a guy named Zacchaeus. He was a tax collector, and in Bible times tax collectors could charge people as much as they could get from them. After paying Rome, they could keep whatever was left over. As a consequence, they were the most hated people in society. But of all people Jesus could have visited, He chose to go see Zacchaeus.

Meeting Jesus changed Zacchaeus's life, and with that life-change, he decided to make restitution for everything he had ever cheated anyone of. In fact, he decided to restore it all fourfold. This guy was willing to put his money where his mouth was by making restitution.

Again, the more serious your offence, the less likely you'll be able to make restitution. There are some things you can't restore. But don't underestimate the power of a sincere apology. Here's what you do: discern the right time, put on the right attitude, be sure making contact is appropriate, then say something like, "I'm sorry. I was wrong. I don't deserve your forgiveness, but is there any way I can make restitution to you?" And you leave it at that.

3. Refocus Your Life

Today can be a new day. Starting today, you can refocus your life on doing God's will in your relationships.

As long as you focus on the past, you allow the past to control you. The good news is this: God wants to deal with all the relational garbage in your life, once and for all. He knows when you can handle it and how much you can handle at a time, so He takes the garbage off one layer at a time. When you committed your life and will to Christ in making Choice 3, a layer came off. As time goes on, God keeps dealing with you, working with you, releasing you from hurts, hangups, and habits.

As you make this sixth choice, forgiving those who have hurt you and making amends to those you have hurt, God begins to recycle the relational garbage of your life and use it for good. How does He do that? In the book of Job, we find three steps to refocusing—and recycling—your life, and with those steps comes one amazing promise: *"Put your heart right. . . . Reach out to God, . . . then face the world again, firm and courageous. Then all your troubles will fade from your memory, like floods that are past and remembered no more."*[23]

"Put your heart right." Refocusing your life begins with your heart. This is where you get your attitude right so you can begin to make amends.

"Reach out to God." If you haven't yet asked God into your life, you can do it today. You do not have the strength to make amends on your own. It's too big a job to handle alone. You need to plug in to Jesus Christ. He can daily give you the strength, wisdom, and humility to face your past and make amends where you can. As you reach out to God, He will enable you to reach out to others and make amends.

"Face the world again." As you make amends and clean your slate, *"as far as it depends on you,"* you resume living. Your eyes are open and looking ahead as you courageously and joyfully face the world. You step out and say, "I'm not a victim anymore." You don't withdraw; you don't hide in a shell; you start looking ahead.

"Then all your troubles will fade from your memory like floods that are past and remembered no more." Here's the promise: as we put our hearts right, reach out to God, and face the world again, the memory of our troubles will begin to fade away. Wow. In those few words is the sound of hope.

Wouldn't you like to be free from all that relational garbage? The choice is yours. Peace and mercy await you.

MAKE THE
Choice

Action 1: *Pray about It*

You've worked through the first five choices of this book; you've made a lot of progress toward becoming the healthy, whole individual God created you to be. The two-part process in this chapter's choice will bring you even closer to your goal, for in it you will find the healing of relationships—and broken relationships lie at the root of so much of our pain. But the choices in this chapter cannot be made alone. You need God's help to follow through. In this action step, we will ask God to help us both forgive those who have hurt us and make amends to those whom we have hurt. The freedom and hope found at the end of this process will bring you great release. Use your own words to ask God's help, or join in the prayer below:

> *Dear God, You have shown me that holding on to resentment for the wrongs done to me and refusing to make right my own wrongs has crippled me—emotionally, spiritually, and even physically. I ask You today to help me be honest about the hurts I feel. I've stuffed some and ignored others, but now I am ready to come clean and tell the truth about my pain. As I do, I ask that You give me the strength and the courage so I can release those who have hurt me and let go of my resentment toward them. Only by Your power will I be able to do this, Lord.*
>
> *I pray, also, that You will give me the courage and discernment*

to know how to make amends to those I have hurt. Help me to be honest as I look back and remember, and guide me as I find the ways to make restitution, where appropriate.

Finally, I pray that I can begin a new life today as I refocus my life on doing Your will in my relationships. Help me set aside my selfishness and set my whole heart on You—I know I have a long way to go. I want the promise found in Job that all my troubles will fade from my memory and be remembered no more. Amen.

Action 2: *Write about It*

Now is the time to get some important issues down in black and white.

Those You Need to Forgive

We'll begin by dealing with those who have hurt you—those you need to forgive. Remember, admitting that someone has hurt you and that you are angry about what he or she has done does not mean you don't love this person. You can be angry with a person whom you love very much.

Here's how you begin: You make a list of those who've harmed you. Write down:

1. his or her name and relationship to you
2. what this person said that hurt you
3. what he or she did that hurt you
4. how the hurt made you feel

Put it down on paper so you can look at it. When you do, it loses its fuzzy quality and becomes real. Think about that teacher who embarrassed you or the parent who said, "You'll never amount to anything; you're a failure." That former boyfriend/girlfriend/husband/ wife/friend who was unfaithful to you. Write it all down, and reveal your hurt. This is your Forgiveness List.

Those to Whom You Need to Make Amends

You made your Forgiveness List of those who've harmed you. Now you need to make an Amends List of those you have harmed. Write down:

1. his or her name and relationship to you
2. what you said to hurt this person
3. what you did to hurt him or her
4. how you think you made this person feel
5. why you are sorry for hurting him or her

Once again, when you write it down on paper or type it on your computer and get it down in black and white, the offense becomes real. It is no longer vague: "I think I may have hurt her with my words when I was angry." When you write it out, it becomes, "This is how I hurt her with my words when I lost my temper that night." Your Amends List makes your responsibility specific. Go back and review once more the names you wrote down in the moral inventory in Choice 4, column 5, page 126.

If you are having trouble thinking of anybody you've hurt, perhaps these questions will get you started:

1. Is there anyone to whom you owe a debt that you haven't repaid? A friend, a family member, a business?
2. Is there anyone you've broken a promise to? A spouse, a child?
3. Is there anyone you are guilty of controlling or manipulating? A spouse, a child, a brother, an employee, a friend?
4. Is there anyone you are overly possessive of? A spouse, a child?

5. Is there anyone you are hypercritical of? A spouse, a child?

6. Have you been verbally, emotionally, or physically abusive to anyone?

7. Is there anyone you have not appreciated or paid attention to?

8. Did you forget a child's birthday or your anniversary?

9. Is there anyone you have been unfaithful to?

10. Have you ever lied to anyone?

That's enough to get you started. If you still do not have anyone on your list, go back to Choice 1 and start all over again!

Action 3: *Share about It*

Offering Forgiveness

It is very important that you share your Forgiveness List with your accountability partner prior to sharing it with the person who hurt you. Your accountability partner can help you develop a plan for safely offering your forgiveness to those on your list. Your accountability partner also knows you and can challenge you to include anyone you may have omitted.

It is vital when offering forgiveness that you do not allow the person to hurt you further. Using your accountability partner as a sounding board will help minimize the risk.

Use the empty chair technique with your accountability partner to offer forgiveness when a face-to-face is not helpful or appropriate. You can also share your unmailed letter with your accountability partner, when you determine that a letter is the best approach.

Making Amends

Be sure to also share your Amends List with your accountability partner. An objective opinion can ensure that you make amends with the right motives. The Bible encourages us to *"consider how we may spur one another on toward love and good deeds."*[24] Just as your accountability partner helped you offer your forgiveness, he or she can help you plan the right time and place to make your amends. If you owe someone money, your partner can help you develop restitution plans.

You need your accountability partner to encourage you to make all the amends on your list. Once that is done, there will be no skeletons in your closet. Then you will have come to the point in your life where you can say, "I have nothing more to hide. I'm not perfect, I have attempted to repair all the harmful things I've done in my past. I have made amends and offered restitution for my part."

Danny's STORY

My name is Danny. I am a believer in Jesus Christ who is in recovery from alcohol, drugs, and anger. I began Celebrate Recovery in prison while serving a fifty-years-to-life sentence.

I grew up in Redding, California, with my mom and stepdad. My mother was sixteen years old when I was born, and when I was two, my biological parents' forced marriage was already over. As a result, I saw little of my father as I grew up. Our home was free from drugs and violence. I had three cool stepbrothers, and when I was fourteen, both my mom's and dad's remarried families provided me two little brothers. Among all my brothers, I was always the very quiet, very shy, and very insecure kid.

I had a lot of freedom as a child. I was a latchkey kid from kinder-garten. By the fourth grade, I spent entire summers by myself. When I was young and always had the house to myself, I thought I was the luckiest kid around! My parents had comfortable homes and nice cars. I always had nice clothes and motorcycles. But I chose a wrong under-standing of these blessings. I thought the goal of life was having nice pos-sessions. I understood love, not as unconditional acceptance, but through getting material possessions. While I had nice things on the outside, on the inside of me I struggled to gain a sense of myself. I didn't know it then, but I was laying the foundations for my own spiritual prison.

When I entered high school, even more shy and insecure, I discovered another mask that I believed gave me acceptance: alcohol and drugs.

When I was sixteen I started partying on the weekends. I discovered how easy it was to make friends if I was the one who had a six-pack, some marijuana, or having a party while my parents were out. Perhaps like some kids, I would have eventually matured out of this phase. But in 1979 a family tragedy took place, and I responded to this event badly.

Shortly after I turned sixteen, I came home from school one day and my mom and stepdad were sitting with a friend and there were stacks of thousands of dollars spread out on the kitchen table. They told me they were going on a business trip to Peru and that I would see them at Christmas. They allowed me to take care of my eighteen-month-old little brother with the help of some family and friends. But my parents did not return. On Christmas Eve I found out that they were arrested in Mexico for smuggling cocaine from Peru.

My parents were not drinkers or drug users. I was in shock! I was angry. I was afraid. I felt guilty because I had been the one partying while they were away. I felt like I was being punished. I drove on Christmas Day, seeking to be with family members. I drove for the entire day. I was struggling to deal with the grief and fear about my mother in prison in Mexico. Today, that experience might be like having a parent captured by a dangerous third-world country.

When I could no longer handle the fear and anger, I pulled over in an empty parking lot and chose to get high. It worked. I felt temporary relief from what I was going through. As a result, I chose a new life of getting high and partying every day. I didn't know it at the time, but that Christmas day I entered my own prison by stuffing my feelings of fear and anger and choosing to escape into a life of drug addiction.

For the next two years, my mom and my stepdad had to sell property and possessions to pay for bribes, lawyers, and living expenses in prisons in Mexico City. I didn't know if I would ever see my parents again. Always in the back of my mind, I feared for my mom. I tried hard not to think about it. And then I felt guilty when I didn't think about it. They sent my eighteen-month-old brother to Oregon to live with family. I moved to my biological father's house. I did not have a relationship with him. I was in a new town and new school. I brought all my baggage with me.

I quickly found a group of kids who hung out in the school back-parking-lot smoking area—kids who were living like me. We made getting high our daily goal. I began a downward spiral of bad decisions. I became more and more impulsive. I started to commit crimes to support my drug habits. In a short period of time, I was expelled from school and then from my new home as well. I take full responsibility for those decisions. There were people around me who loved me. They tried to help. But I was too defensive to let anyone help. I was too insecure to ask for help. My way of dealing with problems was getting high and drunk in the misguided belief that the next day I would do something different and find a solution.

Released from prison after two years, my mother tried to reunite our family. But at eighteen, I was already a dual addict to alcohol and marijuana. Since I was the only kid my age who had an apartment, I daily welcomed all the parties in my house. It didn't take long before I needed all the parties. I began to dread going to sleep at night if I didn't have something to drink and smoke in the morning. I was completely bound. I was living by myself, while drinking every day and using harder drugs. Just like that Christmas day in 1979, I continued stuffing my problems. The more I denied my condition, the more it came out in impulsive decisions.

Like the demon-possessed man who lived in the tombs, cutting himself, hurting himself, and hurting others, my life was out of control. I was an addict because I chose that life. I hurt others because I chose to please myself. My debts piled up, and I was having difficulty keeping myself supplied with my increasing need for alcohol and drugs.

I take full responsibility for what bound me. I was an addict because I chose that life. I didn't worry or think about getting caught for crimes. I didn't consider the consequences to others. I impulsively made decisions for my drug habit. As a result, I was part of a crime in which two men were killed.

After I committed this crime, I got worse. I felt haunted. I couldn't sleep with the lights off. I doubled my efforts to keep my apartment filled with people, parties, alcohol, and now harder drugs like cocaine and hallucinogens to mix with the alcohol. I fought hard to keep my mind off what I had done. *Thankfully*, I was arrested on September 1, 1982, which many of us in recovery call "being rescued." After a short period of detoxing, I saw the look of fear and pain on my family's faces. The weight of what I had done came crashing down on my conscience.

I remember a day when I was looking from the window of a cell door into a hallway where they were escorting a female prisoner. When the female prisoner saw me, she said, "Hey there's a kid in there!" But the jailer said, "That's no kid, that's a murderer!" I realized this was true, and I hit bottom. No hell-and-brimstone preacher could have said it any clearer. I believed I was lost and going to hell. I was, truly afraid.

When you're eighteen and in prison for such a crime, for some reason Christians want to come share the love of God with you. And they did with me. At first their beautiful words went over my head, and I felt they didn't apply to someone like me. How could God love and forgive me after all I had done? I didn't know how to trust. I had lived too long with a hardened outer shell, while being broken on the inside.

Christians continued to come and see me. They shared the stories of Moses, King David, and even the apostle Paul, showing that God wishes to forgive even the worst of sinners and that He could change my heart. It was this message that eventually got through to me. God wanted to give me a new start based on something from the inside, not something external. God was concerned about me, personally, even after I'd made such a wreck of my life. I could hand my life over to Him, so that He could do something good with the rest of what I assumed would be a short life. So I thank God for Monty, Aubrey, and Carol, who shared the message of Christ. On November 7, 1982, I asked Jesus inside, to take over as Lord.

After experiencing God's grace, I rapidly and hungrily grew spiritually. God blessed me with mentors and spiritual fathers and mothers right away, who raised me in the Lord. The message of who we are in Christ became a cherished possession. I had never had an internal sense of who I was. I began highlighting all the passages in the Bible that spoke about how God saw me because of who I am in Christ. Now it would never again be about external validations, but God's work in the secret places of my heart.

When I was sentenced a year later, it was a double life-sentence. I was thankful to be in Christ as I entered the prison system at nineteen. I never expected to be paroled, but make no mistake about it, *I was truly free.*

Because of my addiction to alcohol and drugs, my conscience prodded me to make amends and take care not to relapse. But I didn't understand how. I also struggled to understand how, at age sixteen, I ran my life so completely out of control with alcohol, drugs, and crime. God sent the help I needed in 2003 when Pastor John Baker trained a group of twenty inmates, including me, to begin Celebrate Recovery inside the prison. We could do this through the generous support of Saddleback Church and prison outreach volunteers from the local churches outside the prison.

As we began our Celebrate Recovery ministry inside the prison, I felt like I was on an ocean wave that only God could create. In a facility with fewer than a thousand men, our Celebrate Recovery ministry quickly grew to two hundred participants! One of the points we focused on, even though in prison, was keeping the Celebrate Recovery DNA pure, by keeping the focus on the Cross of Christ, as we worked the recovery steps. This model of ministry had a strong impact on the prison population. With the help of Christian staff members and local church volunteers, we were able to hold two Celebrate Recovery meetings every week, and each meeting included the Large Group and Step Studies. In less than a year, the facility granted us an entire two-hundred-man building cellblock. It was used by those taking part in Celebrate Recovery!

As the Celebrate Recovery ministry continued to grow, the spiritual atmosphere of the prison changed so much that it began to attract the attention of the media. Not only was our CR ministry growing, we were having a positive influence on the prison. Local news stations, a National Christian radio station, and the *New York Times* reported on the impact of our ministry. We'd birthed a Purpose Driven Church and a two-hundred-man Celebrate Recovery ministry in a prison.

This ministry growth and testimony did not come without a price. You cannot expect to have a spiritual revival in a prison without some opposition! The media attention given to our Purpose Driven Church stirred up questions about me and other Christians crossing racial boundaries, which resulted in several assaults on me and our other church leaders. At one point, the prison captain considered moving me from the prison for safety!

Miraculously, God brought me and the other Celebrate Recovery group leaders through that time of opposition. It is a difficult and often frustrating task to preserve a jail or prison ministry, because prisons, by nature, are places of change and turmoil. However, to this day, fourteen years later, the Celebrate Recovery Therapeutic Community in that prison is healthy and continues to help thousands of men live better lives.

I was able to start three Celebrate Recovery ministries in nearby prisons, with the help of church volunteers and prison administrators. While I continued to serve a life sentence, I was often responsible for all the positions of the Celebrate Recovery T.E.A.M. (a team that *Trains, Encourages, Assimilates,* and directs the *Ministry*). More important, I completely worked through five Step Studies. And I worked through the Celebrate Recovery lessons, digging into my inventories. This included openly examining and confessing my faults with a sponsor. Working the steps and the lessons enabled me to dig deep into my underlying issues of fear and anger, which had led to my addictions after my parents' arrest.

The healing and insights I gained by working through multiple Celebrate Recovery inventories was also part of God's miracle when He released me from the physical prison. I say this because state parole boards do not release lifers easily. The process is grueling and requires in-depth psychological clearances. I went through a four-hour hearing before the state's most well-trained experts on when someone is truly ready for release. However, through Celebrate Recovery, I had already done the introspective work for more than a decade before the hearing. Through the many Celebrate Recovery inventories and weekly group sessions, God had already done the work of cutting open my heart for exposure and healing. My truest parole hearing was when I openly examined and confessed my faults to God, myself, and someone else I trusted.

After the hearing panel agreed to my release, I completed one more Celebrate Recovery inventory. In this inventory I faced my fears and stresses regarding what I expected to experience on my release after thirty-two years in prison. I wanted my heart and thoughts prepared for what was ahead, and I did not want to take the gift of grace or those who had loved and supported me for granted. I again confessed to a sponsor and shared my concerns. It was during this inventory that my sponsor helped me gain a better balance toward keeping a spirit of amends about the past and the faith to walk into God's next assignment outside of prison.

CHOICE 6

Repairing RELATIONSHIPS
Evaluate all my relationships.

Offer forgiveness to those who have hurt me, and make amends for harm I've done to others, except when to do so would harm them or others.

The ability to live in this new life would come from keeping the second "R" in our RECOVERY acrostic. *Reserve a daily time with God for self-examination, Bible reading, and prayer in order to know God and His will for my life and to gain the power to follow His will.*

I love Isaiah 1:18: "'Come now, let us reason together,' says the Lord. 'Though your sins are like scarlet they shall be as white as snow; though they are red as crimson, they shall be like wool.'"[25] It is important for me to remember that these words were not written to unbelievers, but to God's people. Through daily time with God, I continuously refocus on God and gain the power to follow His will in each new circumstance. Reserving a daily time with God helps me guard my heart and "take heed when I think I stand lest I fall."[26]

I was released on December 24, 2014, thirty-five years—to the day—after I heard my parents were arrested in Mexico. It is as if God placed a stamp of *grace* on a journey that included healing, forgiveness, and restoration. Since that day I have been riding a wave that only God can create. I thank God for my wonderful wife. I married my wonderful wife a year after my release.

I completed a bachelor's degree while imprisoned and, with my extensive addiction work, I immediately began working as a drug and alcohol counselor at a San Francisco methadone clinic. I still can't believe they gave *me* the keys to a methadone clinic! After a year in San Francisco I responded to *God's call* to serve as a pastor at Saddleback Church.

I understand that Pastor Rick and John Baker had it in their hearts to hire me as a pastor back in 2003 when we formed a Purpose Driven Church and Celebrate Recovery inside the prison. But there was just one problem: at that time I still had a life sentence! I am now the pastor for Celebrate Recovery Inside and have the twenty-thousand-member Saddleback Church and hundreds of pastoral staff as accountability partners!

I am grateful for the Celebrate Recovery ministries that I've been a part of—first while in prison, then in San Francisco, and now at Saddleback Church. It has been an encouragement and strength for me to begin a true DNA CR on the inside and then continue right on in the same ministry after my release. The Bible says,

> *All praise to God, the Father of our Lord Jesus Christ.*
> *God is our merciful Father and the source of all comfort.*
> *He comforts us in all our troubles so that we can comfort others.*
> *When they are troubled, we will be able to give them*
> *the same comfort God has given us.*[27]

Using this verse, I want to encourage anyone still going through the process of healing. Perhaps you are serving jail or prison time, or just now getting out and starting over. You can be free on the inside! If Celebrate Recovery worked for me while still in prison and then worked for me through the huge transition of life on the outside, God can use Celebrate Recovery to help you as you work through your struggles.

I am a grateful dependent follower of Jesus Christ. I struggle with alcohol and addiction, and my name is Ken. I have falsely believed that my greatest strength was being self-reliant, and that belief gave me a great sense of pride. Self-reliance was a tool I used to protect myself from relationships. I didn't grow up in a healthy home, and I had only a few safe people in my life; so I learned early to take care of myself. God has blessed me with some incredible gifts, but it wasn't until I was in recovery that I learned to use them for the purpose described in Romans 8:28: "And we know that in all things God works for the good of those who love him, who have been called according to his purpose."[28]

I was born in 1968 in Boston, Massachusetts. I am three years younger than my oldest sister and fourteen months younger than my older brother. When I was born, my father owned his own stock brokerage firm and my mother was working toward her nursing degree. We lived in a beautiful home in the suburbs of Boston, and from the outside everything probably looked perfect, but it wasn't.

My father controlled our home. My earliest memories of my father were him yelling at my mother and us kids. He demanded the best of us in public or private, and I learned not to do or say anything that made my dad angry. My mom was in school, but she struggled with depression. When I was a very young child, she tried to commit suicide. They admitted her to a psychiatric facility. I remember that my grandma Stella took care of us anytime Mom was "sick."

We moved to Texas in 1973 when my father's business failed. I learned when I was a little older that my father had stolen his investor's money and that he was running away. At this time, my mom was working in nursing, and she was the breadwinner of our home. My father always seemed angry. Anything would set him off. When my brother or I were in trouble, he would discipline us with a paddle. It was bad, but what I hated the most was the way he talked to me. Everything was a lecture.

I was a good student, and school was a refuge for me; but every report card was a lecture. He would say, "A's aren't good enough; they should be A⁺s." I learned not to ask for help with homework because he would tell me how simple it was and that he couldn't understand why I didn't get it. Every school conversation started with him reminding me that he was valedictorian of his high school and that he got a scholarship to MIT. No matter how well I did at something, he was always better, so I quit asking for his help.

It seemed Mom was working or sleeping all the time. Neither Mom nor Dad attended our school functions or Little League games. There were many times when the game or practice ended, and no one picked me up. This first happened when I was six years old. After waiting for what seemed a long time, I walked home in the dark. I remember being scared and crying, but when I got home I found Mom asleep and I didn't want to make her sad. This happened a lot over the years, so I found rides when I could and walked when I couldn't.

I was learning the rules for keeping our home happy. Telling Dad I needed anything makes him mad and telling Mom makes her sad. Basically, I learned that talking about my problems would only make other people upset, and so I shouldn't talk about my problems. I was becoming a people pleaser and very codependent. I'd even take responsibility for things I didn't do just to keep the peace.

We moved again when I was ten, and I got my first job as a paperboy. I was so proud. My dad helped me open my first bank account, and I got to keep five dollars of every paycheck. I deposited the rest in my bank account. I saved all year, and at Christmas I decided to go to the bank and withdraw fifty dollars to buy Christmas presents. I rode my bike to the bank and made out a withdrawal slip. They told me there was no money in my account. I was so sad that I started crying and couldn't stop. One of the bank tellers took me to an office where she explained that my father had withdrawn my money. My father had stolen my money. This was when I stopped trusting or believing him.

We moved a couple more times in and around the Houston area, and when I was thirteen, I had my first drink. I drank two beers and felt the effects. It didn't scare me. It felt good. When I drank, I didn't feel shy, I felt confident. I could talk with girls. What was going on? I had never felt this good. I thought alcohol was a gift to cure my shyness and social anxiety.

It was during this time that my parents divorced. I was thirteen. After the divorce, my dad disappeared from my life. I started drinking regularly and even trying a few drugs. I didn't miss his drama. It was then that a family friend entered my life, seeming to have my best interest at heart. He was a former teacher.

With my mother's approval, he began spending time with me. He was friendly and always willing to spend time with me. He never treated me like a fourteen-year-old, and we did lots of fun things together. He would let me drink, and he introduced other drugs into our time spent together. Since I never had a good relationship with my father, I desperately sought his approval.

He eventually introduced pornography into our time, and then the sexual abuse began. He played on my adolescent desires and manipulated me, but I never told anyone. This abuse lasted for about two years and only ended when I quit being available to spend time with him.

When I would think about this time in my life, I felt irrational rage at him, my parents, and myself. I hated how he used me and that I never told anyone. I remembered the fun we'd had together and that I thought he cared about me. Then I would remember how he'd manipulated me, and I would hate myself even more.

I was brought up believing in God. My mother was raised Catholic, and when we attended church it was with my mom. I was baptized as an infant, and we attended church periodically. As a teen, I accepted Christ as my Lord, and I knew what I was doing when I invited Him into my life; but that was all I did. Since I didn't attend church regularly, I didn't understand that believing in Christ also meant having a relationship with Him. I remember feeling changed for a while, but within a few weeks I was back to my old ways. I would spend the next eleven years with my back to God.

One Father's Day, shortly after I graduated from high school, I was thinking about my dad and missing him. I thought about how much had happened over the past four years. I was crying and told God that I couldn't continue to hope my father would return. I told God that I would give my dad until my eighteenth birthday to make contact, or I was going to write him off. I fully expected to write off my dad but God had other plans. One week before my eighteenth birthday, my dad knocked on our door. He hadn't changed in his manner or personality, but God had answered my prayer/demand. So I didn't write off my dad.

My dad was back in my life, but my alcoholism, addictions, and other problems were just beginning. I was arrested twice over the next two years, once for fighting in public and once for breaking into a car that I thought was mine. After my second arrest, my mother tried to get me into rehab, but I talked my way out of the intervention.

In college I was maybe a little more careful about my drinking and using, but they continued without much control on my part. I met my first wife while in school, and we made the perfect couple to the outside world. We both drank and had train wrecks of family histories but didn't judge each other. We both came from broken homes. I didn't know anything about having a healthy relationship, trusting, or intimacy; and God wasn't in our home. It wasn't six months until we started sleeping in separate rooms and living separate lives. I knew how to put on a happy face for family and friends, but I wasn't a good husband.

I got my first job in business and worked hard; I was promoted to the position of Accounting Administrator. It seemed like we would be set, but within two years I started stealing from the company. I was already spending many nights out drinking at "gentleman" clubs and was pretending to be a big shot. Once I started stealing, the stealing became its own drug. I was miserable at home, and I was enjoying this fake world I had created.

It took almost two years for them to discover my thefts. By then it was seventy thousand dollars. The owner of the company, Royce, confronted me. He wanted to meet with me and my wife to discuss the theft and how to repay it. I told him that she didn't know anything about it and asked for a couple days to break the news to her. He agreed but I had other plans.

First, I knew we had no way to repay the debt and that I would probably end up in prison. How could I explain to Royce what I had used the money for when no one knew about my private life? How was I going to explain to my wife that I wasn't working hard to get ahead but stealing to preserve that life outside our home? I had become an expert at lying, blaming, and manipulating, but I didn't see how I was going to cover this up with a lie.

In what I expected to be my final act of self-reliance, I decided to end my life. I wouldn't tell anyone anything, and once I was gone, who would care? For more than twenty-seven years I had managed to not have even one close personal relationship, including my wife.

That night I came home late and took a bottle of sleeping pills. The next morning, I wasn't dead. I was in the emergency room where I had to ride out the hallucinations. I still remember playing an imaginary game of cards with Christ, as angels flew around the room. I know I was delusional because of the overdose, but the memory of my emergency room visit still gives me comfort today. Even though I didn't have a good relationship with Christ, He was still with me on my worst day.

Today I recognize the truth of Romans 5:8: "God demonstrates his own love for us in this: While we were still sinners, Christ died for us."[29] God did for me what I could not do for myself. He helped reveal the truth of my life when I was too much of a coward to do it myself—and He still loved me.

That morning was the beginning of my recovery journey. I wish I could say that it was easy going, but to be honest I didn't know if I could get clean and sober. I did attend my first AA meeting, and I also met with Royce. That meeting was very uncomfortable, but I experienced a miracle of mercy. Royce was a man of God and demonstrated God's mercy to me. He was direct but told me that against his better judgment, he wouldn't press charges. He did expect full compensation, and he wanted to give me a chance to turn my life around.

I would love to tell you that my life turned around right then, but it has taken some time for me to grow in my recovery and my relationship with Christ. I stayed clean and sober for seven months, only to relapse and find myself wishing to die again. That was my last relapse and my bottom. It was when I realized I wouldn't be able to remain clean and sober without help. I celebrate my recovery beginning on July 24, 1996.

I started attending AA again and got a sponsor and began working the steps. I also began to reconnect with my higher power, Jesus Christ. I have been through many difficult times in my recovery, including divorce from my first wife and taking responsibility for my part. However, I was reading my Bible one evening and came across what is now my life scripture. I was reading about Paul and his thorns, and I realized that my biggest thorn is self-reliance. When I rely on myself I can't experience 2 Corinthians 12:9: "But he said to me, 'My grace is sufficient for you, for my power is made perfect in weakness.'"[30]

When I rely on God, my greatest weakness becomes God's most powerful tool.

During my recovery, I met my wife Tammy. We were both divorced and weren't going to rush into marriage again. We dated and discussed all the things we would do differently, and both of us knew we would be more involved in church. We started looking for a church to attend together and discovered HighPoint Fellowship; we knew that was where we should attend.

I chose to be baptized before the church in 2006. Tammy and I began serving wherever there was a need. I shared my testimony with my pastor and asked if he would allow me to host an AA meeting at the church. He agreed, but asked if I would look at the Celebrate Recovery materials. After I read about the program, we began the process of launching Celebrate Recovery at HighPoint Fellowship. Since beginning Celebrate Recovery, I have experienced an entirely different and wonderful life. I have practiced applying the steps and principles in my daily walk with God.

Working recovery has changed my life and allowed me to reconcile relationships that I thought would be impossible to restore. God had already answered my prayer to bring my father back into my life. My father never became healthy, or even trustworthy; but over the years, we got to know each other as adults and God gave me the opportunity to see my dad's many struggles. I was able to forgive my father and have a relationship with him.

Repairing RELATIONSHIPS

CHOICE 6

Evaluate all my relationships.

Offer forgiveness to those who have hurt me, and make amends for harm I've done to others, except when to do so would harm them or others.

In 2010 my father spent his last days in this world in hospice at my home. I was with him as he took his last breath in this world and his next in heaven. We never had a perfect relationship, but when he took that last breath, his hand was in mine. He knew he was loved by his son. I cherish that memory and am grateful to honor him in my walk with God.

Practicing this choice with my abuser, however, was something I struggled with in early recovery. Today, I recognize the truth that as a child I have no part to own in the sexual abuse I suffered. I don't own any guilt or shame or remorse. I was a victim. Yet I have also discovered another truth: the forgiveness I offer my abuser frees me! Offering my forgiveness to my abuser has also helped me see where I have hurt others. This choice has given me freedom from the rage and self-hatred I suffered in silence for so many years.

It took many years to repay my financial debt to Royce. We would speak on the phone a few times a year, and in many ways he became a mentor. It always seemed strange that he was even willing to talk with me. I was able to ask and receive Royce's forgiveness, and I made a complete financial amends.

God has used my experience to help others, but He had even more planned. On July 12, 2013, Royce's wife, Rose, called me to let me know Royce had died. I was sad but also humbled that she would take the time in her grief to call me. We talked for a few minutes, and she knew I was serving in ministry and would share my testimony. She then asked if I would be willing to share it at Royce's funeral.

I have never been so honored or humbled as when I was allowed to minister to Royce's family and friends in their time of grief and loss. I shared how God placed Royce in my life as an instrument of God's love, mercy, and grace when I felt deserving of none.

I am grateful to now serve with the broken, hurting, and hopeless; and I love watching how God demonstrates His power in weakness. I am amazed to experience this verse from Lamentations.

> *The steadfast love of the Lord never ceases;*
> *his mercies never come to an end;*
> *they are new every morning.*[31]

I am excited to see what God has planned next in my life.

R
E
C
O
V
E

Reserve a daily time with God

Y   for self-examination, Bible reading, and prayer
in order to *know* God and His will for my
life and to gain the power to follow His will.

Maintaining MOMENTUM

The GROWTH Choice

My daughter-in-law, Jeni Baker, shares these words with us:

> *I have always been a fearful person. One of my biggest fears was staying home alone. As a teenager, my whole family would work around my fear, making sure that I was never left home alone after a certain time of night.*
>
> *I carried this fear with me into my adult life and into my marriage. I determined that when I married, my husband would not travel. It was a non-negotiable. When I married Johnny, I thought I was safe. He worked late nights as a restaurant manager and didn't travel. If he needed to be out later than 11 o'clock, my mom would come stay with me. This system worked well for us, and then Johnny changed jobs. He became a pastor and started working for Celebrate Recovery. I loved everything about this job change, until there came a time when he needed to start traveling.*
>
> *This caused stress for both of us. I didn't know how I would manage on my own. It terrified Johnny to talk to me about traveling*

because he knew I would get so upset. Right around that same time, our church's women's ministry theme was "Total Surrender." I was in; I wanted to be totally surrendered! One morning not long after, Johnny came to talk to me about an upcoming trip. As he started telling me about this trip, in my head I was already gathering all the reasons he shouldn't go when the words "total surrender" popped into my head. It took the wind right out of my "fight." I remember telling Johnny, "Okay, if you need to go I'll be okay." I also remember the look of shock on his face. I explained that I wanted to surrender this fear and not allow it to run my life any longer. I knew the only way I was going to be able to conquer this fear was by God's power.

The Word of God is one of the greatest tools we can arm ourselves with. I dove into God's Word and started looking up verses that I could use to combat my fear. I created a list of specific verses that comforted me and gave me the courage I needed. The first night I ever spent home alone, I kept my Bible and that list by my side constantly. I read those verses over and over again. By the strength of God alone, I made it through that first night. The relief and freedom I felt that next morning is something I never will forget. Since then, I continue to work on not allowing that fear to creep back in and get a hold on me.

Reserving a daily time with God has become an essential part of my recovery and has helped me find freedom from all kinds of hurts, hang-ups, and habits.

Only God has the power to take away and keep away our old hurts, hang-ups, and habits. If we revert to trying to do it on our own willpower, we're going to relapse.

In the last six chapters, you've been learning about coming out of the dark and exposing your problems to the light of God's love. At whatever level you've been able to accomplish this, God has been healing the hurts, hang-ups, and habits that have messed up your life. Many of you are already experiencing some amazing changes in your life.

In this chapter we're going to focus on helping you maintain your momentum. The fact is, growth is not smooth. The road to healing is bumpy. Some days it's two steps forward and one step back. Just because you are reading this book and attempting to live out these biblical choices does not mean your journey will be problem free.

If you don't keep your guard up, you can easily fall back into your old self-defeating patterns. This is called *relapse*. The alcoholic starts drinking again. The overeater regains the weight. The gambler returns to the casino. The workaholic fills up his schedule again. We all tend to repeat the patterns of our past. It's easy to slip back into old hurts, old hang-ups, and old habits.

In this chapter we'll begin to understand relapse—its *patterns* and *causes*. Then we'll learn how to *prevent* relapse in the first place. Let's first look at the very predictable pattern of relapse. Regardless of the issue, the pattern is usually the same.

THE PREDICTABLE PATTERN OF RELAPSE

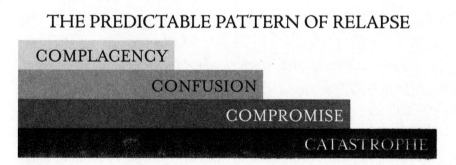

COMPLACENCY

CONFUSION

COMPROMISE

CATASTROPHE

Phase 1: Complacency

Relapse begins when we get comfortable. We've confessed our problem, we've started dealing with it, and we've made some progress.

Then we get comfortable, and one day we stop praying about it, and then we stop working at it. Our pain level has been reduced—not eliminated but reduced—and we think we can live with the reduced level of pain. We haven't thoroughly dealt with our problem, but we don't feel as desperate about it as we once did. We think we don't need to meet with our support group anymore. We don't need to work the choices anymore. We don't need to call our accountability partner anymore. And before we know it, we have become complacent.

Phase 2: Confusion

In this phase we begin to rationalize and play mental games with ourselves. We say things like, "Maybe my problem really wasn't all that bad; maybe I can handle it by myself." We forget how bad it used to be. Reality becomes fuzzy and confused, and we think we can control our problems by ourselves.

Phase 3: Compromise

When we get to this phase, we go back to the place of temptation. We return to the risky situation that got us in trouble in the first place, whether it's the bar, the mall, 31 Flavors, or that "XXX" Internet site. We go back to that unsafe place like the gambler who says, "Let's go to Vegas and just see the shows." But when we place ourselves in risky situations, we'll likely make poor choices. It may begin with little things, but it won't be long before it all unravels and all the ground that's been gained is lost. That brings us to phase four.

Phase 4: Catastrophe

This is when we actually give in to the old hurt, old hang-up, or old habit. The hate comes back, the resentment returns, or we fall back into the old patterns of behavior. But we need to understand this: the catastrophe is not the beginning of relapse. The relapse began in phase 1 with complacency. The catastrophe is simply the end result, the acting-out phase of the pattern.

So why do we fall back? Why do we fall into the predictable pattern of relapse when we know which way to go, when we know the right thing to do? Why do we tend to ignore what we know is right? There are four things that can cause us to relapse.

THE CAUSES OF RELAPSE

1. We Revert to Our Own Willpower

The Bible speaks to our foolish tendencies of trying to make it on our own: *"How can you be so foolish! You began by God's Spirit; do you now want to finish by your own power?"*[1] We got off to a good start:

+ In Choice 1, we admitted that we are powerless to change on our own.
+ In Choice 2, we agreed that only God has the power to help us change.
+ In Choice 3, we made a commitment to turn our life and will over to Christ's care and control.
+ In the fourth choice, we examined ourselves openly and honestly and confessed our faults.
+ In the fifth, we voluntarily submitted to the changes God wants to make in our lives.
+ Then in the last chapter, our sixth choice, we focused on repairing our relationships—offering forgiveness and making amends.

We've submitted, trusted, and committed. We've made room for God to make major changes in our life. But now, if we're not careful, we may start to think, "It's me doing this; I'm making the changes. It's my power."

We revert to relying on our own willpower; but the problem is, it didn't work in the first place, and it's not going to work now! We have a few successes, and suddenly we think we are all-powerful and all-knowing, and can handle everything on our own.

2. We Ignore One of the Choices

Maybe we get in a hurry and try to move through the choices too quickly. Maybe we decide to skip over a difficult choice. Perhaps the amends step seems too hard, and we rationalize that we can do without that one. We think, *Maybe partial recovery and healing will be enough.* But the truth is that we need to follow through on all the choices, or the plan doesn't work. It's been tried and proven countless times over.

There's no quick fix. You didn't get into this mess overnight, and you're not going to get out of it overnight. You need to work through all the choices to the very best of your ability at your own speed. Maintain your momentum. Follow the admonition the apostle Paul gave to some other Christians who had fallen back on their original commitment: *"You were doing so well! Who made you stop obeying the truth?"*[2]

3. We Try to Recover without Support

Since the very first chapter, the very first choice, we've learned the importance of someone to share with, someone to hold us accountable. But some of you may still think, "I can do this on my own. Just me and God—that's all I need to get well. I'll read the book, do the first two action steps at the end of each chapter, and I'll be good to go. I don't need an accountability partner, and I certainly don't need any kind of meetings or small group!" Wrong! It doesn't work that way. You're asking for a relapse.

God's Word tells us why having an accountability partner is so important. We've looked at this verse before, but we need to look at it again: *"Two people are better than one, because they get more done by working together. If one falls down, the other can help him up. But it is bad for the person who is alone and falls, because no one is there to help."*[3] The "Share about It" action step at the end of each chapter puts you in touch with someone who can help you when you fall down. Someone to encourage you to get up and keep trying. Don't neglect this powerful resource. You can't overcome your hurts, hang-ups, and habits alone. When you're tempted and things go bad, who are you going to call? If you do not have anyone to reach out to, you're not going to make it. God created you to be in healthy relationships: *"Let us not give up the habit of meeting together."*[4]

If you try to do these choices on your own, you may see short-term progress and growth, but without the support of others, you will eventually fall into relapse. It's like driving a car at fifty-five miles an hour, then taking your hands off the wheel. You may not crash immediately, but you will eventually. If you don't have a support team when the temptation comes, who will encourage you to do the right thing? If you fall, who will be there to help you up?

4. We Become Prideful

The fourth cause of relapse is our pride. We get overconfident and start to think we've beaten this hurt, this hang-up, or this habit. We think we've got forgiveness all sewed up and that we've closed the door on our past. Be careful. Scripture tells us that *"pride goes before destruction."*[5] We need to stay humble or we'll stumble. Always remember the lesson of the whale: "When you get to the top and are ready to blow, that's when you get harpooned."

Pride always sets us up for a fall. It blinds us to our own weaknesses and keeps us from seeking help. It prevents us from making real amends and from working through all the choices fully.

The biggest problem with pride is that it causes us to blame other people for our own problems; it prevents us from seeing the truth. Don't let your pride blind you to your own faults and responsibilities. The Bible reminds us, *"If you think you are standing firm, be careful that you don't fall!"*[6] You have been working hard on "getting it all together," but you don't have it all together yet. The secret to lasting recovery is to live in humility: *"Humble yourselves before the Lord, and he will lift you up."*[7] Humility is the best protection against relapse.

Pride blinds us to our own weaknesses and keeps us from seeking help.

Your greatest weakness is often an unguarded strength. You may say, "I've got this all together; I haven't had a drink in over a year." Watch out. "I made my amends years ago; my marriage could never fall apart." Watch out. "I could never get addicted to food again." You'd best be careful.

"If you think you are standing firm, be careful that you don't fall!" If left unguarded, the "relapse plane" will fly in and land right in the middle of the very area where you think you're strongest.

PREVENTING RELAPSE

The keys to preventing relapse are found in the words of Choice 7:

CHOICE 7

Maintaining MOMENTUM
Reserve a daily quiet time with God
for self-examination, Bible reading, and prayer
in order to know God and His will for my life
and to gain the power to follow His will.

Developing new habits is not easy. New healthy habits are about making daily choices that put us in a place where God can begin His transformation work in us. Someone has accurately said that the most difficult thing about the Christian life is that it is so *daily*. Jesus knew about daily temptation, and He knew how to fight it: *"Watch and pray so that you will not fall into temptation. The spirit is willing, but the body is weak."*[8]

Relapse is part of our human nature. It is human nature to go back to things that mess us up even though we know they mess us up. It's human nature to let past problems revisit us, to allow old hurts, hang-ups, and habits to haunt us. That's why Jesus tells us to *"watch and pray."* Choice 7 is all about putting those "watching and praying" habits in place in order to prevent relapse.

At the end of this chapter, you'll read the very powerful stories of John and Bill. They learned that they needed the support of like-minded people, along with the three new habits below, in order to maintain their momentum.

Habit 1: Evaluation

The Bible makes it clear that we are to evaluate ourselves: *"Test yourselves to make sure you are solid in the faith. Don't drift along taking everything for granted. Give yourselves regular checkups."*[9] We're also instructed, *"Let's take a good look at the way we're living and reorder our lives under God."*[10]

You've already had some practice evaluating yourself in chapter 4, when you did your moral inventory. In this chapter the focus is on *ongoing* inventories and evaluations of ourselves and our progress. First, we'll look at *what* we should evaluate, then *why* we should evaluate ourselves, and finally, we'll look at *when*.

What You Should Evaluate

1. *Physical:* "What is my body telling me?" Your body is a barometer of what's happening inside you. Are your muscles tense? Guess what? You're under stress. Do you have a headache or a backache? Your body is a warning light, telling you that something may be wrong. Periodically you need to stop and ask, "What is my body saying to me? Am I hungry? Am I tired? Am I fatigued? Am I stressed out?"

2. *Emotional:* "What am I feeling right now?" Are you allowing your real feelings to surface, or are you forcing them down? Repressing your real feelings is like shaking up a bottle of Coke and not taking the cap off; it's going to explode eventually. You need to take time for a "Heart Check."

H – am I *h*urting?

E – am I *e*xhausted?

A – am I *a*ngry?

R – do I *r*esent anybody?

T – am I *t*ense?

Do this check frequently, and respond to your emotional needs.

3. *Relational:* "Am I at peace with everyone?" If not, that internal conflict will hold you back on your road to healing. You know when you're having conflict with someone. It's up to you to resolve the part you've played in the conflict as soon as possible. When you allow a conflict to remain unresolved, you also allow painful memories and the people associated with them to live rent-free in your mind. Aunt Bertha may have hurt you fifteen years ago and live a thousand miles away, but if every day you wake up thinking about her, she is living rent-free in your mind, preoccupying your attention and energy. Soon this preoccupation will grow into a major resentment.

Is someone living rent-free in your mind? Are you holding on to a new hurt? Have you recently hurt someone and not made amends? If the answer to any of these questions is yes, offer your forgiveness or make your amends promptly!

4. *Spiritual:* "Am I relying on God?" Today, moment by moment, are you relying on God? Many of us don't take time to be alone and quiet in the presence of the Lord. We have disconnected ourselves from the most important lifeline we possess. That lifeline is a consistent, regular time with our heavenly Father. How are you doing in your relationship with God? Are you spending time alone with your Father? Are you relying on Him day by day, moment by moment?

Why You Should Evaluate

When you do an inventory at work you count everything. While it's essential to be honest about counting your shortcomings, another important reason to evaluate yourself is to celebrate the positive things in you. "I told the truth at least once today." "Yes, I blew it three times, but I was calm twice." "I at least wanted to be unselfish in that situation." Look honestly at where you are, but always remember to see what's good in your life. Be grateful for what you have done right.

Celebrate any victory, no matter how small, and do it on a daily basis.

The Bible tells us about a good kind of pride: *"Each one should test his own actions. Then he can take pride in himself, without comparing himself to somebody else."*[11] You can be honestly proud of what God is doing in your life, grateful that God is working with you and that you can see progress. Celebrate any victory, no matter how small, and do it on a daily basis.

When You Should Evaluate

Your evaluation, or inventory, is kind of like cleaning house. There are three kinds of house cleaners: neatniks, end-of-day cleaners, and spring cleaners.

Neatniks live with a DustBuster strapped to a holster and like to clean up messes as soon as they happen. They walk around behind the kids, picking up after them, like those waiters at restaurants who take your plate before you've finished your meal.

End-of-day cleaners look around the house, do a daily cleanup, and keep things in order on a fairly regular basis.

Spring cleaners clean house once a year, whether it needs it or not.

These same cleanup styles can help determine when you should do your personal evaluation.

1. Spot-check evaluation: The neatnik can do a spot-check at any time of the day. When you start feeling the pressure build, you say, "What is my body saying to me? What are my emotions saying? Do I have any relational conflict? Am I tuned in to God right now?" You try to deal with it immediately, because the longer you postpone dealing with a problem, the worse it gets.

Spot-check evaluations help you keep short accounts with God. If you keep short accounts, you will never have to do another moral inventory, because you are dealing with your issues as they surface. It's like taking the garbage out every day. There may even be times when you have to take the garbage out more than once a day because something really stinks. If you let it pile up, your life starts to stink. Sometimes you need to deal with your garbage on a moment-by-moment basis.

2. Daily review: This is for the end-of-day cleaners. As your day winds down, find a quiet spot and review your day, confessing your failures and celebrating your victories. Get out your journal and make a list under each of these three headings:

+ Things I did well today
+ Things I messed up today
+ This is how I responded

I have found journaling at the end of each day a key to my "relapse prevention plan." Thank God, I haven't had a drink in over twenty-seven years. But I can't rest on past victories. That is just what the enemy wants me to do. After all these years, I still write down my daily inventory in my journal. I can see the areas where I have fallen short and missed the mark. I can see the daily victories God is giving me. When I sin (not *if* I sin), I write it down and do my best to make the necessary corrections. Over time I can see unhealthy patterns develop, and with the support of God and my accountability partner, I can put together an action plan to get me back on track.

3. *Annual checkup:* This inventory is like a spring cleaning. You take some time off, go away for a day, and do an annual checkup. Look at your life, see what's in order and what's not, and do some deep cleaning. Here are some things to review:

+ Your relationships
+ Your priorities
+ Your attitude
+ Your integrity
+ Your mind
+ Your body
+ Your family
+ Your church

Habit 2: Meditation

Meditation may be a new concept to you, but it really isn't all that hard. Here are two simple keys to get you started: the how-to and the blessings of meditation.

The How-to of Meditation

1. *Reverse worry.* If you know how to worry, you know how to meditate. Worry is just negative meditation. When you worry, you take a negative thought and think about it over and over. When you meditate, you take a positive thought—often a verse of the Bible—and think about it over and over.

2. *Listening.* Meditation is a form of listening to God for His answers and directions. It's a time for slowing down long enough to hear God. The busyness in our lives stifles our recovery and growth. Meditative listening is the secret of spiritual strength.

3. *Memorization.* Having God's Word in your heart is a powerful deterrent to sin. "*I have thought much about your words and stored them in my heart so that they would hold me back from sin.*"[12] How do you store God's words in your heart? You memorize them. As you think about God's Word and memorize key passages, it will keep you from sinning and prevent relapse. Do you want to avoid temptation? Think about God's Word. It is the owner's manual for life. Your life will become a lot easier when you follow the manufacturer's instructions.

The Blessings of Meditation

The key to growth is to have roots deep down in God's Word. The way you grow roots in God's Word is to meditate on it. As you do that, you will be like "*trees along a riverbank*": "*They delight in doing everything God wants them to, and day and night are always meditating on his laws* and thinking about ways to follow him more closely. They are like trees along a riverbank bearing luscious fruit each season without fail. Their leaves shall never wither, and all they do shall prosper."[13] Three blessings of meditation leap out from this passage:

1. Fruit without fail: Those who meditate on God's Word will bear *"luscious fruit each season without fail."* That's quite a bold promise! If we hold God's Word deep in our hearts and meditate on it, we can be sure that our efforts will bear continued healing and growth; we can be sure of God's transforming power in our lives.

2. Health: We also read, *"Their leaves shall never wither."* If you regularly meditate on God's Word, when the heat's on you won't wither away; and when the drought comes you won't dry up and blow away. You will remain strong and tall and healthy. You won't have a relapse.

3. Prosperity: Finally, *"all they do shall prosper."* Knowing and meditating on God's Word leads to success and prosperity. This is not necessarily talking about financial prosperity, but prosperity of *life.* Meditating on God's Word will help you know the right thing to do, and then you will end up succeeding in God's purpose for your life.

Habit 3: Prayer

Prayer is your way of plugging in to God's power. You pray, "God, I can't do it, but You can."

Pray about Anything!

Most people don't realize you can pray about *any* need in your life. You can pray about a financial need, a physical need, a relational need, a spiritual need, or an emotional need. And you can most definitely pray about the struggles in your life: Jesus said to *"watch and pray so that you will not fall into temptation."*[14] You can take any need, any struggle, to God.

The How-to of Prayer

Jesus tells us how we should pray in what is often called the Lord's Prayer: *"This, then, is how you should pray: 'Our Father in heaven, hallowed be your name, your kingdom come, your will be done on earth as it is in heaven. Give us today our daily bread. Forgive us our debts, as we also have forgiven our debtors. And lead us not into temptation, but deliver us from the evil one.'"*[15]

Notice that Jesus says this is *how* we should pray, not *what* we should pray. He has given us a model, not a rote prayer.

When you choose to put these three new habits into practice—evaluation, meditation, and prayer—you are choosing life and health and recovery.

MAKE THE
Choice

Action 1: *Pray about It*

Praying the Scripture may be another new experience for you, but it's a prayer method that brings amazing blessings. In this action step, we'll pray through the Lord's Prayer. You will see how the 8 Choices support this great prayer. Even though you haven't yet come to chapter 8, you'll be able to pray this choice too. As we pray, we'll focus our prayer to avoid the dangers of relapse.

Scripture: "Our Father in heaven, hallowed be your name . . ."

Choice 1: Realize I am not God . . .

Choice 2: Earnestly believe that God exists . . .

Prayer: Father in heaven, Your name is wonderful and holy. I acknowledge that You hold all power—that You are God and that on my own I am powerless. Without You, I will most certainly relapse into my old hurts, hang-ups, and habits.

Scripture: "Your kingdom come . . ."

Choice 8: Yield myself to God to be used . . .

Prayer: I pray that Your kingdom will come in my life—that I will yield myself to be used by You, that You can use me to reach out to others with the Good News of Your kingdom and Your healing. Help me to find ways to serve You and others.

Scripture: "Your will be done on earth as it is in heaven . . ."

Choice 5: Voluntarily submit to God's changes . . .

Prayer: Oh, Lord, I pray that Your will be done in my life. I fight against it so often, but in my heart of hearts, I choose to submit to You. Help me to hold on to that choice. I choose Your will over my willpower; help me not to fall back into old patterns.

Scripture: "Give us today our daily bread . . ."

Choice 3: Consciously choose to commit . . . to Christ's care . . .

Prayer: Supply me with just what I need for today. Help me to take my recovery one day at a time, not looking too far ahead, but committing all my life and will to Christ's care and control—one day at a time.

Scripture: "Forgive us our debts . . ."

Choice 4: Openly examine and confess my faults . . .

Prayer: Forgive me, Lord. I have looked at my life and my heart, and what I've seen is not pretty. You already knew that, and I thank You for loving me anyway and for forgiving me so freely. Thank You for the loving support from others that You have provided along my healing journey.

Scripture: "As we also have forgiven our debtors . . ."

Choice 6: Evaluate all my relationships . . .

Prayer: Soften my heart toward those who have harmed me. Teach me, by Your power, to forgive, as You have forgiven me. And give me the courage, the conviction, and the wisdom to make amends where I have harmed others. Help me not to relapse into old patterns of resentment and bitterness.

Scripture: "And lead us not into temptation, but deliver us from the evil one . . ."

Choice 7: Reserve a daily time with God . . .

Prayer: Help me to daily spend time with You. I know that time with You is my best defense against relapse and my best offense toward growth. May my time with You create a hedge of protection around me. Amen.

Action 2: *Write about It*

One of the habits we talked about in the Preventing Relapse section is the habit of *evaluation*. Spend some time writing about the four areas we discussed there: *physical, emotional, relational,* and *spiritual.* Use these questions to guide your writings:

1. *Physical:* What is your body telling you? Remember, your body serves as a warning light, alerting you to things that are wrong.

2. *Emotional:* What are you feeling? Try to be honest as you write and not repress or stuff your feelings. Use the H-E-A-R-T check to identify what's going on inside of you:

H – am I *h*urting?
E – am I *e*xhausted?
A – am I *a*ngry?
R – do I *r*esent anybody?
T – am I *t*ense?

3. *Relational:* Am I at peace with everyone? Do I need to make amends to anyone? Do I need to forgive anyone? Write honestly about any conflicts you're having and what your responsibility in the conflict may be so you don't relapse into your old habits.

4. *Spiritual:* Am I relying on God? Take a moment to write about where you are in your relationship with God and what you can do to move your relationship to the next level.

Action 3: *Share about It*

Share what you wrote in your "Write about It" section with your accountability partner. You can share with him or her daily if you're going through a tough time. Your accountability partner can help you develop a godly plan to resolve each problem promptly. If you acted out and owe someone an amends, share that with your accountability partner too. This person can help you see your part and pray with you about making your amends.

As you share your evaluation and journal with your accountability partner, ask him or her to help you see any unhealthy patterns that are developing and any old hurts, hang-ups, and habits that are resurfacing.

Review the patterns of relapse with your accountability partner: *complacency, confusion, compromise,* and *catastrophe,* and ask him or her to help you look honestly at your life to see if any of these patterns are there. Listen openly, and talk together about ways to turn things around and prevent relapse in the future.

John's STORY

My name is John, and I am a grateful believer in Jesus Christ who struggles with codependency.

My first memories are of a home filled with love and warmth, a family intact and idyllic. Summers were packed morning to starry evening with fishing and bike riding, fort building and campfire s'mores. The long, cold winters were highlighted by the annual chopping down of a twenty-foot-tall balsam fir found deep into our property in northern Minnesota. We'd drag it back as a family, tumbling, laughing and rosy cheeked, pulling the giant evergreen through the front door of our log home. We listened to scratchy old Christmas records while stringing popcorn late into the night.

We attended and were extremely involved in a young, growing, vibrant Pentecostal church. My three siblings and I had just started school at the church's private academy when, with no warning, the church imploded—revealing scandal, lies, cover-ups, and shame. Not long after, my parents' marriage ended, and my childhood as I knew it was gone with an alarming suddenness and finality.

In what seemed to be mere weeks after the divorce, I found myself, with my older brother and two younger twin sisters, on a dairy farm with a new father and four new siblings. In a hastily thrown-together marriage, my mother and stepdad packed the eight of us into a tiny farmhouse in Kettle River, Minnesota. This is where I had my first taste of hard work, first taste of milk straight from the bulk tank, first taste of poverty, and my first taste of household chaos. The marriage was a disaster from the start.

This began a time in my life that was without predictability or security. My mom moved us on and off the farm several times, eventually ending the marriage and moving us back to her hometown. Changing schools and being uprooted from one community after another became commonplace. Mom was lost, and we got lost with her.

Depression took me like a fog in middle school, like a thick, smothering blanket. A once happy, active extrovert, I retreated into eating and inactivity, becoming overweight and reclusive. Bullies became a terror to me. My peers tortured me physically and emotionally in and out of school. In my sophomore year of high school, I came out of my shell enough to try out for the football team. In football I discovered something I was good at, something I received praise for, something that, I felt, gave me purpose. I also began attending a church youth group at the invitation of my older brother. It was there, in that drafty brick youth annex every Wednesday night, that the seeds of faith planted early in my childhood began to grow.

A few colleges showed interest in my performance on the football field. But my performance in the classroom was so abysmal that I wasn't worth a second look. I barely graduated. I convinced myself that I would never cut it academically at any institution of higher learning. So I never applied. I was still depressed, still afraid, still lost in my family dynamic.

Following graduation, I lived with my mom and sisters in Minneapolis. My stay in Minneapolis ended abruptly when my mom bailed a con man out of jail who had stolen almost everything she had. When she came home with him, I gave her an ultimatum. Either he went or I would. Her choice confirmed my worthlessness, and again I was set adrift in depression.

I did finally register at a community college in Virginia, Minnesota, that had a football program. I played ball and made the grades. But the depression worsened as I isolated myself more and more. Taking part in my church youth group had helped me resist attending parties and drinking in high school. But now I didn't have that support.

A few months into my college experience, lonely and looking to gain acceptance from my friends and desperate to find relief from my depression, I said, yes again to the parties and drinking. In alcohol I discovered a new sidekick of depression that took my insecurity to breathtaking lows.

After a promising year of football, a large college in central Minnesota invited me to try out. After my visit, the head coach showed more concern about my well-being than my performance at the tryout. I remember him looking hard at me as I halfheartedly thanked him for inviting me to the tryout. He answered me by asking, "Son, are you okay?"

I was not okay. I was empty and lost, and I was beginning to feel like my life was not worth living. I dropped out of college and moved into an apartment with a friend. We drank and partied until I stopped partying and just drank. All I saw or felt was darkness.

Jesus tells us about this darkness: "The eye is the lamp of the body. If your eyes are healthy, your whole body will be full of light. But if your eyes are unhealthy, your whole body will be full of darkness. If then the light within you is darkness, *how great is that darkness!*"[16]

I based my view of my circumstances, my interpretation of my life's events, and my beliefs about myself on what others said to me. The lies I believed about my worth and my purpose for living clouded my soul's understanding. I could not see the truth. A haze of pitch-black deception clouded the way I saw myself and God . . . and *how great was that darkness.*

Late one night, lost in depression and self-hate, I picked up a double-barreled shotgun my grandfather had given me. I had it in my lap for what seemed like hours. I finally loaded it and began to peek down the barrels to see what it would be like to look at death. I was so sick and tired of being sick and tired.

"God, are You there?" What started as whisper grew in volume and desperation.

"Where are You!!!?? I am dying! I am already dead, and You don't care!"

I remember spitting a halfhearted prayer toward the ceiling—an almost sarcastic dare, an ultimatum of sorts.

"If you don't answer me, I am going to do it . . . I am going to pull the trigger."

In that darkness, the Lord answered me. He gave me a vision I will never forget. It was of me as Jonah lost in the belly of a fish at the bottom of the ocean, running from the call God had on my life. He gave me these verses out of that vision that night, and these words will ever be the story of my salvation:

> In my distress I called to the Lord,
> and he answered me.
> From deep in the realm of the dead I called for help,
> and you listened to my cry.
> You hurled me into the depths,
> into the very heart of the seas,
> and the currents swirled about me;
> all your waves and breakers
> swept over me.
> I said, "I have been banished
> from your sight;
> yet I will look again

> *toward your holy temple."*
> *The engulfing waters threatened me,*
> *the deep surrounded me;*
> *seaweed was wrapped around my head.*
>
> *To the roots of the mountains I sank down;*
> *the earth beneath barred me in forever . . .*
> *But you, Lord my God,*
> *brought my life up from the pit.*[17]

I lowered the shotgun to the floor, completely disarmed by the Holy Spirit, and I once and for all surrendered my life to Jesus Christ.

Months later I enrolled in a Christian college in Springfield, Missouri, ready for whatever adventure God would call me to.

As a young man armed with a renewed faith and a zealot's confidence, I convinced myself that all my problems were behind me. I believed the path before me was laid smooth by my decision to commit my life to God. I have since learned, through many trials and tests, that full recovery from life's hurts, hang-ups, and habits requires a decision followed by a process. I have learned that this process of change and refining is hard. It is painful, but it is worth it. In one of my favorite books, *Great Expectations,* Charles Dickens writes, "Suffering has been stronger than all other teaching. . . . I have been bent and broken, but—I hope—into a better shape."

The years that followed my recommitment to God's purpose bent and broke me in ways I never imagined. But I believe it was to shape me into the man He wanted me to be.

The Bible says, "Yet you, LORD, are our Father. We are the clay, you are the potter; we are all the work of your hand."[18]

In college I fell in love with the most beautiful woman God has ever breathed life into. We hurdled toward marriage as recklessly as two people in love ever have. While dating she told me of her struggle with an eating disorder. In a courageous moment, fearing my response but sharing it anyway, Jennene described to me how bulimia and anorexia had governed her life since late in high school. Her tearful confession only made me love her more. I just knew that I could fix it! I knew my love for her would be enough and that once we married, all would be well. Of course, it wasn't. In fact, her eating disorder only got worse, and my response to her struggle soured over time.

We married in the summer of 1998. Less than a year later, I graduated from college. We moved to Delaware, and I dove into a career in social work and counseling. I also began laboring through a graduate program, while volunteering any extra time I had at church. I helped run the church food pantry, started a children's clothing closet, and launched a program my pastor had told me about called Celebrate Recovery.

I loved helping people work through their problems. I loved being a part of the process of healing individuals and families in Celebrate Recovery. I loved witnessing the emotional breakthroughs folks experienced week in and week out in therapy and in their recovery. I *hated* that recovery was happening everywhere except in my own home.

The more I tried to fix my wife, the more she spiraled into her disorder. I would cajole, rage, plead, scream, threaten, bargain, lecture, and beg my wife to change. Nothing worked, so I did. I *worked* to escape what was happening at home. I reasoned that my time was better served with people who would listen to me, people who would benefit from my expertise, people who appreciated and responded to my encouragement and guidance.

Four daughters were born into the midst of our tumultuous marriage. Each brought hope that maybe this new life would inspire the needed change we both so desperately wanted. However, not even these precious souls had the power to mend the brokenness in our relationship. I withdrew further from my family and into my own coping strategy of people-pleasing and approval-seeking. I desperately needed to be needed.

About six years into our marriage, I received an opportunity to enter full-time ministry as an outreach pastor in West Virginia. Besides my counseling duties and oversight of the church's benevolence programs, I received the task of starting and facilitating Celebrate Recovery. Despite the change in location and vocation, Jennene fell deeper into the darkness of her eating disorder. I fell further into the darkness of my resentment and anger.

Through the Celebrate Recovery program, I had a good understanding of what codependency looked like. What I didn't have was an understanding of how much I looked and acted like a textbook codependent! As a pastor, I felt that my calling was not only to help people, but to *save* people. Though I made efforts to work my program, and though I did begin to identify myself as a codependent, inevitably I would fall back into my old patterns of dysfunction. I would rarely say no to anything put in front of me. I continued to get my worth from the praise of others. I favored identifying myself as the savior of man rather than a man in *need* of a Savior. I labored for nearly a decade in social work, counseling, and ministry to help "those people." Unfortunately, it took almost losing my wife and family to realize that I was, and am, one of "those people."

In the winter of 2009, my wife finally reached her breaking point and told me she was willing to do anything to find freedom from the hell she was putting herself and her family through. Weeks later she was tearfully kissing our girls good-bye, steeling herself for a forty-day stay at a treatment center in Arizona. Her courage was jaw-dropping, yet my heart was so hard toward her. My attitude was so self-centered that all that went through my mind was, "It's about time!" I dropped her off at the airport like a man bringing a broken-down car to be serviced. They needed to fix her, whatever it cost, and if they didn't, I wasn't sure she would be worth keeping. What a selfish fool I was. I was about to learn that marriage is not expecting your spouse to be the person you need her to be. Marriage is being the spouse God has called *you* to be.

I flew out to join my wife three weeks later at the treatment facility for what they called "Family Week." Jennene had been working hard, but the eating disorder would not let go of its hold without a fight. I became quickly discouraged by what I saw as a lack of progress on her part. I felt she was not taking this experience seriously. I felt she wasn't grateful for the sacrifices made by me and others to get her into treatment.

On top of my disappointment, they asked me to take part in intensive family therapy. They asked me to explore my part in my wife's struggles. I resented it. She was the problem! I was the martyr who had put up with this behavior since the beginning of our marriage! I sat in those sessions stubborn and unmoving. I was stuck. Even though I had been running Celebrate Recovery for several years, I had, in my pride and self-righteousness, abandoned a continued process of prayerful self-examination that this life-changing ministry calls for.

CHOICE 7

Maintaining MOMENTUM
Reserve a daily quiet time with God
for self-examination, Bible reading, and prayer
in order to know God and His will for my life
and to gain the power to follow His will.

I was powerless, but I was still desperately trying to control everything and everyone around me. Locked in a stalemate in the last session of

Family Week, I sat unmoved, staring at the floor. I was resigned to the sad fact that, after all I had done for her, after all she had put me through, she still refused to change. I felt my heart growing cold and heavy. If she didn't care enough about me to salvage our marriage, to protect our children, to love me the way I deserved to be loved, well . . . I was done caring too.

All of these thoughts rolled through my mind as the words of the therapist echoed against the walls of his office, barely registering. Then, quietly at first, but growing in intensity, I heard him say something odd. Something about how, he hated to do it, but it was time we heard directly from the eating disorder itself.

He suddenly had my complete attention as his voice dropped to an icy baritone uttering the words I feared more than anything else in the world. The therapist, representing the eating disorder, shared in horrifying detail how he was going to destroy our family. How he was going to poison our minds and eventually invade the lives of each one of our sweet little girls. Finally, how he was going to slowly kill my wife right in front of them, right in from of me.

A storm of fury built up to a fever inside my chest that was about to burst out in violence on the therapist. Suddenly, with breathtaking clarity, I looked at my wife and saw her for the first time the way I always ought to have seen her. Scared, wounded, and alone in the fight of her life against this murderous, insidious evil. I could barely get out the words through my heavy, choking sobs, "I am sorry . . . I am so sorry. You are not your eating disorder. All this time I have been fighting you when I should have been fighting the eating disorder."

That was a turning point for both of us. We both came back from that experience with a common enemy. We attacked it together through the process found in the 8 Principles and the 12 Steps of Celebrate

Recovery. By working my program honestly and fervently, I have learned my part in waging battle against the common enemy of my wife and marriage. I follow Paul's instructions to the Ephesians by loving my wife as Christ loved the church and gave Himself for her. In fact, in many ways, I have learned that this is my part to play in *all* I do as a father, as a friend, as a minister, and as a neighbor. Love, not fix. Love, not save. Love, not control. Love.

Today Jennene and I celebrate what God continues to do in our marriage and in our entire family. We are growing closer to each other and closer to Him through a continued, daily process of self-examination, prayer, and spending time in His Word. Thanks be to Jesus Christ, and thank you for letting me share.

Bill's STORY

I am a faithful follower of Jesus Christ who struggles with sexual addiction, alcoholism, and anxiety. My name is Bill. I grew up in a typical Western New York Irish and Italian Roman Catholic home. I have two sisters, four children, two grandchildren, and enough baggage to fill a Greyhound bus. My parents are still married and tried to give me the most loving home they knew how to. I have many fond memories of my childhood, and God is teaching me, through my daily time with Him, to be appreciative of those good memories. We were never poor, but sometimes we were broke.

My father was a public servant to the core and worked very hard as a civil engineer. I always had to explain to my friends, "Not trains but streets and water." My mother was a homemaker who gave us a safe place to grow up and feel loved and meet God. We always had breakfast, dinner—and in the summer, lunch—together as a family at the table. My mother eventually became the Queen of the school bus drivers, and I am certainly glad she did not drive while I was in school.

Like I said, we were Catholic, so my sisters and I went to Catholic school. The kids mostly teased me because I wore homemade pants to school until about fifth grade. Don't get me wrong; those pants were great. They had the pockets sewn on the outside and everything. This was the beginning of me needing to feel loved by others. It hurt to be the last one picked in team sports. I was very athletic and good at sports, so I knew why they picked me last. It was because I wasn't good enough to be their friend.

One day when I was seven, I went to the barbershop with my father and saw some *Hustler* and *Playboy* magazines on the waiting room counter. My father did not look at them, but when he was getting his hair cut, I did. For some reason, the imagery stirred something in me that was exciting and scary all at the same time. Eventually my curiosity got the best of me, and I started snooping in my uncle's bedroom to look at his pornography. It was at this time that I was sexually abused by one of my uncles. He was ten years older than me and told me we would both get in trouble if I told on him. I never spoke of this until I earnestly worked the principles of recovery; and one day, during my daily time with God, He revealed it as the root of my addictions.

The sexual abuse changed my view of sex forever. I began to see it as a way to rebel; after all, my uncle was a role model to me, and he was doing it. It began to consume me at a young age in a very negative way. I would steal my uncle's pornography magazines and hide them in an old van in the junkyard down the railroad tracks from my house. This was where my addiction to sex began. It went from looking at pornography to full-blown sexual addiction when I was thirteen.

I was not the best-behaved kid at Catholic school because I used the Word of God to rebel at a young age. I always believed in Jesus and knew that He died for my sins and rose from the dead so we may have eternal life. Sister Margret Mary convinced me in kindergarten that God was real. My Papa died and went to heaven, and she sweetly assured me that he was with Jesus in heaven. Nevertheless, I was the kid who would not listen to the nuns and priests at school and asked why our Bible was different from the one at VBS. That's right, Vacation Bible School. This is where I truly met Jesus, was justified by grace, and chose to be baptized. This was a sore spot to my Catholic family, but they respected my belief in this new "religious system."

I got kicked out of Catholic school for misbehavior and sent to public school. I began to seek girls for sex, all the while looking for something

I was missing. This became an obsession, in which I started using girls for my pleasure. This is when I also started to drink alcohol to numb the pain of the abuse and to lower my inhibitions so I could engage in my sinful lifestyle.

My parents saw this drastic change in my attitude and blamed the influence of my new friends. During this time, I was acting out toward my parents as well. My father would try to discipline me, and my mother would emasculate him in front of me like he had no right to do so. This caused me to have resentment against all women and to think my dad was weak. I vowed never to be like him, and now my sexual exploits increased to having sex with multiple partners almost daily.

But then the dynamic changed. Now it was to exert my power over women. I continued to drink every weekend and hide my drinking from my parents and even some of my friends. On my seventeenth birthday, the school administration kicked me out of high school for smoking. It was my tenth offense. I took and passed my GED and started college in Rhode Island that April.

While I was there, my sexual appetite increased as well as my drinking. I began to drink almost daily, because of my lack of accountability. My first son was born while I was in college. I had no idea that this woman, who was a one-night stand, was even pregnant. Then the child support papers arrived, and I knew he was mine. Poor kid looks just like me. Meanwhile, my now first wife was pregnant with our first of two children as well.

She and I started out in the swinger lifestyle. This was just what I thought I needed to complete me and my huge sex drive. I was wrong and it eventually led to a divorce because of infidelity. I walked in on my wife doing the very thing I was okay with and I lost it. I beat that poor man within inches of his life and was arrested for felony assault. The judge gave me a break by giving me the choice to join the Marines or go to jail. So I joined the Marines.

I spent sixteen years in the U.S. Marines doing reconnaissance. During this time, I embraced the lie that my sexual addiction was "part of who God made me to be." I had no respect for myself or for women. I started to hang out at clubs to pick up "loose women." Little did I know I was the prey and not the predator.

I was now drinking all day, every day and could not function without alcohol. My lifestyle brought me into the seediest places in the red-light districts to satisfy my flesh. I was looking for something to fill an empty space in my life. All of this said I was still empty and lonely.

I met a woman who was also a Marine and married her, but she was not on board with my "ambivalence" toward women or my drinking. Eventually, the way I treated her was too much for her. She also was unfaithful and left me. I know now that I was not faithful to God through all of this, so why would I expect anyone to be faithful to me?

The Marines transferred me to Okinawa, Japan, in the mid-nineties, and I was happy to go. Once there, I started to embrace the idea of using prostitutes. After all, I told myself that they were providing the service for which I was looking. I went to Thailand for the summer of 1999, and my sin hit a peak. I was soliciting prostitutes daily and living my life as far from God as I could get. I thought I was invincible and that there was nothing I couldn't do. I used people for my personal pleasure and discarded them as quickly as I found them. I would use my anger and imposing stature as a Marine to keep people at a distance, never letting anyone get close enough to hurt me.

I contracted HIV in July 1999 from a Thai prostitute. The sad thing is there is no way of knowing who gave it to me because of how rampant my sin and insanity had become. I was sent back to the States after my diagnosis to finish my career on nondeployable instructor duty. While I was waiting to transfer back to the States, I met a woman, married, and had my fourth child. We moved back to the States, and life became a blur of alcoholism and sex. We made a deal with each other: we would never mention that the alcoholism was an issue and our marriage would be just fine. That did not work at all. Just hearing myself say that today makes me realize how deep my denial and insanity had become. This marriage ended as fast as it began, and this time I decided I was never getting married again. So here I am waiting to die while on instructor duty.

I was on patrol on a Tuesday morning, September 11, 2001, with eighteen recon students, when we got the word that the United States had been attacked. The Marine Corps forgot about me being nondeployable, and ten days later sent me out with the teams to carry out the mission of vengeance against our enemies. I could live recklessly and dangerously, all the while hoping to die in a hail of gunfire.

God had different plans. I deployed for most of the next five years. I took two weeks off to come home and visit at the end of 2002. While I was home, I continued my sinful ways and had another series of one-night stands and alcoholic binges. Then I went back to the Teams.

In September 2006, I retired and went home to Buffalo to die of the disease my sin had bought me. I had full-blown AIDS and only sixteen T cells left. I began to attend a small church plant and Alcoholics Anonymous. I was able to shed my obsession for the booze, but there was something missing in my recovery plan. I got a sponsor and worked the steps of Alcoholics Anonymous. I also engaged in a Christian small group where I met a man named Aaron. I referred to him as my spiritual-battle buddy. Aaron was a guy with the faith of the centurion. I stopped my sinful behaviors and started to heal with the help of my battle-buddy, my sponsor, and most important, Jesus Christ. God had big plans for me. I stopped being just a believer and started following Jesus and His teachings. I started serving at church as the chair guy and as the video guy. I met this nice woman at church, and we started dating. I started to work through my resentments and becoming the man God made me to be.

This new relationship was the first pure relationship that I have ever had. I explained to her that we would never get married. She laughed at me, and we married a few months later.

God could have stopped blessing me after He put Lillian into my life and that would have been enough. But like I said, God had plans for me. I started to work with the youth as their pastor. God was doing a work in me that I couldn't explain. I started focusing on God and His Word, I began to pray and meditate daily. My church elders asked if I would check out a program called Celebrate Recovery. I looked into it and that's when the lights turned on. This is exactly what my recovery was missing: deep intensive work with Jesus Christ and the recovery principles based on His Beatitudes from the Sermon on the Mount. Lillian and I attended our first One Day and learned how to start a program of our own. We returned and took our leaders through the Step Study and the leaders training from the Advanced Leadership Training Kit.

When I completed my first of many Step Studies, I learned that God didn't want me to live with the pain and regret of my past. I am now happy and love how it changed my recovery and walk with Christ forever. I have since forgiven my uncle and introduced him to Celebrate Recovery. He was my guest at the premiere of the movie *Home Run*. I gave him the Celebrate Recovery participant guides and a Celebrate Recovery Bible as a gift of amends for the bitterness I harbored against him. The men from my Step Study are some of my closest friends. We still get together and hold one another accountable today.

You know how I said earlier that I was looking for something through my sexual addiction and despair? What I was looking for was Jesus Christ. Only Jesus could fulfill the emptiness and loneliness in my life.

My life today looks different. I did not realize how unhappy I was until I stepped out of denial and into the light of my Lord and Savior Jesus Christ. I have accepted the forgiveness He has freely offered me and have begun to move forward in service to my King and His Church.

My favorite step is the Step 12. I like the way it is worded: "Having had a spiritual awakening as the result of these steps, we tried to carry this message to others, and to practice these principles in all our affairs." "A spiritual awakening" . . . that's the part I love. Jesus Christ is the reason I woke up.

I want to be clear when I say this: Jesus was what I needed, not the pleasures of the flesh or having my ego fed so I wouldn't act out. Just Jesus. His example of how to live is all I crave. I am no longer dead in my sin, but I am alive in Christ, for He was the One I required all along. Jesus has His own version of Step 12, found in Matthew, where Jesus said:

> *Go therefore and make disciples of all the nations,*
> *baptizing them in the name of the Father*
> *and of the Son and of the Holy Spirit,*
> *teaching them to observe all things that I commanded you;*
> *and lo, I am with you always, even to the end of the age.*[19]

I have embraced Choice 7 as a way of life today.

CHOICE 7

Maintaining MOMENTUM
Reserve a daily quiet time with God
for self-examination, Bible reading, and prayer
in order to know God and His will for my life
and to gain the power to follow His will.

Every day when I wake up, I pray the most dangerous prayer. I ask God to use me. Then I ask Him to give me serenity, recovery, and grace just for today. I spend time reading the Word to remind me Whom I belong to, and I pursue righteousness for the sake of Christ.

I am so inspired by what God does and how He works through and in every one of us every day. Never in my life had I experienced true Gospel community until God brought Celebrate Recovery into my life. The people you meet in this fellowship are the best friends you could ever have. I am eternally grateful that God has added me to this Forever Family.

If you are new to recovery, my only advice is to hang in there. If you are new to a relationship with Jesus as your Savior, my advice is to hang on, because He is going to take you for a ride that will last for an eternity. I know that God is still creating a new me. It is my pleasure to be the clay in His hands.

R
E
C
O
V
E
R
Y

"Happy are those who are persecuted because

they do what God requires."[1]

Yield myself to God

to be *used* to bring this Good News to others,
both by my example and by my words.

Recycling PAIN

The SHARING Choice

Mac Owen, who is our Celebrate Recovery national director, shares this message:

> One fact I know about people who have been rescued is that they can't keep quiet about what happened to them. The apostle Paul was no different. He said, "For he has rescued us from the dominion of darkness and brought us into the kingdom of the Son he loves, in whom we have redemption, the forgiveness of sins."[2]
>
> This is what God did for me. He rescued me from a life of drug addiction and alcoholism. I found the hope that I had only dreamed about, and I can't keep it to myself. It seems as though the reason God made me was to share this hope and then another person . . . and then another. The hope God gave me is there for others as well.
>
> I was at a marriage retreat when I noticed him, someone from our church whom I didn't recognize. Even though he was in a crowd of people, he looked alone. So I went over and introduced myself,

asking, "How's it going?" It was like this was the question he had been waiting for his whole life. Immediately, he told me about his life of failure—failure as a husband, as a father, as a person. For as long as he could remember, he never measured up. Was life even worth living? Maybe just giving up was the answer.

As I sat and listened, it was obvious that here was a man who needed to be rescued, to hear about the hope that someone had shared with me.

So I asked if he would be willing to meet with me for coffee. He said yes.

Over the next three weeks, I shared about my encounter with Jesus and how my life of hopelessness had turned into a life filled with hope. I shared that he too could experience that same hope, but it came with a cost. It required surrender, giving up control, and turning his life over to Jesus. I will never forget his words, as tears streamed down his face: "I want to, I really do; but I don't deserve it. How could He love a failure like me?" In that moment, my heart broke for him and I said, "Me too! That's the beauty of it. God only rescues broken people."

As relief came over his face, he said, "I surrender. Can I be baptized?" I replied, "Not only can you, but we can go do it right now." I gained a brother that day because God had taken my greatest weakness and turned it into my greatest strength. I was sharing with one other broken person that there is hope for them too!

Your greatest contribution to this world—your greatest ministry—will not be found in your strength but in your weakness. It will come from your pain. The very thing you want least to talk about, the very thing you want to hide in the closet, is the very thing God wants you to share. One of the great things about God is that He never wastes a hurt. And He doesn't want to waste yours.

In this, the last chapter and the last choice, we'll see that the "Y" in R-E-C-O-V-E-R-Y stands for *yield*. It also stands for *you*. God wants *you* to yield to Him and allow Him to recycle the pain in your life for the benefit of others.

Most of us are under the misconception that God uses only the really gifted, extraordinarily talented people. That's not true. God uses ordinary people. In fact, He does His best work through weak people: "'My gracious favor is all you need. My power works best in your weakness.' So now I am glad to boast about my weaknesses, so that the power of Christ may work through me."[3]

People are not helped when we talk about our strengths; they're helped when we're honest about our weaknesses. When we share our strength, they say, "Big deal, I'll never have what he has." Or, "My faith is not as strong as hers." But when we share from our weaknesses, they say, "I can relate to that!"

I have the honor of giving my testimony several times a year. Every time I give it, people say, "Thank you for sharing your struggles and weaknesses with me. It is exciting to see the things God has done in your recovery." They do not thank me for my strengths. They thank me for being open and honest with my weaknesses. God gets the glory. They see that if God can restore a sinner like me, He can and will help them find freedom from their hurts, hang-ups, and habits.

When you understand that God uses your weaknesses and your pain, life takes on a whole new meaning and you experience genuine recovery. The proof that you are truly recovering is when you begin to focus outside yourself, when you stop being absorbed with *your* needs, *your* hurts, *your* problems. Recovery is evident when you begin to say, "How can I help others?"

In this final chapter, we'll answer two important questions: Why does God allow our pain? And, How can we use our pain to help others?

WHY DOES GOD ALLOW PAIN?

Why God allows pain and suffering is a universal question. There are several reasons, but here we'll share the big four.

1. God Has Given Us a Free Will

God created us with the right to choose. In the Book of Beginnings, Genesis, we read, *"God created man in his own image."*[4] One of the ways God's image is shown in you is in your freedom to choose. Simply considering the creation of the universe, we see that God made millions of choices. You too have the right to choose. You can choose good or bad, right or wrong, life or death. God says to us, "You can reject Me or accept Me. It's your choice."

God could have created you without a free will so that you always did right and never did wrong, but God didn't want a bunch of puppets. He wants you and me to love Him voluntarily. You can't really love someone unless you have the opportunity not to love that someone. You can't really choose good unless you have the option to choose bad.

Our free will is not only a blessing; it can also be a burden. As you have read in the courageous stories in this book, poor choices cause painful consequences. We all make choices that bring pain to ourselves and others. If we choose to experiment with drugs and get addicted, then it's our own fault. If we choose to be sexually promiscuous and get a sexually transmitted disease, we bear the consequences of our own bad choice. Do you see the dilemma? God will not overrule your will. God doesn't send anybody to hell. We choose to go there by rejecting His will for us. God loves you and wants you to be a part of His family, but if you thumb your nose at God and walk away from Him, you can't blame anyone but yourself. That is free will.

There's one more thing to consider about the free will God has given us. Not only does God give *you* free will, He gives it to everyone else too. So this means that sometimes others choose to do wrong, and you may get seriously hurt as an innocent victim. Many of you

The proof that you are truly recovering is when you begin to focus outside yourself.

have been deeply hurt by a parent, spouse, teacher, friend, relative, or someone you didn't even know. God could have prevented that hurt by taking away that person's free will. But if He had done that, in order to be fair He would have had to take away your free will too. Pain is part of the free-will package.

2. God Uses Pain to Get Our Attention

Pain is not your problem. Your depression, your anxiety, and your fear are not even your problems. These are simply warning lights, telling you that something is wrong and you need to deal with it. Pain is God's wake-up call: *"Sometimes it takes a painful experience to make us change our ways."*[5]

Sometimes pain is severe, like the pain of a burn on our skin or the internal stab of a heart attack. Without these painful sensations, we might just go about our business, unaware of life-threatening dangers.

But the "blessing" of pain is that it gets our attention and lets us know something is seriously wrong. Paul said this about the benefit of pain: *"I am glad . . . not because it hurt you but because the pain turned you to God."*[6]

Your problem may be low self-esteem, loss, abandonment, or abuse. Your pain is telling you that these issues need your attention! Nobody likes pain, but God uses pain to get your attention.

Do you remember the story of Jonah being swallowed by a great fish? Jonah was going one way, and God said, "I want you to go the other way." And at the bottom of the ocean, Jonah finally said, *"When I had lost all hope, I turned my thoughts once more to the Lord."*[7] Isn't that a great verse? God uses pain to get our attention.

3. God Uses Pain to Teach Us to Depend on Him

The apostle Paul was well acquainted with pain, and out of his experience, he tells us, *"We were really crushed and overwhelmed . . . [and] saw how powerless we were to help ourselves; but that was good, for then we put everything into the hands of God, who alone could save us."*[8] You will never know that God is all you need until God is all you have. When it's all falling apart and you've lost it all, that's when you can see clearly the only One who is remaining beside you. Without problems, you'd never learn that God is the only real problem solver. God allows pain to teach you to depend on Him. *"The suffering you sent was good for me, for it taught me to pay attention to your principles."*[9]

The truth is, some things we only learn through pain. You've seen this demonstrated over and over in the stories of the courageous men and women at the end of each chapter, and you've seen how each of them learned to depend on God through pain, one of life's greatest teachers.

4. God Allows Pain to Give Us a Ministry to Others

Pain actually makes you humble, sympathetic, and sensitive to others' needs. It prepares you to serve. When we turn to God for healing from the source of our pain, He comforts us and gives us the help we need. *"Why does he [God] do this? So that when others are troubled, needing our sympathy and encouragement, we can pass on to them this same help and comfort God has given us."*[10] Being used by God for the benefit of others is what Choice 8 is all about:

CHOICE 8

Recycling PAIN
Yield myself to God
to be used to bring this Good News to others,
both by my example and by my words.

Everyone needs recovery of some type: mental, physical, spiritual, social, or relational. We all have hurts, hang-ups, and habits. Nobody's perfect. And when we're hurting, we want someone who understands, someone who's been through what we've been through—not someone whose life is all together.

Who better to help an alcoholic than someone who has struggled with alcoholism? Who better to help someone dealing with the pain of abuse than one who also suffered abuse? Who can better help the person who lost a job and went bankrupt than somebody who's experienced the same thing? Who can better help the parents of a teenager who's going off the deep end than a couple who had a child who did the same?

God wants to use and recycle the pain in your life to help others, but you've got to be open and honest about it. If you keep that hurt to yourself, you're wasting it. God wants to recycle your hurts, your hang-ups, and your habits to help others.

There's a beautiful story in the book of Genesis about Joseph. Family and others did terrible things to Joseph—and he was a good guy! He didn't deserve the pain in his life. One day his brothers decided to gang up against him and sell him into slavery. Then they went back home and lied to their dad and said that Joseph had been eaten by a lion. Now that's a dysfunctional family!

Joseph was sold into slavery and taken from Israel into Egypt. He faithfully did his job as a slave, minding his own business, when all of a sudden, his master's wife tried to seduce him. Joseph refused her advances, and she cried, "Rape!" Of course the husband sided with his wife, and Joseph was thrown into prison. This guy's whole life went downhill fast. He was at his bottom. But God had a plan and a purpose for Joseph.

Through a series of events, Joseph was promoted to second in command over Egypt. God used Joseph to save not only Egypt but other nations as well from destruction and famine. Later, during the famine, his brothers came to him to get food—only they didn't know they were standing before the very brother they had betrayed. When Joseph revealed himself, they expected to have their heads cut off, but Joseph surprised them: *"You meant to hurt me, but God turned your evil into good."*[11]

God is bigger than anyone who hurts you. No matter what other people have done to you, God can recycle it and use it for good. God never wastes a hurt. But you can waste it, if you don't learn from it and share it. Others will be blessed and encouraged if you share the problems and struggles you've gone through. God can and will use your pain to help others, if you let Him.

HOW CAN WE USE OUR PAIN
TO HELP OTHERS?

The simple answer to the question, "How can I use my pain to help others?" is to *share your story*. That's it. It's that simple! You share your experiences, your journey, your weaknesses, and how God has gotten you where you are today. As you share, you'll discover a blessing for yourself in addition to the one you pass on to others. When you share your story, it not only gives hope to others, it brings healing to you. Every time you share your story, you grow a little bit stronger, you experience another measure of healing.

At the end of this chapter you'll read the final two stories of the book—the stories of Mac and Mary, who have allowed God to recycle their pain and use it for the benefit of others. God wants to recycle your pain too, so He can use you to help others. The following scripture encourages you to share your story and even offers you some instruction as to how: *"Always be prepared to give an answer to everyone who asks you to give the reason for the hope that you have. But do this with gentleness and respect."*[12] You need to be prepared to give an answer to the questions, "How did you make it? How did you keep from relapsing? How did you recover?"

Accept Your Mission

God has a mission for you. It's called the "Great Commission," and it's found in the Bible: *"Go and make disciples of all the nations, baptizing them in the name of the Father and the Son and the Holy Spirit."*[13] The moment you step across the line and become a believer, you become a missionary. You become a part of God's great plan of reaching out to hurting, lost people.

Do you realize there are only two things you can't do in heaven? One is sin; the other is share the Good News with people who have never heard it. Which of those do you think is the reason God is leaving you on earth? Obviously, sinning isn't the reason.

Sometimes in your mission of storytelling, God wants you to take the initiative. This is called intervention. *"If someone is caught in a sin, you who are spiritual should restore him gently. But watch yourself, or you also may be tempted. Carry each other's burdens, and in this way you will fulfill the law of Christ."*[14] If you are a believer, it is your responsibility to share in the problems and troubles of other people.

This is where our beatitude for this chapter comes in: *"Happy are those who are persecuted because they do what God requires."*[15] Reaching out to others with the Good News of how God has changed our lives is not always easy—or welcome. But we are blessed when we carry out the mission God has given us.

"Life is worth nothing unless I use it for doing the work assigned me by the Lord Jesus."[16] What is that assignment? It is telling others the Good News of God's mighty love and kindness. There is no greater accomplishment in life than helping somebody find the assurance of heaven.

The world has far more people who are ready to receive the Good News than those willing and ready to share it. There are people who need to hear your story. You don't have to be a biblical genius. You can simply tell what happened to you. That's the most powerful kind of story. You can say, "I don't know where all the verses are, but this is what happened to me." Nobody can refute that—it's your personal experience.

God wants to use you. Share your story.

Tell Your Story

In the "Write about It" action step, we'll get your story down on paper. Following are guidelines to consider as you prepare:

1. Be Humble

We're all in the same boat; we're all fellow strugglers. When you share your story, when you witness, it's basically one beggar telling another beggar where to find bread. You're not saying, "I've got it all together," because you don't. You're getting it together. You're on the road to healing, but you're not there yet. Getting there is a lifelong journey.

2. Be Real

Be honest about your hurts and faults. The men and women who have shared their stories in this book have modeled how to do this. They opened themselves up; they were transparent, vulnerable, and real. Can you imagine the courage it took for those people to have their struggles printed in black and white, for the world to see? Draw from their courage and open up your heart as well. You too can help other people by being honest about your hurts. When you are honest about your hurts, the honesty spreads and helps those who hear your story to open up too.

3. Don't Lecture

Don't try to argue or force people into heaven. Just share your story. God wants you to be a witness, not a defense attorney. You may be the only Bible some people will ever read. Some people wouldn't be caught within a hundred yards of a church, so they would probably never hear a sermon. But you have a story that can reach them, a story they can identify with. You can reach people a pastor never could. Just share what God has done for you, and they will want what you have!

Consider Your Beneficiaries

Who could best benefit from hearing your story? The answer is people who are currently experiencing what you're already recovering from, people who need to know Christ and the freedom found in Him and who need to know the 8 Choices found in this book. They might be your peers, your neighbors, or your family. Tell God you're available, then get ready. If you are prepared and willing to share the Good News of how God has worked in your life, God will wear you out.

Can you imagine getting to heaven and someone saying to you, "I'm in heaven because of you, and I just want to thank you for sharing your story with me"? Do you think that sharing your story will have been worth it? It will far outlast anything you do in your career, anything you do in your hobby. We're talking *eternal* implications—getting people from darkness into light, from hell into heaven, from an eternity without God to an eternity with God. People will be thanking you the rest of eternity. There is nothing more significant in life.

MAKE THE
Choice

Action 1: *Pray about It*

Ask God to lead you to somebody to share your story with, the Good News of how God made a difference in your life and how He can make the difference in theirs.

You can begin each day with a prayer something like this:

Dear God, help me be ready to share with someone today the victories You have given me. Help me find the right words and the right time to share my heart with someone who is hurting and doesn't know where to go or how to stop the pain. I pray that I can share the ways you freed me from my hurts, hang-ups, and habits. Let me do so with gentleness and respect. Thank You for letting me serve You today in this way. Amen.

Action 2: *Write about It*

If you prayed the prayer in the first action step, you need to prepare in advance to share your story. How do you get prepared to share your story? Review the three guidelines we presented earlier in the chapter under the heading "Tell Your Story." The following are some suggestions to help you get started:

1. Make a brief list of all the experiences that have significantly impacted your life to this day—positive and negative. Write

down the ones you caused and the ones you didn't. Looking back at your moral inventory, found in Choice 4, will help you remember these experiences.

2. Next, write out what you learned from each experience.

3. Write about how God helped you make it through the tough times.

4. Make a list of the people who need to hear your story.

5. Write your story out on paper.

Why is it so important to write out your story? Remember, thoughts disentangle themselves when they pass through the lips to the fingertips. Write it out.

Action 3: *Share about It*

After you have written out your story, your testimony, share it with your accountability partner. He or she can serve as a good sounding board. Your accountability partner has been with you from the start of your healing journey and knows you and your story. Your partner can help you review your story to ensure that you haven't left out any important events that would be helpful to others. Your accountability partner can also help you share your story in a way that is humble, real, and not lecturing.

Mac and Mary's STORY

Mac: I'm a believer in Jesus Christ who has struggled with drugs and alcohol for much of my life. My name is Mac. I can say "much" of my life instead of "most" of my life because of Jesus. I've lived to see a milestone in my recovery. After more than twenty-eight years in recovery, I have now been sober longer than I was using.

My childhood was pretty uneventful, in terms of abuse. My parents loved me and set good standards to live by, even though they were very strict. So try as I might, I can't look back and blame others for my actions—actions that brought great shame and guilt to me and my family. But today, because of Jesus Christ, I don't have to live in the past anymore. I am free!

Ironically, though, my earlier life was spent searching for freedom in all the wrong people, places, and things. My dad was in the military. By the time I was fifteen, I had moved from California to Germany to Washington. Then, back to Germany, to Georgia, and back to California. Then to Virginia, and finally ended up in Louisiana. Moving so often, I learned how to blend in and make friends quickly. I had to, in order to survive.

My dad preached wherever he was stationed. So I knew about God, heaven, and hell. I learned that unless you were a Christian, you would go to hell, and that scared me. I remember fear being the motivating factor for being baptized when I was twelve. I was baptized at a church summer camp, and besides the fear, the fact that there were some good-looking girls who decided to do this first made my decision easy. I appeared to enter a relationship with God, but it was for all the wrong reasons.

Two weeks later at that same summer camp, I was introduced to marijuana by one of the Christian counselors. I found a group of people who looked to be having a lot of fun, so that's when I decided, "Who needs to live in fear? These people aren't worrying about anything!" I jumped in headfirst. This was in the late sixties and early seventies, and all kinds of drugs were available. It was my mission to try them all, and I did. I became fearless—I believed I was invincible—not realizing I had set the pace for eventual destruction.

When my dad retired from the military, we moved to West Monroe, Louisiana. He went there to go to the School of Biblical Studies and to become a full-time pastor. I was fifteen and didn't want to move because of all the friends I had made in Virginia. How would I ever find others who liked to do what I did now? Amazingly, within a week after moving, I found the same people in Louisiana, only with different names. I never even ran out of drugs, and the acceptance was immediate.

Once we arrived in Louisiana, my parents sent me to summer church camp, where I met Mary. At the end of that week of camp, I was courageous enough to ask Mary out through somebody else.

Mary: I'm a believer in Jesus Christ who struggles with codependency. My name is Mary. I grew up an elder's kid in our church, cutting my baby teeth on the pews. My dad was a preacher, teacher, worship leader, and writer. My parents lived out the Deuteronomy verse that says to "tie God's word as symbols around your hands and teach them to your children as you walk by them day after day."[17] There were always guests at the dinner table in our home. Missionaries from foreign countries stayed with us for recharging, while others flocked to our home seeking wise counsel, Bible study, and to repair wrecked marriages.

During my childhood, my mother would write Bible verses on three-by-five cards and tape them up all over our bathroom walls. As I would get dressed in the morning, there staring me in the face were several verses that I would read over and over. It became a habit, without me even realizing. My sister and I would throw our heads under the covers at night and giggle, thinking how silly it was when our mama recited those verses to us—never realizing the impact they would have on me in years to come. I grew up feeling totally cared for in love and security.

I confessed Jesus as Lord of my life when I was twelve years old and was baptized telling myself, "I will never sin again!" I wanted to please God with all my heart. But just as Satan tempted Eve to doubt God's goodness, I listened to him also.

Mac: A new school year began: Mary was a senior and I a junior. Life was great! We continued dating and, after a few months of "close fellowship," we skipped school one day and went to Mary's house. Mary's mother was in the hospital and her dad out of town. I talked her into having sex, the first time for both of us, by using the manipulative if-you-love-me line. Two weeks later, she didn't start her period; but we thought, "No way, surely one time can't get you pregnant?"

Mary: Four months later, I finally consulted a doctor, and yes, I was pregnant. To my knowledge, no one had ever been pregnant outside of marriage in our church, so we had a big secret. I felt all alone and was convinced Mac couldn't support us. He was only sixteen.

By the time I was five months pregnant, I decided it was confession time—I had to tell my dad. During my childhood, my mother had a mental illness, and doctors had put her through experimental procedures, including electric shock treatments. She suffered in mental hospitals and was a test subject for drugs that kept her debilitated for much of my childhood. So needless to say, my sweet mother, who loved me the best she knew how, didn't notice I had a growing belly.

I had always been able to talk to my dad, and now I knew I couldn't keep my secret from him any longer. I walked into the den where my dad was taking a nap. I had snuggled up next to him many times throughout the years on that big ole flowered sofa, while he read Bible stories to me and we talked about God's love. I knelt down next to him, eye to eye, and said softly, "We need to talk, Daddy."

I was prepared for him to point his finger and say all kinds of harsh words, but the exact opposite transpired. Tears began streaming down his cheeks as he said he would support and love me always. I told him my plans to move out of town and place my baby for adoption.

I left home for my secret "summer trip." Three months later, on August 17, 1975, the doctor left me in a tiny room all by myself. (Remember that date, as it's significant later in our story.) My labor lasted for twelve hours, with no anesthesia and no family. As they rushed me into the delivery room, a nurse shoved a gas mask over my face. I thought they were suffocating me to punish me for what I had done.

I awoke later in bed, my sheets soaking wet from perspiration and tears. I was experiencing emotions that were alien to me. A time that was supposed to be the happiest time of my life was my saddest. I asked the lawyer if I could see my baby just one time, but he said no. I went back home two weeks later and moved to a Christian college out of state. My dad was hoping to get me away from Mac.

Mac: But I followed. My parents thought that by sending me to a Christian college, they could fix me. But guess what? On my first day on campus, I found those same party people. Matter of fact, I found the guy who first introduced me to pot six years earlier at the church camp. I started off as a freshman rooming with seniors. Not a good place to be. Halfway through the semester, I was kicked out of college after sneaking out of the dorm past curfew to smoke a joint with a friend. Mary and I both came back home and married three weeks later.

Married life was great. We partied all the time. Later I would come to understand that our partying helped us mask the guilt of giving up our baby. After three years of marriage, we started trying to have another baby. Mary told me she was quitting the partying. I said, "Go ahead, but I'm not. This is how you married me. This is how I'll be until the day I die." But even in the midst of my addiction, I set a boundary and decided to quit everything except smoking pot. I convinced myself that wasn't so bad.

As I continued down the road of drug addiction, the conflict began between Mary and me. Our two daughters were born during this time. Mary and I were living under the same roof, but living two different lives and growing further apart. I stayed away from the house as much as possible, working overtime to pay for my drug habit. By this time, methamphetamine had become my drug of choice.

Mary: In time, I came to the realization that our marriage was totally unmanageable and that I wouldn't survive unless I turned my life and hurts over to God. I had to quit trying to be Mac's Holy Spirit and fix him, and instead work on my own shortcomings. I started seeking the pathway to peace, while Mac continued to run down the path to destruction. This pattern continued for seven years.

I held on to the verses I read as a child on my bathroom wall. In the Bible, it says that when God's Word is spoken, it will not come back empty but will accomplish what He desires and achieve the purpose for which He sent it.[18]

I repeated this verse to myself the way I remembered my mother quoting it—slowly and distinctly: "Do not fear for I am with you. Do not be afraid for I am your God. I will strengthen you and help you. I will uphold you with my righteous right hand."[19] And when I said these words, I felt God was speaking to me. His spoken word did not come back empty.

All those scriptures I'd heard as a child came back to me, comforting me during the dark and lonely nights. Now I carried two secrets. We had a son we would never know, and now I had an insane husband! I say *insane* because I didn't know that his destructive behavior was fueled by all the drugs he was doing. The last thing I ever expected was for him to be using meth. He was happy one day and a bear the next—to put it mildly.

So I walked on eggshells to keep peace. I wore my mask to church every Sunday. I just wanted my insides to feel like everyone else looked on the outside—perfect, I thought. Mac was at church many Sundays warming the pew, while I poked him discreetly to wake him up.

My feeble prayer at the time was that Mac would just stay awake and hear the message. Never in my wildest dreams did I think of better things—like Mac becoming an elder in our church, one day starting a

Celebrate Recovery ministry, or becoming the CR National Director. The only reason I share these things with you is to confirm that God takes broken lives and does exceedingly more than we can ask or imagine!

Mac: Even as a drug addict, there was one line that I said I would never cross—I always said I would never use needles. But during the last two years of my addiction, I shot up ten to twelve times a day. I wore long-sleeve shirts all the time, so no one would notice the marks on my arms. I slept only about sixteen hours a week.

But one Sunday morning, God gave me a great gift: *a moment of clarity.*

I was crashed out in the bed and Callie, then four years old, stood beside the bed and said to her mother, "Why doesn't Daddy go to church with us anymore?"

Mary in her codependency said, "He's been working hard. He needs sleep."

Callie stood her ground. Stubborn and defiant, just like me, she said to Mary, "If he ain't going to church, I ain't going either."

That sassy little thing, hands on her hips, her four-year-old determined self, wouldn't leave the bedroom. Mary ordered her out and they left for church. Mary had no idea that I'd heard every word.

After they left, I suddenly felt like I had run into a brick wall. God used a little girl to break my heart. I realized I was killing everybody I claimed to love. It was as if my eyes were opened for the first time, seeing the insanity of it all. So I collected all my drug paraphernalia—drugs, scales, and needles—and burned it all. Then I started writing down what

I wanted to tell Mary. For some reason, I knew that I wouldn't be able to say out loud the things I needed to tell her.

Mary: As I left for church that morning, I was crushed, realizing that our children were being affected. That Sunday the sermon was on confession. I put on a good face and acted like everything was perfect in my life. Yet I couldn't hold back the tears when we sang the last song of the day, "It Is Well with My Soul."

I thought of the man I'd left in our bed, a man I no longer knew, a shadow of the man I'd married. It wasn't well with his soul, and because of that, it wasn't well with mine either. And it wasn't well with our daughters.

Back home, God was finally waking Mac up and breaking down his stubborn, strong-willed spirit.

Arriving home, I found Mac sitting in his recliner. I had never seen him shed a tear, so I was disturbed to see his eyes red and swollen. I had no idea what he was about to say.

Mac: I had been raised on "Who's a man?" and "Men don't cry," and "Men show no weakness." But what I found in those tears that morning was relief like I'd never known. I told Mary all that I had done and that I wanted to start a new life. Then something different happened.

Mary for the first time stepped out of her codependency and said, "Well, now, who are you going to call? I'm tired of keeping secrets."

I said, "I told you I'm through with that life. What more do you want?"

But Mary replied, "We need someone to help us. Would you talk to Ray?"

Ray, our minister, had been coming to my cabinet shop for years—getting me to build things for him—only to find out later they were things he really didn't need. He was selling them! But he saw something in me that nobody else did. He saw someone worthwhile, while others saw someone worthless—at least that's what I thought. He reached out to me, and it worked. I said I would talk to Ray. So he came over that day to pray with us; and from that day forward, Ray became my mentor. Ray said I didn't have to confess before the whole church, but I may help someone else if I did. I knew I needed to be held accountable.

For the first time in my life, I realized I had to surrender everything in my life to God. I couldn't do this on my own anymore. Even though I didn't yet know anything about Celebrate Recovery and the 8 Choices, my first choice was crystal clear to me: "Realize I'm not God. I admit that I am powerless to control my tendency to do the wrong thing and that my life is unmanageable."

So Mary and I went down front that Sunday night at church, expecting to be shunned by people when they learned the truth. But the whole church—about four hundred people—came down afterward and hugged us and cried with us. They didn't know what to do with me—I was their first drug addict—but they loved me and encouraged me to keep coming back.

There was one little lady who came up to me that night and said that I needed to go to AA. I thought she was talking about some kind of car club. She said, "Not triple A, double A." Mary wanted me to talk to someone at a rehab center the next day. I told her I wasn't crazy and didn't need that. I finally agreed to talk with someone, but nothing more. But after much discussion with the head guy at the center, I said, "Okay, I guess I'll stay. Let's go home and get my stuff."

Mary said, "That's okay, your stuff is in the trunk!"

Our life became a whirlwind with rehab—ninety meetings in ninety days, Bible studies, and making new friends. A whole new life had begun for us. We started a group called Overcomers two years later, which we led for fourteen years. Approximately twenty to thirty people came on a regular basis, and many were brought to the Lord.

Mary: The only other people who knew about our son were my dad; my brother, John; and his wife, Chrys. Fast-forward to spring 1988. One month after Mac yielded to God, God gave us a surprise gift. Our church youth group was attending a youth rally five hours away, and my sister-in-law was one of the chaperones.

The lawyer who handled our adoption would never tell us our son's name. But then he—the lawyer—found out he had terminal cancer. He felt that before he died, he needed to tell us our son's name, which was Heath.

Back to the youth event: As groups were assigned to stay in homes for the night, the event organizers ran out of homes by the time they got to Chrys's group. So they asked if her group would mind staying in a nearby town. As the suitcases were being loaded into the car of a very friendly couple, Chrys asked if they had any children. When the woman said they had a son named Heath, a funny feeling come over her. So she asked his age. Heath's mother said he was twelve. So she went one step further and asked, "When is his birthday?" Heath's mother said August 17—the date Heath, our son, had been born—August 17, 1975!

At two in the morning, our phone rang. There was no such thing as cell phones then, so Chrys called me from the family's kitchen phone, collect. She whispered, "You'll never imagine where I'm at right now!"

I said half asleep, "Where?"

She replied, "Heath's bed!"

A family at our church had the last name Heath, so I questioned her: "What are you doing in Mr. Heath's bed?"

She exclaimed, "No, no—Heath, your son!"

Mac and I laughed and cried.

At that time, Heath's parents didn't find out who Chrys was. We believe that God gave us that gift at that time in our lives to reassure us that our son was loved and cared for in a Christian home.

Seven years later, in August 1994, we got the call we always hoped we would get. When Heath was about to turn nineteen, his parents contacted us and said he would like to meet us on his birthday. My stomach still flip-flops just recalling that day. My dad was in charge of videoing the momentous occasion, but as we sat down later to view it, the whole reunion part of the video showed the ground! My dad was so excited he forgot he was holding the camera!

It's been over twenty years, now, since we first met Heath. We didn't get to experience Heath's natural birth together, but we were blessed to witness his spiritual birth when Mac baptized Heath in 1995.

In 2008, Heath's parents moved to our hometown in Louisiana, and Heath's mother and my mom became best friends, as she took care of my mom after my dad died. We also attended the same church and celebrated holidays together. Our family continues to grow as God has blessed us now with ten grandchildren!

Mac: After leading the Overcomers recovery ministry for thirteen years, Mary's brother, John, "happened" (coincidence—I think not) to visit Saddleback Church in California. He told me about a ministry called Celebrate Recovery and said I ought to check it out. But in my mind,

I knew everything about recovery. So what else was there to know? But I'd learned in AA that this kind of thinking was "contempt prior to investigation," and John would not stop and kept asking us to go see what Celebrate Recovery was all about.

Finally, I said okay in 2004, thinking I would go to California, have a little vacation, and attend some of the Summit. The first day we got there at 8:00 a.m. so we could leave early to get on with what was really important—checking out southern California. We ended up staying until 9:00 p.m. The next day we arrived at 8:00 a.m. and didn't leave until 10:00 p.m.

At the end of that second day, I turned to Mary and said, "We're stopping what we're doing and starting this! Look how many more people we can help—more than just drug addicts and alcoholics." After 120 days of prayer and preparation, we started Celebrate Recovery in West Monroe, Louisiana, on December 31, 2004.

I have loved watching God's plan for our life unfold. One of the many adventures God has blessed us with included a pastor named Sam. Sam had been a pastor for forty years when he tried to commit suicide.

The critics in his church were persistent, and the only way he thought he could get through the pressure was by doing something he said he would never do—take a drink. That one drink turned into drinking every Monday to get over what had happened on Sunday. After drinking for ten years, with no one knowing except his wife, Sam decided he couldn't take the hypocrisy of his own life anymore, and that's when he attempted suicide. So along with some alcohol, Sam took a handful of pills.

That's when I got the call to go visit him. I immediately went to see him in ICU, and even though he was unconscious, I prayed over him and told him, "Don't give up. God still has a plan for you." When the leaders of Sam's church found out what he'd done, they removed him from the position of pastor, and he became one of "those" people.

But over the next few weeks, I shared with him about the hope that God still had for him. Sam became a part of our CR ministry, and while at one of our small groups, Sam shared with me that he had just met our son's parents at church on Sunday.

I said, "Sam, everybody has, they go to church here now!"

And he said, "No, no, you don't understand. Forty years ago when I first became a pastor, I performed their marriage ceremony."

That's right! Before our son was conceived, God had a plan to use Sam to marry the couple who would adopt our son! And then later allow me to be instrumental in giving Sam the hope that not only could his relationship with God be restored, but that God would continue to use him. So, no matter where you're at today or what you're going through, hang on . . . God always sees the big picture, and He is always right on time.

Mary: Mac and I have been through many fun adventures coming up on forty years together this year. But the most exciting adventure of all was when Mac said, "I'm giving my life to Christ. I can't do this on my own anymore."

I thought our adventures were going to slow down after that, and that we would live a nice, calm family life. But God had a much bigger plan. Over the years, we've seen Him weave together His plan for us to help others find the hope we found.

Amazingly, John and Cheryl Baker were healing in their recovery at the same time Mac and I were. God worked in both of our families' lives for sixteen years before He brought our paths together. He had planted a seed in all of our hearts of helping others find healing through recovery; and God has been growing this ministry one step at a time, one day at a time, one person at a time.

Mac: We love giving back to God, while giving others hope. Several years ago, while speaking at Saddleback Church at a Celebrate Recovery Summit, I looked out over the audience and was so encouraged to see leaders from all walks of life gathered together to share their strengths and struggles, hopes and victories. As I introduced myself I said, "Hello, my Forever Family!" That's how I see our Celebrate Recovery family. Many people have grown up in families that weren't safe. Now in Celebrate Recovery, people get to learn what safe family is all about. We will get to spend eternity with our Celebrate Recovery family.

Mary: Remember when Mac said that twenty to thirty attended our Overcomer's group? It was a ministry that was already working! But now the Celebrate Recovery group we started in West Monroe, Louisiana, has grown to an average attendance of four hundred every Friday night!

We are in awe, as we see God's favor on the CR movement. Groups now meet all over the world, led by passionate people who are on a mission for *Him*.

Our children have been a part of Celebrate Recovery too, serving in roles of State Representative, Ministry Leader, Training Coach, and Open Share Group Leaders.

And our son, Heath—you know, the one God gave back to us?!

Heath worked with the teens in our church for several years, and his office was two doors down from Mac's.

In 2012, we moved to Colorado because seven of our grandchildren now live there. The house we lived in for thirty years in Louisiana has now been turned into a men's recovery home called Awaken514. We are grateful that men live there today, in the house that Mac built long ago, working to carry forth a new legacy of recovery in their own families.

We are blessed to continually witness changed lives, as we see God doing His best work through weak people. In 2 Corinthians God told Paul, "My grace is all you need. My power works best in weakness."

And Paul responded, "So now I am glad to boast about my weaknesses, so that the power of Christ can work through me."[20]

Twenty-eight years ago, I prayed that God would just keep Mac awake in church. God has truly taken the ashes of our lives and turned them into something beautiful. I believe what God said in Joel 2: "I will repay you for the years the locusts have eaten."[21] I've learned nothing is impossible with God!

Isaiah 59:21 says,

"As for me," God says,
"this is my covenant with you [and Mac]:
My Spirit that I've placed upon you
and the words that I've given you to speak,
they're not going to leave your mouths
nor the mouths of your children
nor the mouths of your grandchildren.
You will keep repeating these words and won't ever stop."
God's orders.[22]

If there is restoration for Mac and me . . . there is hope for you too! Never let go of hope. Put your faith into action by making *Life's Healing Choices.*

Mac: We are grateful for CR, as it continues to affect more people and as it continually enriches our lives. One of the character studies in the CR Bible shows us that many of the great men and women in the Bible were also in recovery: Abraham—liar. Moses—anger problem. David—adulterer.

And Paul was so distracted by religion that he became a murderer. Peter had anger and abandonment issues. Mary Magdalene had so many demons they didn't even name them all. And then there's Rahab—she was self-employed . . . And that's just a few of God's leaders!

As our journey continues in CR, our road is filled with peace and joy as we see *one more person* come to know the hope we've found in our Savior Jesus Christ! We get to live out Principle 8 daily:

CHOICE 8

Recycling PAIN
Yield myself to God
to be used to bring this Good News to others,
both by my example and by my words.

In Celebrate Recovery, we get to live out all 8 Principles that God laid out in the Beatitudes, giving hope to all who have hurts, hang-ups, and habits.

Which, last time *I* looked, was everybody I see . . .

First and foremost . . . starting with me.

I've been working the 12 Steps for over twenty-eight years and have never found another program or ministry that moves people through the steps—and even more important, through the Beatitudes—like CR does. Being on the front lines of what I believe is *the* outreach ministry of the church, we are able to bind up the brokenhearted. We proclaim *freedom* for the captives of sin in Jesus's name and release from darkness the prisoners of hurts, hang-ups, and habits.

> Now the Lord is the Spirit,
> and where the Spirit of the Lord is, there is freedom.
> And we all, who with unveiled faces
> contemplate the Lord's glory,
> are being transformed into his image
> with ever-increasing glory,
> which comes from the Lord, who is the Spirit.[23]

How can we repay the Lord for His goodness? If anybody will give us two minutes of their time, we will share the hope and joy we've found in Jesus!

Today we are making *Life's Healing Choices* and that's Celebrate Recovery!

Mac and Mary's story is a true example of what the eighth choice is all about—recycling our pain. Each time they share what God has done in their lives, they help others. Each time they share what God has done in their lives, they receive further healing from their own hurts, hang-ups, and habits. The same can be true for you. Be ready to share with others what God has done in your life through completing the 8 Healing Choices!

R
E
C
O
V
E
R
Y

Closing THOUGHTS

As we come to the end of the 8 Choices, I want to congratulate you on taking this healing journey with me. If you completed each choice to the best of your ability, you have already begun to see some amazing changes and healing in your life. And this is only the beginning of what God has planned for you.

I would like to share one more prayer with you. It is called the Prayer for Serenity:

God, grant me the serenity
to accept the things I cannot change,
the courage to change the things I can,
and the wisdom to know the difference.
Living one day at a time,
enjoying one moment at a time,
accepting hardship as a pathway to peace,
taking, as Jesus did, this sinful world as it is,
not as I would have it;
trusting that You will make all things right
if I surrender to Your will;
so that I may be reasonably happy in this life
and supremely happy with You forever in the next. Amen.

—REINHOLD NIEBUHR

301

In this prayer, we are asking God that we *be reasonably happy in this life*. That's what we have been really striving for as we've worked through these 8 Choices—a reasonable, healthy way to live life in the reality of today. We are no longer looking for or expecting perfection in ourselves or others. Through your making the 8 Healing Choices, it is my prayer that your definition of happiness has changed. I hope you have found that true happiness is having a personal relationship with Jesus Christ. Happiness is being free from your hurts, hang-ups, and habits. Happiness is having honest and open relationships with others.

The greatest loss would be for you to go all the way through this book, to read these great truths and the hope they bring, but take no action. Have you stepped across the line? Have you given your life to Christ? If you haven't done so, do so today. You can go back and reread chapter 3, and it will help you in making your commitment.

Just reading this book is not enough for recovery from your hurts, hang-ups, and habits. It takes commitment, and it takes relationships. Commit yourself to a church family for support. If you do not already have a church family, find one that has a Celebrate Recovery program. That is a good indication that it is a healthy, safe, and caring church. (Go to www.celebraterecovery.com to find a church and program near you.) You will be able to continue your recovery journey there, and you will find people there to love and support you. Celebrate Recovery started in 1991. Millions and millions of struggling people, like you and me, have found God's love and healing in a Celebrate Recovery group. If you already have a church family, start attending their Celebrate Recovery. If they do not have one yet, make an appointment with your pastor, share this book, and help start one! You have experienced firsthand the changes

God has made in you. Now God wants to use you to help others change their lives! It's your choice!

I promise to continuously pray for all of you as your healing journey continues.

God bless you.

John Baker

Notes

Abbreviations Used in the Notes

Copyright and permissions information appears on the copyright page.

ESV	*English Standard Version*	NET	*NET Bible*
GW	*God's Word*	NIV	*Holy Bible, New International Version*
JB	*Jerusalem Bible*	NLT	*Holy Bible, New Living Translation*
KJV	*Holy Bible, King James Version*	Phillips	*The New Testament in Modern En-*
MSG	*The Message*		*glish*
NASB	*New American Standard Bible*	TEV	*Today's English Version*
NCV	*Holy Bible, New Century Version*	TLB	*The Living Bible*

INTRODUCTION: Finding FREEDOM from Your *Hurts, Hang-ups,* and *Habits*

1. Romans 3:23 NIV
2. Isaiah 57:18–19 TEV
3. Matthew 5, portions of verses 3–10 TEV & NIV
4. Matthew 5:3 TEV
5. Matthew 5:4 TEV/NIV
6. Matthew 5:5 NIV/TEV
7. Matthew 5:8 TEV
8. Matthew 5:6 TEV
9. Matthew 5:7 TEV
10. Matthew 5:9 TEV
11. Matthew 5:10 TEV

CHOICE 1: Admitting NEED—The REALITY Choice

1. Matthew 5:3 TEV
2. Proverbs 14:12 NIV
3. Romans 7:15–17 NLT
4. See Genesis 3
5. Matthew 5:3 TEV
6. Genesis 3:10 NIV
7. Romans 7:21, 23 TLB
8. Psalm 32:3 TLB
9. Psalm 32:4–5 TLB
10. Proverbs 28:13 TEV
11. 2 Corinthians 12:10 MSG
12. Matthew 5:3 TEV
13. James 4:6 NIV
14. Psalm 70:1 MSG

305

15. Ecclesiastes 4:9–10, 12 NIV
16. Romans 7:15–17 TLB
17. Psalm 40:12 TLB
18. Luke 12:2–3 TEV
19. Colossians 2:14 TLB
20. Deuteronomy 30:4 NLT
21. Psalm 32:3–5 TLB
22. Romans 2:4 NLT
23. Ephesians 2:10 NLT
24. Jeremiah 29:11 NIV

CHOICE 2: Getting HELP—The HOPE Choice

1. Matthew 5:4 TEV/NIV
2. Matthew 5:4 TEV/NIV
3. Isaiah 61:3 NLT
4. C. S. Lewis, *The Problem of Pain* (New York: Macmillan, 1944).
5. Hebrews 11:6 NIV
6. Romans 1:20 NIV
7. Psalm 31:7 TLB
8. Matthew 6:8 NIV
9. Psalm 34:18 NIV
10. Psalm 56:8 TEV
11. Job 13:27 NIV
12. Psalm 69:5 NLT
13. Psalm 103:13–14 NIV
14. Jeremiah 31:3 NIV
15. Romans 5:8 TLB
16. John 15:13 NIV
17. Ephesians 1:19–20 NLT
18. Luke 18:27 NIV
19. 2 Timothy 1:7 TEV
20. Philippians 2:13 Phillips
21. Isaiah 43:2 NLT
22. Isaiah 43:2 NLT
23. Proverbs 27:17 NCV
24. Hebrews 11:6 NIV
25. Ephesians 4:21–24 NLT
26. Galatians 5:19–21 NIV
27. Romans 8:35–39
28. Psalm 23 NIV
29. Matthew 5:4 TEV/NIV

CHOICE 3: Letting GO—The COMMITMENT Choice

1. Matthew 5:5 TEV/NIV
2. Matthew 11:28–30 Phillips
3. Proverbs 18:12 TEV
4. Proverbs 10:8 TLB
5. Psalm 40:12 TLB
6. Isaiah 44:22 NLT
7. Mark 5:6, 15 NLT
8. Mark 8:36–37 TLB
9. Matthew 17:20 NIV
10. Ephesians 1:13 NIV
11. Philippians 1:6 TLB
12. Acts 16:31 NIV
13. 2 Timothy 3:16 Phillips
14. Psalm 40:8 NCV
15. Philippians 4:13 TLB
16. Revelation 3:20 NLT

17. 1 Corinthians 15:2–4 NIV
18. Romans 3:22 NIV
19. Mark 1:16–18; Romans 12:2 NIV
20. Romans 10:9 NIV
21. Matthew 11:28–30 MSG
22. 2 Corinthians 5:17 NLT
23. Matthew 11:28–30 NIV
24. 2 Corinthians 5:17 NLT
25. Romans 10:9 NIV
26. Romans 8:11 NET

CHOICE 4: Coming CLEAN—The HOUSECLEANING Choice

1. Matthew 5:8 TEV
2. Isaiah 1:18 NIV
3. Psalm 32:1–2 TLB
4. Psalm 139:23–24 TLB
5. Proverbs 20:27 TEV
6. 1 John 1:8 NIV
7. 1 John 1:9 Phillips
8. Isaiah 1:18 TLB
9. James 5:16 TLB
10. Paraphrase, James 5:16
11. James 5:16 TLB
12. John 8:12 NIV
13. Romans 3:23–24 NCV
14. Hebrews 4:16 NCV
15. Romans 3:24 NCV
16. Romans 8:1 NIV
17. Lamentations 3:40 NIV
18. Matthew 19:26 NIV
19. James 1:19 NIV
20. 2 Corinthians 1:4 GW
21. 2 Peter 1:5–7 NIV

CHOICE 5: Making CHANGES—The TRANSFORMATION Choice

1. Matthew 5:6 TEV
2. Romans 12:1–2 TEV
3. John 8:44 NCV
4. John 8:32 NIV
5. Romans 12:2 NIV
6. Proverbs 17:24 TEV
7. Matthew 6:11 NIV
8. Matthew 6:34 TLB
9. Jeremiah 13:23 TLB
10. Philippians 4:13 NIV
11. Philippians 4:8 TLB
12. Mark 14:38 MSG
13. Galatians 5:16 JB
14. 1 Corinthians 15:33 NCV
15. Ecclesiastes 4:9–10, 12 NIV
16. Philippians 1:6 NLT
17. Proverbs 27:17 NIV
18. Matthew 5:37 NCV
19. Jeremiah 29:11 MSG
20. John 10:10 NIV
21. Psalm 37:5–7 NIV

NOTES

CHOICE 6: Repairing RELATIONSHIPS—The RELATIONSHIP Choice

1. Matthew 5:7 TEV
2. Matthew 5:9 TEV
3. 2 Corinthians 7:10a NIV
4. Matthew 5:7, 9 TEV
5. Colossians 3:13 NLT
6. Ephesians 4:31–32 NIV
7. Job 5:2 TEV
8. Job 18:4 TEV
9. Job 21:23, 25 TEV
10. Matthew 5:7 TEV
11. Matthew 5:9 TEV
12. Mark 11:25 TLB
13. Matthew 6:12 KJV
14. Matthew 18:21–22 NLT
15. Romans 14:10–12 NIV
16. Colossians 3:15 NIV
17. Matthew 5:23–24 NLT
18. Hebrews 12:15 TLB
19. Romans 12:18 NIV
20. Luke 6:31 NIV
21. Ecclesiastes 8:6 TEV
22. Proverbs 12:18 MSG
23. Job 11:13, 15–16 TEV
24. Hebrews 10:24 NIV
25. Isaiah 1:18 NIV
26. Paraphrased, 1 Corinthians 10:12
27. 2 Corinthians 1:3–4 NLT
28. Romans 8:28 NIV
29. Romans 5:8 NIV
30. 2 Corinthians 12:9 NIV
31. Lamentations 3:22–23 ESV

CHOICE 7: Maintaining MOMENTUM—The GROWTH Choice

1. Galatians 3:3 TEV
2. Galatians 5:7 TEV
3. Ecclesiastes 4:9–10 NCV
4. Hebrews 10:25 TEV
5. Proverbs 16:18 TLB
6. 1 Corinthians 10:12 NIV
7. James 4:10 NIV
8. Mark 14:38 NIV
9. 2 Corinthians 13:5 MSG
10. Lamentations 3:40 MSG
11. Galatians 6:4 NIV
12. Psalm 119:11 TLB
13. Psalm 1:2–3 TLB
14. Mark 14:38 NIV
15. Matthew 6:9–13 NIV
16. Matthew 6:22–23 NIV 2011, emphasis added
17. Jonah 2:1–6 NIV 2011
18. Isaiah 64:8 NIV 2011
19. Matthew 28:19–20 NASB

CHOICE 8: Recycling PAIN—The SHARING Choice

1. Matthew 5:10 TEV
2. Colossians 1:13–14 NIV
3. 2 Corinthians 12:9 NLT
4. Genesis 1:27 NIV
5. Proverbs 20:30 TEV
6. 2 Corinthians 7:9 TLB
7. Jonah 2:7 NLT
8. 2 Corinthians 1:8–9 TLB
9. Psalm 119:71 NLT
10. 2 Corinthians 1:4 TLB
11. Genesis 50:20 NCV
12. 1 Peter 3:15 NIV
13. Matthew 28:19 NLT
14. Galatians 6:1–2 NIV
15. Matthew 5:10 TEV
16. Acts 20:24 TLB
17. Paraphrase, Deuteronomy 6:8
18. Isaiah 55:11
19. Isaiah 41:10
20. 2 Corinthians 12:9 NLT
21. Joel 2:25 NIV
22. Isaiah 59:21 MSG
23. 2 Corinthians 3:17–18 NIV 2011

About the Author

John Baker is the founder of Celebrate Recovery, a ministry born out of the heart of Saddleback Church in Lake Forest, California. Since Celebrate Recovery's founding in 1991, more than four million people have gone through the Christ-centered recovery program. There are currently more than 35,000 churches that have weekly Celebrate Recovery meetings. John is an ordained elder of the Saddleback Church and also oversees five Signature Ministries at Saddleback Church: Celebrate Recovery, Mental Health, Daniel Plan, HIV/Aids, and Orphan Care.

John and Cheryl have been married for more than four decades and have served together in Celebrate Recovery since 1991. They have two adult children, Laura and Johnny, and five grandchildren.